# Transfer Spending, Taxes, and the American Welfare State

# Transfer Spending, Taxes, and the American Welfare State

by
Wallace C. Peterson, Ph.d.

**Kluwer Academic Publishers**
Boston / Dordrecht / London

Distributors for North America:
Kluwer Academic Publishers
101 Philip Drive
Assinippi Park
Norwell, Massachusetts 02061 USA

Distributors for all other countries:
Kluwer Academic Publishers Group
Distribution Centre
Post Office Box 322
3300 AH Dordrecht, THE NETHERLANDS

Library of Congress Cataloging-in-Publication Data

Peterson, Wallace C.
    Transfer spending, taxes, and the American welfare state / by
Wallace C. Peterson.
        p.   cm.
    Includes index.
    ISBN 0-7923-9077-6
        1. Income distribution—United States.    2. Transfer payments—
United States.    3. Tax expenditures—United States.    4. Welfare
state.    5. United States—Economic policy—1981–   I. Title.
HC110. I5P44    1991
338.973–dc20                                                          90–40457
                                                                         CIP

*Printed on acid-free paper.*

Printed in the United States of America.

To Bonnie

# Contents

# List of Tables

## List of Tables

# Acknowledgments

In any serious work, it is never possible to acknowledge all those who have in some way contributed to the writing. But there are always some to whom a special thanks is due. For this book I am especially indebted to my friend and colleague John Munkirs of Sangamon State University, who first suggested to me the direction this book has taken. Special thanks, too, are due John Kenneth Galbraith, who has been especially supportive of the approach taken in the book to the problems of America's welfare state. Marc Tool, editor of *The Journal of Economic Issues*, has encouraged and supported my writings along the lines found in this book. At the University of Nebraska–Lincoln, my colleagues George Rejda and Jerry Petr have been helpful and supportive. George's generosity in sharing his expertise in the arcane realm of Social Security economics is much appreciated. Joyce Richter was extremely helpful in getting the manuscript into final shape for the publisher. Finally, I want to thank my wife Bonnie for patience and understanding during the book's actual writing. Being the wife of an author is not an easy role. I accept responsibility for any errors in fact or judgment that remain in the book.

Wallace C. Peterson
Lincoln, Nebraska

# Introduction

In 1989 the federal government spent $1197 billion, a mind-boggling sum that is almost impossible to visualize. Since there were 248.8 million people living in the United States in that year, the government spent an average of $4811 for every man, woman, and child in the nation. For a hypothetical family of four, federal spending in 1989 amounted to an average of $19,244. To put this sum in perspective, the money income of an American family averaged $35,270 in the same year.

To finance spending $1197 billion, the government collected taxes from American citizens and residents in an amount of $1047 billion. Because of a shortfall between what it spent and what it took in taxes, the government had to borrow $150 billion, partly from individuals, but mostly from banks, insurance companies, and foreigners.

How, where, and on whom did the federal government spend all this money? Since federal spending in 1989 totaled 23 cents in comparison to every dollar spent for the buying of goods and services, finding an answer to this question is not a trivial matter. Spending by Washington reaches into every nook and cranny of the economy, touching the lives and fortunes of almost everyone in the nation. Thus, answers to these questions are of more than academic interest. The main purpose of this book is to provide answers, ones that will not only surprise many people, but that will probably change their perspective about how our national government works and what it really does with all that it borrows and collects in taxes.

A sizeable chunk of federal spending involves the government going into the marketplace and buying goods and services. Goods purchased by Washington range from paper clips to missiles, while the services bought are mostly labor, including pay to the military and the civil services as well as to the Congress, all political appointees, and the President himself. All told, the federal government in 1989 spent $404 billion in the marketplace buying goods and services. This amounted to slightly more than one third —33.8%, to be exact—of all the money spent by the federal government in 1989. In this spending, the federal government acts no differently than do consumers or business firms; it enters the marketplace and buys goods, goods which for the most part are produced by private firms. It also enters the marketplace to hire labor, much in the same fashion as any business firm. A major difference between the government and the rest of us— consumers and business firms alike—is that the federal government has nearly unlimited power to get the money it needs, either by taxing us or by borrowing. No private persons or firms have such power, and lesser units of government—states, counties, and cities—have far less taxing or borrowing power than does the federal government.

Where and for what purpose did the government spend the rest of the money? The sum of $404 billion is large, but it is still only a bit more than one third of total federal spending. The balance of $793 billion was spent for what are technically called *transfer payments*. The term is well chosen. The federal government pays out billions of dollars every month and year to millions of people and thousands of businesses, sums for which it receives nothing in return. Unlike the government's marketplace transactions, it does not get goods or services in exchange for the money it pays out. The federal government is simply transferring either money income or services (like Medicare) to people, to businesses, to other government units, and even to foreigners without a quid pro quo—an equivalent value in exchange. Simply put, the federal government taxes the population at large, including business firms, or borrows money, and then transfers a part of the money received as either income or services to people and other entities entitled by law to receive the income or services. The latter point is important. The federal government does not do this in willy-nilly fashion, paying out such huge sums just to be big-hearted. Persons, businesses, and other governments, including foreign governments, that are on the receiving end of federal largess are there by virtue of laws—duly enacted, constitutional laws that create legal claims for income or services from the national government.[1]

For example, Census Bureau data show that in 1987 (the latest year for which full data are available) over 33 million families—50.8% of all families—got some form of cash income from the federal government. The kinds of income received ranged from Social Security benefits, the largest single type of transfer payment, to cash assistance for mothers with dependent children (AFDC) and unemployment compensation. Noncash assistance or services—what economists call *income-in-kind*—went to almost as large a proportion of the nation's families. In 1987, an estimated 30 million families got in-kind help, from food stamps to school lunches to medical care in the form of Medicaid or Medicare. The billions of dollars paid out in subsidies to business, including $24 billion in farm aid in 1988, as well as the $151 billion for interest on the federal debt in 1988 are also forms of transfer spending.

Basically, this is what the *welfare state* is about—the use of the taxing and borrowing power of the national government to transfer either cash or in-kind income to people, businesses, and other units of government. That, too, is what this book is about. Since the transfer and redistribution of income has become the major activity of the federal government, at least insofar as the federal government's activities are measured by how it spends its money, it is important to explore and seek answers to questions such as these: Who benefits and who pays for the structure of transfer spending that constitutes America's welfare state? How did this structure come about? How has it evolved? What has been its impact upon poverty in the nation? Does federal transfer spending make the rich less rich and the poor less poor, or does it make the rich richer and the poor poorer? What was the impact of the Reagan "Revolution" on America's welfare state? And what of the future? Is the system, or some parts of it, such as Social Security, facing collapse, or is the system basically healthy? These are but a few of the questions that this book seeks to answer.

Specifically, the discussion will proceed as follows. In the first chapter the meaning of the *"welfare state"* is examined, including comment upon its historic origins and development in the United States. By showing in this chapter the explosive growth in transfer spending in the post-World War II era, especially in the 1970s, the stage is set for a detailed analysis in chapter 2 of the structure of transfer spending in the country. Here we get to the heart of the matter: who benefits and to what degree from the contemporary transfer spending by the federal government.

Chapter 3 looks at the redistributional activities of the federal government from another perspective, namely through the impact of *tax expenditures* on the income of people and businesses in our society. Tax expenditures are little known to the public, yet like direct income transfers, they have a major impact upon the distribution of income and wealth. Briefly put, tax expenditures represent tax revenue lost to the federal government because of favored or special treatment of some income in the tax laws. From an economic perspective, tax expenditures have the same impact as direct money-income transfers, since persons or businesses who benefit from them end up with more income than otherwise would be the case. The picture that emerges from the analysis in chapters 2 and 3 is that of a three-tiered welfare state, one tier for the rich, one for the middle class, and one for the poor. This picture will surprise many, for it runs counter to the popular view that the welfare state takes from the rich and gives to the poor. But this three-tiered structure is the reality.

Chapter 4 moves in a different direction. It contains a detailed analysis and critique of the conservative "revolution" launched by the Reagan administration, a revolution directed not only at the basic concept of the welfare state, but also at the overall role played by the federal government in the nation's economic life. This chapter examines what the Reagan Revolution sought to accomplish, how well it succeeded, and what its effects mean for the future of America's welfare state.

Chapter 4 sets the stage for the book's final chapter, which is an exercise in social and economic forecasting. Here some of the problems confronting our complicated welfare state are discussed, and an attempt is made "through a glass darkly" to foresee the future dimensions of the welfare state. Reforms are also suggested.

Wallace C. Peterson

## Notes

1. Other governmental units in our society—states, counties, and cities—do this also, but since most of their transfer-type spending is financed ultimately by the federal government, the focus in this book will be almost entirely upon what Washington does in this realm.

# 1 ON THE MEANING OF THE WELFARE STATE

Like many things in economics, there is no precise definition of the *welfare state*. Even though its antecedents stretch back into the nineteenth century, modern usage of the phrase grew out of the Beveridge Report on social insurance, a document presented to the British government in November 1942.[1] This document, with its call for sweeping reforms in British social legislation, became the basis for a system of "cradle-to-the-grave" social insurance for the people of Great Britain. When the Labour government came into power after Winston Churchill's defeat in 1945, the party used its nearly 150-seat majority in the Parliament to develop Britain's postwar welfare state.

## The Beveridge Report and the Welfare State

The Beveridge Report asserted that the prime objective of social policy in Britain after the war should be "the abolition of want." This was to be achieved by establishment of a system of "social insurance" designed to guarantee that no citizen's standard of life would fall below a minimum level of material subsistence. How could this be done? Studies of life in a

1

number of the principal towns in Britain before World War II showed that loss of earning power was the primary cause that plunged people and families into poverty. Further, income was lost mostly because of unemployment, disability resulting from sickness or accidents, the premature death of a family's principal breadwinner, or insufficient pension income upon retirement. In this view, "want" (or poverty) resulted essentially from events beyond the control of the individual, events tied up with the workings of an industrial economy. Poverty, in other words, was seen as a social phenomenon rather than the result of any personal failing on the part of the individual or the family. Therefore, it was felt that compassion should be extended to those who fell out of the system into poverty through no fault of their own. This was the philosophic outlook held by the liberal architects of the modern welfare state, a view that many conservatives accepted only grudgingly, if at all.

Given this perspective, the answer to the problem of want necessarily must come from social rather than private action. Such was the stance taken by the Beveridge Report. What is required, the Report said, is a system of "social insurance" that will protect the individual and the individual's family against the "interruption or destruction of earning power" because of any of the special circumstances described earlier. Furthermore, the Report argued, because all families confront extra expenses arising from birth, marriage, and death, the scheme for social insurance should cope with these needs in addition to meeting the threat of poverty because of income loss.

Before describing more fully the details of the Beveridge *Plan for Social Security*, a word is in order on the use of the term *social insurance* in the Report. This is important because the label *insurance* is attached to practically all contemporary variants of the welfare state, including our own Social Security system. The words *transfer expenditures* do not appear in the Report. Lord Beveridge argued that what made his scheme one of insurance was its adherence to several key principles. These included, first, a flat-rate compulsory contribution (or tax) to be paid by every person covered by the scheme, as well as by that person's employer; second, provision of a flat-rate benefit without a means test, irrespective of the amount of earnings interrupted by unemployment, disability, or retirement; and, third, benefits sufficient to provide the minimum income needed for subsistence in all normal situations. Contributions from the covered persons and his or her employer were to be paid into a Social Insurance Fund, out of which benefits would be paid. These benefits are what we now describe as transfer expenditures or income transfers. Any shortfall in the fund because of benefits paid out would be made up by general revenues flowing into the British Treasury.

The structure is similar to the system now used in this country for Social Security. In the United States, the payroll taxes used to finance Social Security benefits (sometimes euphemistically called "contributions") are paid into so-called Trust Funds, the proceeds of which must be "invested" in U.S. government obligations. The practical import of this is that money collected from employees and their employers becomes a part of the general revenue of the government. In the Beveridge Report it was argued that because of the contributory principle, the proposed scheme could properly be described as one of insurance, and because contributions were mandatory for all persons covered, the name *social insurance* was justified.

A key, controversial point, still unresolved by economists and insurance scholars,[2] is whether schemes for income maintenance like that proposed in the Beveridge Report and America's current Social Security system should be described as systems of insurance. No attempt is made in this book to resolve this controversy. The fundamental difference between private insurance and various social insurance arrangements is this: for a private insurance plan to succeed, a fund must accumulate out of which future obligations can be met. Without such a fund, the insurance company simply fails. In the case of social insurance systems, however, this is not the case. Though the term *fund* may be used, as with the Social Security Trust Funds, the reality is that through the device of "investing" money collected under the system in government obligations, the "contributions" for social insurance become a part of the revenue stream of the government. The long and short of the matter is that all such schemes are basically systems for the transfer of income from persons and businesses subject to the mandatory contribution—payroll taxes in the United States—to those who may be the beneficiaries of the system. Stripped of rhetoric about insurance, these systems tax the working population in order to finance the benefits paid out to those eligible to receive benefits under the system. In this sense, the Beveridge plan, our own social Security system, and similar arrangements in other nations are fundamentally income transfer programs. They are also "pay-as-you-go" systems.

Let us return now to the more specific proposals of the Beveridge Plan. The plan consisted of four essential elements. First, and at the heart of the plan, was the arrangement whereby each British citizen (and his or her employer) paid a weekly sum into the Social Insurance Fund, out of which benefits were paid for unemployment, disability, and retirement. Second, the extra expenses arising from marriage, birth, and death were to be met, respectively, by a marriage grant to women, maternity leave benefits and a system of children's allowances, and a funeral grant for all covered persons. These features gave the plan its cradle-to-the-grave character. Third, the plan called for establishment of a national health service to make available to every citizen medical and dental care as needed. The report did not call for the socialization of all medical services, only for a system of national health insurance. Finally, there was a commitment to maintaining employment and preventing the reemergence of mass unemployment like that of the Great Depression of the 1930s. This was a major and logical part of the plan, given the basic underlying assumptions that poverty (or want) results primarily from a loss of income, and that unemployment is the major reason for such a loss in the modern industrial economy. As the Report stated,

> ...income security which is all that can be given by social insurance is so inadequate a provision for human happiness that to put it forward by itself as a sole or principal measure of reconstruction hardly seems worth doing. It should be accompanied by an announced determination to use the powers of the state to whatever extent may prove necessary to ensure for all, not indeed absolute continuity of work, but a reasonable chance of productive employment.[3]

There is yet another important point to note about the Beveridge proposals, one that has an important bearing on both the nature of the modern welfare state and, more specifically, how it has evolved in the United States. The Report baldly stated that the abolition of want in modern society required a redistribution of income and wealth. In contrast to what has probably been the majority and more popular view in the United States that, as President Kennedy said, a "rising tide lifts all boats," the Beveridge Report explicitly said, "Abolition of want cannot be brought about merely by increasing production, without seeing to a *correct* distribution of the product..."[4] Further, both "social insurance and children's allowances are primarily methods of re-distributing wealth,"[5] something not to be feared, according to Lord Beveridge, since a better distribution can increase wealth by "maintaining physical vigor." The conservative opposition to the whole idea of the welfare state stems primarily from this, namely that it is redistributive in intent as well as in fact. The great conservative fear is that any tampering with the market-determined distribution of income and wealth will affect incentives adversely, thus damaging production and the creation of new wealth.

All the foregoing is, of course, history. Not only did the Labour government in 1945 enact into law the main feature of the Beveridge Report, but by its action also established the broad contours for the modern welfare state, in Britain and throughout the western economic world. The welfare state has become a part of contemporary market capitalism. In its bedrock essentials, the welfare state involves the use of the power of the central government to protect people from income losses inherent in an industrial economy—especially income losses arising out of unemployment, accidents and illness, and retirement—and to provide for a minimun standard of material well-being for all citizens, irrespective of circumstances. Taxes and transfer spending (or income transfers) are the primary means used by modern governments to construct and administer the welfare state.

The foregoing represents the classic definition of the welfare state, one rooted in the abolition of personal want as perceived by the Beveridge Report. This classic definition of the welfare state is crucial to the entire analysis of this book. We shall subsequently examine the transfer spending structure of the American government in terms of this definition, one basic objective being to demonstrate the extent to which total transfer spending by the federal government has exploded far beyond the boundries established by the basic, classic definition of the welfare state. Further, the use of an analytical structure built around this definition enables us better to come to grips with the problem of poverty in our society and particularly to understand how and why some kinds of poverty persist and remain untouched by the formal apparatus of welfare state spending. First, however, we need to examine briefly the major features of America's welfare state and to explore how they came into being.

## America's Welfare State

Although many critics would argue that America's welfare state is niggardly by British and European standards, lacking both children's allowances and a system of universal medical care and insurance, a structure of taxes and benefits roughly conforming to the classic definition of the welfare state explained above exists in the United States. It was created in two stages that were separated by three decades and that were responses to drastically different economic circumstances.

Although at the federal level there are about 40 separate programs that provide income support in one form or another, the bulk of them fall into two major categories: Social Insurance programs and Public Assistance programs. The nature of these categories and the basic distinction between them is best understood by a brief review of their history.

The key element in the legislative structure of America's welfare state is the Social Security Act, passed on August 14, 1935. This landmark legislation grew directly out of the recommendation of a Committee on Economic Security created by President Franklin D. Roosevelt in 1934, the major purpose of which was to study the problem of economic insecurity in the

United States. From a broader perspective, the economically catastrophic effects of the Great Depression finally pushed the federal government toward actually doing something beyond emergency relief measures in the way of income maintenance programs. In the jargon of Washington, the Social Security Act has five major titles, or, in plain English, parts. Title I provided grants to the states for assistance to the aged; Title II established the Social Security system; Title III provided grants to the states for administration of a system of unemployment compensation; Title IV established the Aid to Dependent Children (ADC) program; and Title V provided grants to the states for aid to the blind. Basically, the Act set up a system of old-age pensions based upon compulsory "contributions," a system of unemployment compensation, and a structure of aid (or public assistance) to persons sometimes characterized as *the deserving poor*—mostly the aged, the blind, and children. This was America's welfare state in the beginning, a development that came far later in this country than in most European states. Even though the term *welfare state* did not come into popular usage until after the Beveridge Report, Britain—along with most of the major European nations, including France and Germany—had the rudiments of social welfare systems in place at the turn of the century. Germany under Bismark pioneered in establishing old-age and survivors pensions in 1889, followed by Denmark in 1891, France in 1905, and Britain in 1908.

Of the five American programs established by the 1935 legislation, only one, the Social Security system, is wholly under the administrative control of the federal government. The other four are administered by the states, even though the bulk of the financing comes from the federal government. From the beginning, the states have determined eligibility for and amount of assistance. In the Congress the southern bloc had its way in this matter, fearing that too much federal generosity in benefits would undercut the low wage structure of the South and threaten the black–white caste system.[6] A major consequence of giving the states so much power in administration of the programs has resulted not only a wide diversity between the states in benefit amounts for unemployment compensation and public assistance, but also slow growth in the size of benefits and slow progress in the elimination of poverty. An unstated but implicit assumption of the 1935 legislation was that poverty, as the Beveridge Report later assumed, resulted primarily from the loss of income because of risks peculiar to an industrial society, namely, unemployment, insufficient income after retirement, or premature death and disability of the family breadwinner. Yet a quarter of a century after the enactment of the Social Security Act, 22% of Americans still lived in poverty,[7] and, as the Kennedy Administration was soon to discover, poverty had causes other than those assumed by the architects of the Social Security Act.

Another important and enduring characteristic of the American approach to social spending that was established by the landmark 1935 Act was the division of income support programs (transfer spending) into two major categories. These are Social Insurance programs and Public Assistance programs. The former category includes all cash and in-kind benefits paid out through the Old Age and Survivors and Disability Insurance program (OASDI)—what the public popularly thinks of as Social Security—and unemployment compensation. Social Insurance programs *are not* means tested—that is, having a low income is not a prerequisite to receiving benefits. Furthermore, the benefits are linked to one's prior employment status. The intent of programs falling under the Social Insurance rubric was not to reduce poverty as such; rather, it was to protect workers and their dependents from a loss of income because of retirement or unexpected events such as mass unemployment, illness, or premature death of the breadwinner, events over which the worker often has little control. In other words, these programs are designed to keep workers and their families from falling into want (or poverty) because of the foregoing threats to income. In contemporary usage, the benefits under Social Insurance programs are often called *Entitlements*. The Social Insurance programs reflect the assumption that the major source of poverty in capitalism is an income loss because of events that thrust people out of the job market.

Public Assistance is different. Programs in this category aim at poverty and are designed to increase either the money incomes of the poor or their real incomes through in-kind benefits. These programs are means tested, meaning that recipients must have incomes below a certain level to qualify. The 1935 Social Security Act established basically two programs in this category—Aid to Dependent Children (ADC)and aid to the blind and the aged. Subsequently, as discussed below, new programs have been added. Public Assistance fits the popular conception of welfare because it is means tested, it is directed to the poor, and no prior record of either employment or contributions is required for eligibility.

Old age pensions, unemployment compensation, disability and survivors insurance, and some public assistance to the deserving poor—mostly children, the blind, and the aged—was the structure of American's welfare state until the 1960s. In the early 1960s, several things happened to set the stage for a new burst of social welfare legislation that enlarged significantly the scope of America's welfare state. First, the civil rights movement focused not only on discrimination and the overall plight of blacks in the south, but also on the fact that millions of Americans, black and white, were desperately poor, largely outside and unhelped by the formal apparatus of the welfare state. Reinforcing this was the exposure that John F. Kennedy got to grinding poverty and hunger during the 1960 presidential campaign, especially during the West Virginia primary election battle. Then in 1963 Michael Harrington published a remarkable short book, *The Other America*.[8] Harrington carefully documented not only the broad extent of poverty in America, but the equally important fact that much of it had become invisible to the roughly two thirds of Americans described by John Kenneth Galbraith in his influential 1958 book, *The Affluent Society*.[9] Because of Harrington's book,[10] President Kennedy shortly before his death directed Walter Heller, the Chairman of his Council of Economic Advisers, to lay the groundwork for a full-scale assault on poverty. This was done. Chapter 2 ("The Problem of Poverty in America") in the 1964 *Economic Report of the President* provided the statistical evidence and basis for the all-out *war on poverty* launched by President Lyndon Johnson in his first State of the Union message in January 1964.

President Johnson's war on poverty was a part of his vision for a "Great Society," the bundle of social and reform legislation that he put together during his 1964 campaign for election to the presidency in his own right. The wave of remorse and sorrow that swept over the nation after President Kennedy's assassination, in combination with Lyndon Johnson's smashing landslide victory over Barry Goldwater, enabled Johnson early in 1965 to push an array of measures through the Congress comparable in scope to what Franklin D. Roosevelt accomplished in his famous 100 Days. Major civil rights acts were passed, and the Voting Rights Act became law, along with the Economic Opportunity Act, the cornerstone of the war on poverty, Medicare and Medicaid, federal aid to education, and the food stamp program. Although the thrust of many of these measures was toward the poor, the package of Great Society legislation had something for almost every interest group in the nation. There were tax cuts for big business, air and water pollution standards for environmentalists, truth in packaging for consumers, a model cities program, funds for low-cost housing, federal assistance for mass transit, higher subsidies for farmers, money for major additions to the national park system, establishment of a national foundation for the arts and humanities for intellectuals, and many billions for regional economic and social development projects.

How was all of this Great Society legislation to be paid for? This part of the Great Society story has been largely forgotten, save perhaps by some of the supply-side ideologues of the Reagan Administration. By the end of 1964, the Kennedy-Johnson Administration had presided over more than a doubling of the economy's real growth rate, from 2.2% in 1960 to 5.3% in 1964. This increase in growth rate occurred before the impetus to growth that came with the Vietnam war buildup, and it gave rise to a "social dividend," as Walter Heller called it—an excess of federal tax revenues over federal spending that would amount to $7 to $8 billion per year. Heller made his rosy forecast in March of 1966 in the Godkin Lectures at Harvard University.[11] At the time, there was ample justification for such a scenario, since money was pouring into the federal treasury because of the accelerating growth rate. Unfortunately, this happy vision of an expanding social dividend to finance new spending programs without new taxes was blown completely out of the water by the billion of dollars in new military spending generated by the Vietnam war. Much of the Great Society became a casualty of the unwinnable war in southeast Asia.

## America's Welfare State from 1965–1988

To understand how the structure of America's welfare state was affected by the agony of Vietnam and the turmoil of the 1970s, we need to sift through several related ideas and developments. These include the links between the war on poverty and the structure of the welfare state as it existed in the early 1960s; the enlargement of this structure through Great Society legislation, which expanded social welfare spending and programs in education, public housing, vocational rehabilitation, and child nutrition; and the impact of the Nixon Administration on America's welfare state.[12] It was during Richard Nixon's presidency (1969–1974) that the contours of the welfare state as it exists today were finally shaped, and it was also during his presidency that an unprecedented explosion in welfare state spending took place. Moreover, this explosion, partly triggered the Reagan Administration counterassault on the welfare state.

There are two important things to be said about the war on poverty, undoubtedly the best-known and best-remembered of all the Great Society programs. The first is that this "war"—which in reality was more like a small skirmish—developed largely outside the structure of the welfare state as inherited from the New Deal. This was a deliberate policy decision by the architects of the poverty war.

As indicated earlier in this chapter, the classic concept of the welfare state assumed the root cause of poverty to be income losses from unemployment, the premature death or disablement of the family breadwinner, or insufficient income in the retirement years. But as Michael Harrington discovered, the poverty that persisted into the 1960s—a condition mocking the idea of an Age of Affluence—did not fit readily into any of these categories. Its roots had to be elsewhere.

The real explanation was thought to be the low labor productivity of the poor. For a variety of complex reasons, some personal but most social, the poor were poor because they did not have sufficient job skills to command a livable wage in the market economy. Even when they worked hard, as many did, they could not lift themselves out of poverty. The poor were also believed to be relatively powerless as they confronted the institutions that shaped their lives at the community level—the schools, local governments, welfare agencies, and political machines. In the jargon of the social sciences, there existed an *opportunity theory* of poverty, a belief that the causes of poverty—its pathology, in other words—lay in the community rather than in the individual.[13]

These basic explanations for the newly discovered poverty of the 1960s shaped the fundamental approach of the poverty battle, namely, its emphasis on job training and community action programs. The legislative vehicle for the war on poverty was the Economic Opportunity Act (EOA), signed into law by President Johnson in August 1964. Job training was to be the centerpiece of the EOA, concentrated in programs such as the Job Corps, the Neighborhood Youth Corps, and the Work Experience Program. Community Action programs were supposed to oversee and coordinate the work of the array of existing agencies that provided social services at the state and local level. Through the community action programs, the poor were also supposed to have "maximum feasible participation" in the shaping of the antipoverty programs that affected their lives.[14] The general thrust of the EOA toward job training—the idea that the poor could work their way out of poverty—appealed not only to Lyndon Johnson's intense dislike for welfare, but also to the fundamental hostility in American opinion to programs that give money directly to the poor.[15] Further, the jobs approach meshed with the confidence of the Kennedy–Johnson economists that, through the appropriate fiscal and monetary policy actions, they could fine-tune the economy, bringing about a full-employment situation relatively easily. Under these circumstances, and newly trained for jobs, the poor could be brought into the economic mainstream.

The second major point about Johnson's war on poverty involves its cost. It is a well-established part of the conventional wisdom that in the 1960s almost unlimited amounts of money were spent fighting poverty, but with only limited or meager results. As Ronald Reagan quipped in one of his famous one-liners, "In the sixties we fought a war on poverty and poverty won."[16] Yet the reality is quite the opposite. Between 1965 and 1974, the year in which Nixon abolished the Office of Economic Opportunity (OEO was the administrative arm of the war on poverty), spending on programs under the umbrella of the poverty war never exceeded 2.5% of all social welfare spending at the state and federal level.[17] Nevertheless, and in spite of relatively limited direct spending for OEO programs, the late 1960s and early 1970s saw a substantial reduction in poverty. In 1964 the poverty rate for families was 17.4%; by 1974 this rate had fallen to 9.9%, a decline of 43%.[18] How are these seemingly paradoxical results to be explained? There is no great mystery to this development. Along with the much more highly publicized, not to mention more controversial, antipoverty programs carried out through the Economic Opportunity Act, other legislation during the 1965–1974 decade significantly expanded the basic structure of the New Deal welfare state. Most of the progress made during this period in reducing poverty came through increased transfer spending, not through job training.

The most important Great Society legislation during these years was amendments in 1965 to the Social Security Act creating Medicare and Medicaid. Medicare created a system of subsidized health insurance for elderly persons who had participated in the Social Security program. Medicare is essentially an in-kind type of transfer program—medical services being the in-kind benefit received—that is not-means tested and that therefore falls under the classification of Social Insurance. Medicaid, on the other hand, is a program of medical assistance—also an in-kind transfer —directed to the poor, funded primarily from the federal treasury, but operated jointly with the states. Medicaid comes under the category of Public Assistance, since it is a means-tested program.

In a sense, the Medicare and Medicaid amendments to the Social Security Act were the last major additions to the formal structure of the welfare state created in 1935.[19] Other legislation passed in the 1960s and 1970s modified, expanded, or improved this structure without changing it in any fundamental way. Programs affected by such legislation included food stamps, Aid to Families with Dependent Children (AFDC), Supplemental Security Income (SSI), and unemployment insurance. A brief word on each of these is in order.

The food stamp program, which has become a major in-kind transfer program in the Public Assistance category, actually started under President Eisenhower as a modest program to distribute surplus agricultural commodities to the needy. It was expanded under President Kennedy in 1961 on a pilot basis and was given permanent status by the Congress in 1964. In 1971 uniform national standards were established, and in 1974 Congress extended the food stamp program to all the states. In 1985, 7.7% of all households received food stamps, but 72.9% of all poor households—households below the poverty level-got food stamps.[20]

The program that to the public is practically synonymous with welfare— Aid to Families with Dependent Children (AFDC)—began modestly as Title IV in the original Social Security Act. The purpose was to provide assistance to children whose parents were dead, disabled, or absent. It was originally called Aid to Dependent Children (ADC), but in 1960 the act was amended to enable states to extend benefits to the parents (usually the mother) of dependent children. At that time the program name was changed to AFDC, and a further amendment in 1961 permitted the states to extend benefits to some poor, two-parent families. Between 1965 and 1975, the number of families receiving AFDC assistance more than tripled. After that, however, the number stabilized at around 3.5 million.[21] Children have always made up about 70% of AFDC recipients. This explosive growth in AFDC assistance was not solely due to legislation; it also came about because the civil rights movement and the war on poverty made many poor Americans aware that they were eligible for benefits under this program.

The original Social Security Act was amended again in 1972 when Congress passed the Supplementary Security Income (SSI) program. SSI, which went into effect in 1974, was designed to replace Title I (aid to the aged not covered by Social Security) and Title V (aid to the blind and disabled) by a guaranteed, national minimum income for any citizen aged, blind, or disabled. SSI is a cash income transfer, coming under the category of Public Assistance in the basic welfare state structure. The last important change in welfare state transfers coming during this period (1965–1974) involved unemployment insurance, a program in the Social Insurance category. In 1970 its coverage was extended, and a new and permanent program was established for persons who exhausted their benefits during any period of high unemployment.

Table 1-1 is constructed in such a way as to show America's basic welfare state structure from 1960 through 1988. It shows expenditures by the two major categories, Social Insurance and Public Assistance, for 1960, 1970, 1980, and 1988. The objective of the table is to show the evolution of the classic welfare state structure over the past three decades. Presenting these data in this form offers a useful way to contrast as sharply as possible what we have termed the classic definition of the welfare state with an enlarged and alternative structure, one described later in this chapter and one that more accurately describes the reality of our society and how the federal government actually spends its income.

At this point, comments are in order about the data in table 1-1. We

Table 1-1.  Classic Federal Welfare State Spending: 1960, 1970, 1980, 1988
(in Billions of Current Dollars and in Percent)

| Programs | 1960 | 1970 | 1980 | 1988 |
|---|---|---|---|---|
| Social Insurance[a] | | | | |
| 1.  Social Security | $12.1 | $32.8 | $119.4 | $215.2 |
| 2.  Unemployment Compensation | 2.9 | 3.9 | 20.3 | 15.9 |
| 3.  Medicare | — | 7.5 | 35.6 | 88.8 |
| Subtotal | $15.0 | $44.2 | $175.3 | $319.9 |
| Public Assistance | | | | |
| 4.  AFDC | 0.9 | 3.2 | 7.3 | 9.3 |
| 5.  Aged, Blind, and Disabled | 1.2 | 2.0 | — | |
| 6.  SSI | — | — | 5.9 | 10.7 |
| 7.  Food Stamps | — | 0.6 | 8.2 | 11.2 |
| 8.  Medicaid | — | 3.7 | 14.3 | 31.5 |
| Subtotal | $2.1 | $9.5 | $35.7 | $62.7 |
| Total classic welfare state spending | $17.1 | $53.7 | $211.0 | $382.6 |
| Total federal expenditures | $93.1 | $205.1 | $602.1 | $1,118.3 |
| Classic welfare state spending as a percent of all federal spending | 18.4% | 26.2% | 35.0% | 34.2% |

[a] Totals for Social Insurance include administrative expenses, so they differ slightly from
the figures in table 2-2.

Sources: U.S. Department of Commerce, *Survey of Current Business*, July issues, selected
years. U.S. Department of Health and Human Service, Social Security Administration, *Social
Security Bulletin, Annual Statistical Supplement*, selected years.

spoke earlier of a transfer "explosion." Table 1-1 clearly reflects this.
Between 1960 and 1988, total spending for Social Insurance and Public
Assistance programs jumped by a factor of 22, whereas total federal spending increased only 12-fold and gross national product (GNP) in current
dollars increased 9.5-fold. As between the two basic welfare state spending
categories, spending under the Social Insurance rubric rose 21-fold, while
Public Assistance spending jumped 30-fold. This does not mean, however,
that the poor benefited most from the explosion in classic welfare state
spending during these two decades. They did not, primarily because the
lion's share of all spending within the classical framework of the welfare
state goes to recipients of Social Insurance. In 1960, Social Insurance spending accounted for 88 cents out of every dollar of welfare state spending. By

1988, this percentage had fallen to 84 cents per dollar of welfare state spending, primarily, of course, because the Public Assistance category grew faster than Social Insurance spending.

This explosion in welfare transfer spending is also reflected in the fact that, by 1988, spending for the eight different programs included in the two basic categories shown in table 1-1 accounted for 34.2% of total federal spending. Contrast this with the 18.4% of federal spending absorbed by welfare state spending in 1960. In current dollars, classic welfare state spending soared from $17.1 billion in 1960 to $382.6 billion in 1988.

Who benefited primarily from this welfare state spending explosion? How much went to the poor and how much went to the nonpoor? Exact answers cannot be found for these questions, but enough major research on poverty and its persistence in this country has been done to give us some reasonably accurate answers. The fact that there was a relatively sharp decline in the poverty rate during part of this period (1965–1974) suggests there was at least some impact on poverty from the manifold increase in transfer spending. But the matter is more complicated; we cannot simply assume a simple and direct correlation between more transfer spending and less poverty. Other factors are involved.

Changes in the proportion of the population characterized as being below the poverty line depend basically upon two broad factors. There is, first, the general state of the economy, whether times are prosperous or depressed. Good times lift families and persons out of poverty, while bad times thrust them back into this state. Second, there is transfer spending by the national government, spending that also plays a key role in lifting people out of poverty. But to assess the relative importance of transfers in reducing poverty, it is essential to know (if possible) how much transfer spending is targeted toward the poor. Painstaking and extensive research at the prestigious Institute for Research on Poverty at the University of Wisconsin has yielded some solid answers to these questions.

To solve the problem, researchers at the University of Wisconsin's Institute for Research on Poverty developed a pretransfer measure of persons in poverty.[22] This measure shows the percentage of people who fall below the official—that is, federal—poverty line because they do not receive enough income from the private market to lift themselves and their families out of poverty. These were the people targeted primarily by the war on poverty. If that war had been 100% successful, this poverty measure would have dropped to zero. This, of course, did not happen. The pretransfer measure of persons in poverty can then be compared to the official poverty measure, which reflects both the impact of economic conditions and transfer spending on the poverty rate. This comparison is made in table 1-2, which shows

Table 1-2.  Pretransfer and Post-transfer Poverty: 1965–1980 (Percentage of Persons in Poverty)

| Year | Pretransfer Poverty | Change | Post-transfer Poverty[a] | Change |
|------|---------------------|--------|--------------------------|--------|
| 1965 | 21.3% | — | 17.3 | — |
| 1966 | — | — | 14.7 | d |
| 1967 | 19.4 | d | 14.2 | d |
| 1968 | 18.2 | d | 12.8 | d |
| 1969 | 17.7 | d | 12.1 | d |
| 1970 | 18.8 | i | 12.6 | i |
| 1971 (R) | 19.6 | i | 12.5 | d |
| 1972 | 19.2 | d | 11.9 | d |
| 1973 (R) | 19.0 | d | 11.1 | d |
| 1974 (R) | 20.3 | i | 11.2 | i |
| 1975 | 22.0 | i | 12.3 | i |
| 1976 | 21.0 | d | 11.8 | d |
| 1977 | 21.0 | — | 11.6 | d |
| 1978 | 20.2 | d | 11.4 | d |
| 1979 | 20.5 | i | 11.7 | i |
| 1980 (R) | 21.9 | i | 13.0 | i |

[a] Official measure of poverty.

(R) = Recession; d = decline in the rate; i = increase in the rate.

Sources: Sheldon II. Danziger and Daniel H. Weinberg, Editors, *Fighting Poverty: What Works and What Doesn't* (Cambridge, MA., Harvard University Press, 1986) and U.S Department of Commerce, Bureau of the Census, Current Populaton Series, P-60, *Poverty in the United States*, 1987.

the percentage of persons falling below the official poverty line according to these two measures for the period from 1965 (data on poverty are not available before 1965) up to and including 1980. We also need to know the proportion of welfare state spending that goes to the poor. This proportion varies significantly between different types of transfer programs; however, for social welfare spending overall, Institute of Poverty scholars estimated the ratio to be between 42% and 44%. In other words, almost 42 to 44 cents out of every dollar of welfare state spending went to the poor for the period under review.[23]

The data in table 1-2 fall into three approximately equal periods: 1965–1969; 1970–1974 and 1975–1980. In the first period, the economy expanded at a rapid rate—real GNP grew at annual average rate of 4.2%—as did welfare state transfer spending. Consequently, both the pretransfer and the official (or post-transfer) poverty rate fell, the former from 21.3% to 17.7% and the latter from 17.3% to 12.1%. Transfer spending seems to have been a somewhat stronger influence than improving economic conditions in reducing poverty during these years. From 1970 through 1974, pretransfer poverty rose, reflecting the general deterioration in the economy that came after 1970. Recessions came in 1970 and again in 1973–1974, thrusting, as always, people and families into poverty. Welfare state transfers continued to expand, thus offsetting to a degree the rise in pretransfer poverty. Overall the poverty rate fell until 1973, and then began to inch upwards. After 1975 there was a slight decrease in the pretransfer poverty rate, primarily because of the recovery from the 1973–1974 recession, but overall the posttransfer poverty rate remained almost stable through 1979, then rose in 1980 as the economy again entered a recession.[24]

On balance, welfare state transfer spending played a decisive role in the reduction of poverty from the mid-1960s to the mid-1970s. After the mid-1970s and into the 1980s (as we shall examine in detail subsequently in dealing with the Reagan Revolution), the rate of growth in transfers slowed, and the economy experienced in the early 1980s its worst recession since the Great Depression of the 1930s. Consequently, the poverty rate for persons jumped upwards in 1983 to 15.2%, almost the level that prevailed in 1965. The recovery from and long expansion following the 1981–1982 recession brought the rate down, but not as low as the level reached in 1973, the best year on record in the antipoverty struggle. The greatest success in the entire 20-year period (1960–1980) was attained in reducing the poverty of the elderly. The percentage of persons over 65 classified as poor went from 35.2% in 1959 to 15.7% in 1980. By 1987 the poverty rate for the aged had fallen further to 12.2%.[25] Social Security benefits, which reach most persons over 65, poor and nonpoor alike, are the major reason for this achievement. At the other end of the spectrum, the story is less happy, for after an initial decline between 1965 and 1970, the poverty rate for children under 18 has been climbing back to the levels of the late 1950s. In 1960, the poverty rate for children under 18 was 26.9%; by 1970 this rate had dropped to 15.1%, but after 1970 it began to climb, reaching 18.3% in 1980 and 20.6% in 1987.[26] Nearly one out of every five American children now lives in poverty.

To conclude this section, some brief comments are in order on the growth during the 1960–1988 period of other forms of social welfare spending by the federal government and the impact of the Nixon Administration on the structure of America's welfare state. Social welfare spending in this context means programs dealing with income assistance, jobs, food, medical care, housing, and education. The overwhelming proportion of federal spending for social welfare purposes is spending for Social Insurance and Public Assistance programs. But aside from the $382.6 billion that Washington spent in 1988 for these programs, an additional $22.6 billion was spent for the other programs that fall under the social welfare label. Where did this money go? The largest chunk ($14.7 billion) went to state and local governments to finance social programs and spending at the state and local level. The balance ($7.9 billion) was used for direct funding of such programs by the federal government. Specifically, this money went to programs for maternal and child health care, public housing subsidies, vocational education and rehabilitation, educational institutions and aid to students, foster care payments, and assistance to nonprofit institutions, to name some of the most important of the scores of social programs that do not fall directly under the New Deal-created welfare state structure. We shall look more closely at some of these programs in chapter 2, when we examine in detail the structure of federal transfer payments to people and families.

During the Nixon Administration (1969–1974), three developments affecting the welfare state structure took place. Unlike Ronald Reagan some years later, Richard Nixon did not come into office with an implacable hostility to the idea of the welfare state, determined to scale it back, if not dismantle it altogether. On the contrary, he went along with congressional initiatives for significant increases in spending for standard welfare state programs—Social Security, AFDC, food stamps, and disability payments. Most of the explosion in transfer spending in these areas came under Richard Nixon, not Lyndon Johnson.[27]

Nixon also proposed what would have been a new and major addition to the classical welfare state structure if he had gotten his proposal through the Congress. This was his Family Assistance Plan (FAP), a proposal for a guaranteed annual income. The plan, which was the brainchild of Daniel Patrick Moynihan, former Harvard professor and now U.S. Senator from New York, failed because of an unlikely combination of liberal and conservative opposition. Liberals opposed the plan because the minimum income guarantee proposed ($1600) was too low, while conservatives opposed the concept in principle, seeing any guaranteed income as an expansion of welfare, which, in turn, would lead to greater dependency. Aside from George McGovern's Demogrant scheme proposed during his ill-fated 1972 presidential campaign, there has not been any serious consideration of a guaranteed income since Nixon's FAP was defeated in the Congress.

Although Nixon was not basically hostile to the New Deal-based welfare state apparatus, the same cannot be said about his feelings toward the war on poverty and other Great Society programs. These he disliked intensely, proceeding to dismantle them as rapidly as time and politics permitted.[28] At its height, the OEO oversaw at least 24 separate programs, including the Job Corps and other job-related programs, emergency health and medical services, VISTA (the domestic version of the Peace Corps), and the popular Head Start. By 1974, when the OEO officially went out of business, most of these programs had either been terminated or transferred to other agencies of the government. Only Head Start survives as a major remnant of Johnson's war on poverty. Many of the of the job training programs of the war-on-poverty era and the early 1970s were consolidated in 1973 in the Comprehensive Employment and Training Act (CETA), which also made provision for public service jobs. CETA was eliminated in 1981 by the Reagan Administration, leaving the economy with no public jobs program.

## A Primer on Government Spending

The description and analysis of social welfare spending in the prior section is appropriate and accurate within the context of the classic definition of the welfare state. This structure was created by the Beveridge Report and is also reflected in America's welfare state legislation. Unfortunately, this model is no longer adequate as a framework for understanding just what the federal government really does within the context of our complex, mixed economy, because income support spending—transfers—has burst the boundaries of this classical structure. We need to work with a broader concept, one that takes into account the full range and distributional impact of transfer spending by the national government. To set the stage for this, it is necessary to review briefly some fundamentals about how governments —all governments—spend their money. This review leads to a broader, more up-to-date and accurate concept of America's late twentieth century welfare state, one which we shall employ for analysis in the rest of this book.

Few subjects in American life are more publicized and more controversial than government spending and taxation, especially spending and taxing by the federal government. Ronald Reagan built his remarkable political career almost wholly on castigating the evils of federal spending and big government. In the *Program for Economic Recovery* that he sent to the Congress on February 18, 1981, newly inaugurated President Reagan said that the "uncontrolled growth of federal spending has been the primary cause of the sustained high rate of inflation experienced by the American economy." Further, the President went on to say, his policies will "restore the Federal government to its proper role in American society."[29]

Well and good. But the problem with the Reagan view was that it was too simplistic and narrow, given the complexities of our society and economy. Everyone, no doubt, would like the federal government to carry out its "proper" role, but the precise nature of this role is by no means self-evident. Much of the controversy about the national government centers on two basic questions. First, how big should the federal government be? Second, what should it be doing? Obviously we cannot come up with precisely correct answers to these questions, but by examining data from the past that bear on them, we can come closer to getting some reasonable answers. Further, this approach will permit us to formulate an appropriate framework for the broadened concept of the welfare state, a main theme of this book.

## The Size of Government

At first glance, one might suppose that basic questions about the size and growth of government were matters of simple measurement. Because Ronald Reagan steadfastly maintained in his long campaign for the presidency (1976–1980) that the federal government was too big, the leading edge in his program for economic recovery was "a comprehensive reduction in the rapid growth of Federal spending."[30] This reflects a widely used method for measuring government's size: *total spending*! This approach is the basis for the belief held by many people besides Ronald Reagan that government in our society has grown rapidly—too rapidly, in the eyes of many. There is truth in this view. If we look at government spending at *all* levels (federal, state, and local) for *all* purposes, there is little doubt that it has grown at a brisk pace. In the 40 years from 1948 to 1988, the nation's GNP (in current prices) grew 18.5-fold; but in the same interval government spending at all levels grew 32-fold, or more than one-and-one-half times faster than overall output and spending.

This fact of growth does not tell us, however, how big the government is in our society, and more important, whether it has become "too big." For this we need more information. The data supplied in table 1-3 cannot answer the latter concern, but they can give us useful answers to the former. The size of gvernment is not as obvious as many may think, but without a useful and reasonable estimate we cannot even begin to consider whether it is "too big."

Table 1-3 contains three sets of figures on government spending for the period 1948–1988. For each set it shows the annual average dollar value of government spending in each of the four subperiods contained in the 1948–1988 period, and also shows the same data as a percent of the GNP. The

Table 1-3. Government Spending and the Economy: 1948–1988 (Annual Averages in Billions of Current Dollars and in Percent)

| | Total Spending[a] | | Total Spending For Goods and Services | | Nonmilitary Spending For Goods and Services | |
|---|---|---|---|---|---|---|
| | (1) Dollar | (2) Percent | (3) Dollar | (4) Percent | (5) Dollar | (6) Percent |
| Period | Value | of GNP | Value | of GNP | Value | of GNP |
| 1948–1959 | $93.2 | 25.3% | $69.8 | 18.9% | $34.6 | 9.2% |
| 1960–1969 | 199.0 | 28.9 | 146.5 | 21.2 | 88.9 | 12.9 |
| 1970–1979 | 506.1 | 32.1 | 328.6 | 20.8 | 244.5 | 15.5 |
| 1980–1988 | 1286.6 | 34.2 | 750.3 | 20.0 | 518.8 | 13.8 |

[a] Goods and services plus transfer expenditures.

Source: *Economic Report of the President* (Washington, D.C., U.S. Government Printing Office, 1989).

figures shown are for total spending for all purposes by federal, state, and local governments; total spending for goods and services only by these same governments; and, finally, nonmilitary spending for goods and services by these governments during the periods indicated. These percentage data enable us to answer questions about the size of government.

The figures shown in the first two columns in the table are ones often used as "proof" that government is big and getting bigger all the time. These figures tell a story, but not the whole story. If we look simply at the averages for government spending at *all* levels for *all* purposes as a percent of the GNP, it is true that government has grown significantly in size relative to the national output. In the 1948–1959 period, government spending for all purposes averaged 25.3% of the national output. By the 1980s, however, this average had climbed to 34.2%, an increase of 8.9 percentage points, or 35%, in the relative importance of government spending.

It is easy—much too easy—to jump from the foregoing statistics to the conclusion that government is now taking slightly more than one third of the nation's output. Government, it seems, is getting bigger and bigger, a trend that if not checked means that government will dominate and swallow up everything in its path. This was the fear that lay behind the Reagan Administration's campaign against "big government." However, this conclusion is not correct, although the statistics found in table 1-3 and the percentages cited above are correct. Now we encounter what may seem to be a puzzling paradox: on the one hand, the statistics show undoubtedly that government, spending has grown significantly in relation to the GNP, but, on the other hand, it is asserted that this does not necessarily mean an increase in the size of government. Is something awry? Is some sort of statistical sleight of hand being pulled? Not really. But to resolve the paradox, we need to examine in detail the two fundamental ways in which governments —all governments—spend their money.

## How Governments Spend Their Money

Adam Smith, the founder of modern economics as well as a great philosopher, said in his masterwork, *An Inquiry into the Nature and Causes of the Wealth of Nations*, that the sovereign—that is, the government—has but three principal duties. They are 1) to protect the society from "the violence and invasion of other independent societies"; 2) to protect "every member of the society from the injustice or oppression of every other member"; and 3) to erect and maintain "those public institutions and those public works... which are of great benefit to society but which are too costly to be maintained by any individual or group of individuals."[31] In modern prose, Smith's duties add up to those commonplace activities most people think of when they hear the word *government*—maintaining armies, navies, and airfleets, building roads, running school systems, operating courts, delivering the mail, providing police and fire protection, creating parks, and doing many other things that private business cannot do or chooses not to do on a scale adequate to the needs of society. This we shall term the *Smithian* view of government, one with which the Reagan administration was quite comfortable.

This Smithian view of what the government should do also offers a way to resolve the paradox involved in the assertion that increasing government expenditures do not necessarily involve an increase in the size of government. Let us see how. In order to do the many different things falling under the Smithian umbrella, governments must have resources (that is, people and materials), just as private firms must when they produce goods and services to sell in markets. A major difference between governments and private firms, however, is that governments get the money to purchase resources mostly from taxation, whereas private firms must depend upon selling what they produce for their revenue. Now we are close to the crux of the matter. The goods and the services (mostly labor services) that governments buy from the private economy to carry out their Smithian duties are the most meaningful and practical measures of just how much of the economy's total output is being used by government. The goods and services that governments purchase are in a fundamental sense the resource inputs that they need to carry out their duties. At this point one might ask: what is it that governments produce? Or do they produce anything? The answer to the latter question is yes, and to the former is that governments produce a wide variety of things and services that people want and value, ranging from national defense to the street before your house or the park down the road. Government output, or production, is social or collective, whereas market output is private and individual. Our right to a share of social output comes from being citizens of a political body, such as a city, state, or nation, whereas our right to a share of output produced privately depends upon having enough income to buy what is being produced.

Now if we look at the question of the size of government from this perspective, that is, in terms of the share of the economy's output that governments acquire by buying goods and services from the market economy, we get a different perspective on how big government really is. Return to the data in table 1-3. Columns 3 and 4 show, first, the dollar averages of government spending for goods and services for the periods indicated, and, second, the average proportion of the GNP that such expenditures took in the same periods. Dollar expenditures rose significantly in this 40-year span, but the proportion stayed nearly constant, being 18.9% in the 1948–1959 period and only 20.0% in the 1980s. This is the important statistic. It tells us what has happened, or has not happened, to the *real* size of government in our society over these four decades. Government in the Smithian sense has been constant in size over these years, using around one fifth (20%) of the nation's output for its manifold purposes. If we liken the gross national product to a gigantic pie baked annually to satisfy all our wants, the relative size of the government's slice of this pie has remained the same![32]

The figures in column 6 of table 1-3 are also instructive, since they illustrate how much of the nation's output has gone to the public sector once military spending is removed from the totals. There was some increase from 1948 through 1988, but the overall share is now on the order of 14%. How does this compare with the pre-World War II situation? In 1929, the eve of the Great Depression, public spending for goods and services by all governments in the economy was equal to 8.5% of the GNP. By 1933, the low point of the depression years, this figure had climbed to 14.3%, but by 1939, ten years after the crash, government spending for goods and services had dropped back to 13.4% of the GNP.[33] These figures tell us that the big change in the nonmilitary role of government in the economy came during the depression years, not after World War II. Even more interesting, perhaps, is what has happened in the 1980s. Overall, there was no shrinkage under Reagan in the *real* size of the public sector (column 4), but the nonmilitary size of the government's output did fall. This reflects the priority the Reagan administration placed upon building up the military sector.[34]

Let us now return to the other part of our paradox, the statistical fact of a sustained rise in government spending for *all* purposes measured as a share of the GNP (column 2 of table 1-3). This brings us to the second major way governments spend money, one that is fundamentally different from spending money to buy goods and services as discussed in the previous paragraphs. This second way involves *transfer expenditures*, a form of spending referred to several times earlier in this chapter but not discussed in detail. Transfer expenditures are a type of government spending virtually unheard of in Adam Smith's day, and surely undreamed of in his philosophy. Today, however, and especially for the federal government, they have become the primary way in which governments spend money. Unless we grasp this fact, it is perhaps impossible to fully understand the drastic, perhaps even *revolutionary*, change that has taken place in the role that government plays in our society. It is also because of changes in this form of spending that the classic welfare state structure defined earlier is no longer adequate for describing the true dimensions of America's welfare state.

So what precisely is a transfer expenditure? It is a governmental outlay that provides a person, an organization, or even another unit of government *income* in either a monetary or an in-kind form,[35] and for which the government *does not* require in exchange a product, a service, or an asset. Further, the person or entity receiving the income has no obligation to pay that income back to the government in the future. To illustrate, if the government hires a secretary, this is *not* a transfer expenditure; it is the purchase of a labor service, and in return for its financial outlay the government gets work from the secretary. However, when the government pays out unemployment compensation to a jobless worker, we have a transfer expenditure or income transfer. No work is required from the unemployed person, and there is no obligation to repay the government when, or if, the jobless person goes back to work.

The word *transfer* is well chosen with respect to this kind of government spending. The government is the instrument—the means—whereby income is obtained from some, or all, citizens, usually by taxation but also by borrowing, and transferred by the government to other citizens and entities in the economy. Transfers differ from goods and services expenditures because they do not directly use resources—there is no quid pro quo. Transfers also have a much more direct effect upon the distribution of income and wealth in the society. This is not to say that government buying of goods and services does not affect income and wealth; it does, but transfers are normally undertaken with the deliberate intent of affecting incomes somewhere in the economy, which is not the primary purpose of other government activity.

Now we are able to reconcile the paradox reflected in the data in table 1-3. Since the percentages shown in column 4 in the table assure us that there has not been any major change in the Smithian role of the government in the post-World War II era, the growth in government activity reflected in column 2 in the table must reflect the growth of transfer-type spending. And this is exactly what has happened. Earlier in the chapter, mention was made of the *transfer explosion*; this is the explosion that pushed total government spending from roughly one quarter of the GNP in the decade immediately after World War II to slightly more than one third of the GNP in the 1980s. This is the little-understood revolution that has taken place in our society, a revolution that has dramatically transformed the federal government's role in the economy.[36]

## The Changing Role of the Federal Government

Throughout much of the post-World War II era, the primary focus of public interest in the federal government has been on its role as a stabilizer. People look to the national government to keep the economy near full employment, to stabilize prices, and to tame the worst excesses of the business cycle. This is what the postwar Age of Keynes has been about. By the careful and judicious use of its monetary and fiscal powers, the federal government is supposed to be able to do these things. And by and large, the government in Washington has been reasonably successful in this role, notwithstanding the fact that the economy suffered severe inflation in the 1970s and several recessions, two of which were quite severe (1974–1975 and 1981–1982). Overall, however, the near half century since World War II ended has been a remarkable economic success story, a success that is largely a legacy of the Keynesian Revolution.

Less heralded and less well understood, however, a different kind of quiet revolution was also taking place during these years, one that culminated in the transfer explosion of the last two decades. This has been the persistent, steady growth in the government's role in providing income through transfer spending to an ever widening segment of the population. It is this development that has brought about far-reaching changes in the federal government's role in the economy, changes that even today are but dimly perceived by most citizens. Tables 1-4 and 1-5 document these changes.

Table 1-4 shows in percentage form for the postwar decades the proportion of total federal outlays used for the purchase of goods and services,

Table 1-4.  Federal Government Purchase of Goods and Services, Military Spending, and Transfer Payments: 1948–1988 (Annual Average Percent of Total spending for Indicated Periods)

| Period | (1) Purchase of Goods and Services[a] | (2) Military Spending | (3) Transfer Payments | (4) Column 2 Plus Column 3 |
|---|---|---|---|---|
| 1948–1959 | 63.2 | 53.2 | 36.8 | 90.0 |
| 1960–1969 | 55.1 | 43.0 | 44.9 | 87.9 |
| 1970–1979 | 36.4 | 24.9 | 63.6 | 88.5 |
| 1980–1988 | 34.8 | 25.7 | 65.2 | 90.9 |

[a] Including military spending.

Source: *Economic Report of the President* (Washington, D.C., U.S. Government Printing Office, 1989).

for military spending, and for transfer payments. These figures, stark in their simplicity, contain a powerful message. Specifically, they tell us three critical things about the *real* role of the federal government in our society.

1. In the 41-year period from 1948 to 1988, the federal government's economic role has shifted dramatically from being concerned with the Smithian functions of government to providing income in money or in kind to more and more people and entities in the economy. In the immediate post-World War II era, 63.2% of all federal spending went for the purchase of goods and services to carry out Smithian activities. By the 1980s, this percentage had dropped dramatically to 34.8%, while transfer spending had jumped from 36.8% to 65.2%. If we measure what the federal government does by how it spends its money, the rearrangement of incomes through transfer spending has become its primary activity.

2. A second and perhaps surprising fact for many is the changes in the *relative* importance of military spending taking place over these years. In absolute amount, military spending has grown enormously—from $11.3 billion in 1948 to $298 billion in 1988—but the proportion of federal spending directed to the military has dropped steadily over the period. In the years immediately after World War II (1948–1959), military outlays consumed more than half of all federal spending, but by the 1980s, the military's share had dropped to one quarter of the total. True, there were wars during the 1950s and 1960s, but it has been the growth in transfer spending more than the ending of these wars that accounts for the relative decline in military spending in the 1970s and 1980s. The Reagan Administration's

Table 1-5.   Federal and State and Local Government Spending for Goods and Services: 1948–1988 (Annual Average Percent of GNP for Indicated Periods)

| | (1) | (2) | (3) |
|---|---|---|---|
| | | | *Combined Federal,* |
| | *Federal* | *State and Locol* | *State, and Local* |
| *Period* | *Spending* | *Spending* | *Spending* |
| 1948–1959 | 11.0 | 7.9 | 18.9 |
| 1960–1969 | 10.7 | 10.5 | 21.2 |
| 1970–1979 | 8.1 | 12.7 | 20.8 |
| 1980–1988 | 8.2 | 11.8 | 20.0 |

Source: *Economic Report of the President* (Washington, D.C., U.S. Government Printing Office, 1989).

stress on more armaments did boost the percentage figure in the 1980s slightly as compared to the 1970–1979 decade.

3. Finally, if we combine the percentage for military outlays and transfer spending into a single figure, as is done in column 4 of the table, we come up with a quite remarkable statistic. Over the whole of the post-World War II era, approximately 90% of the federal government's activities, measured by how the government spends its money, has consisted of either 1) re-arranging incomes in society, or 2) nourishing the military economy! Out of the total of federal spending for *all* purposes, barely more than 10% on the average has gone for what was described earlier as the "Smithian" tasks of government, excluding, for this comparison, the national defense role that Smith envisaged for government.

What are we to make of these findings? If we dig a bit further into fig-ues showing the relative decline in the proportion of federal spending represented by the buying of goods and services, another interesting per-spective on the federal government emerges. Earlier, in reference to the data in table 1-3, the point was made that, overall, the *relative* size of government in a real or Smithian sense has remained practically unchanged since World War II. But as the figures in table 1-5 show, the size of the fed-eral government when measured in this way has actually shrunk since the end of World War II. In the 1948–1959 period, federal purchases of goods and services averaged 11.0% of the GNP. But by the 1980s, the federal goods and services slice of the GNP had shrunk to 8.2% (column 1) but state and local spending for goods and services had jumped from 7.9% to

11.8% of the GNP. The real growth in government after World War II took place at the state and local level.

This brings us back to transfer spending, which is where most of the growth in federal activity has taken place. Why has this happened? There is no immediate, simple, all-encompassing explanation for this development, but it does accord with a basic fact about our economic life, something that also undergirds a major theme of this book: namely, most people do not gladly or without protest accept the verdict of unrestrained market forces in determination of their incomes. People may do this in the pristine academic world of pure theory, but they do not do so in reality. As John Kenneth Galbraith has pointed out so clearly, people want control over their own lives, and a major factor in achieving this is getting control over their incomes.[37] If they do not like the terms on which they can get income from the private market, they will try to organize to better those terms, and if that fails they will turn to government.

There should be nothing especially novel nor surprising in this fact. It has been true since the founding of the republic—the government has always been involved in the distribution of income, willingly or unwillingly, wittingly or unwittingly. The older and somewhat better-understood aspect of this centers upon government intervention into the workings of the market system, interventions ranging from the antitrust laws to the minimum wage. Ultimately the purpose of all such interventions is to bend or modify market forces in ways that are favorable to particular individuals, groups, or business firms. There is nothing abnormal in this; it is a part of the political process. However, it has led to a vast and heterogeneous collection of nonmarket controls, regulations, and extramarket arrangements—some good, some bad—all of which modify and change the way in which people get incomes from market transactions.

The growth in transfer expenditures is simply the most recent, and, perhaps the most powerful, manifestation of this strain in our national economic life. What characterizes the transfer explosion is that the power of government is being used to provide income directly to people and businesses by outright income transfers on a scale unheard of in our national life until relatively recently. Government is also doing this indirectly through the tax system, an aspect of the transfer revolution we shall analyze in chapter 3. What the Reagan Administration attempted in its revolution ran counter to this powerful trend, a fact that David Stockman ruefully admits in his account of why the Reagan Revolution failed.[38]

Now we come to the final point of this chapter, the need for a broadened definition of America's welfare state, one that not only better describes what is actually happening in this realm in America, but that also provides an appropriate framework for the discussion and analysis in the rest of this book. Early in this chapter, we pointed out that the classic notion of the welfare state that sprang from the Beveridge Report involved the use of the power of the central government to protect people and their families from income losses arising out of conditions inherent in industrial societies. Taxes and transfer spending are the instruments to accomplish this. This bedrock definition is still true. It is also true, however, that the scope of welfare state activities of a tax and transfer nature has exploded far beyond the boundaries set down by the Beveridge Report concept of the welfare state. Unfortunately, no appropriate term or phrase has emerged that describes the vastly enlarged income transfer system we now have in the United States. For better or for worse, we are, therefore, stuck with the term *welfare state*, but we must broaden the concept to include the entire range of transfer spending by the federal government.

We shall do this in the following way. First, we shall classify as transfer expenditures all federal spending other than purchases of goods and services. This follows from the fundamental distinction drawn earlier with respect to the two primary ways in which governments spend money, buying goods and services and transferring income. Second, we shall break down the overall category of transfer expenditures into five major subcategories. These follow the classifications used in the national income and product accounts for federal expenditures, and include 1) transfers to people in both money and in kind form; 2) grants from the federal government to state and local governments; 3) net interest on the public debt; 4) subsidies to business; and 5) a catch-all *Other* category, consisting mostly of transfers by the federal government to foreign governments. If each of these subcategories is examined, it is apparent that they all have the characteristics of transfers as described earlier. Third and most important, we shall determine what people or other entities benefit from the vast sums spent by the federal government as transfers. This is a must if we are to discover how these outlays affect the distribution of income and wealth in our society. These are the tasks we now turn to in chapter 2.

## Notes

1. Sir William Beveridge, *Social Insurance and Allied Services* (New York, Macmillan, 1942).

2. George E. Rejda, *Social Insurance and Economic Security* (Englewood Cliffs, NJ, Prentice Hall, 1988), pp. 9 ff.

3. Beveridge, *op. cit.*, p. 163.

4. *Ibid.*, p. 167 (italics added).

5. *Ibid.*

6. Harrell R. Rodgers, Jr., *The Cost of Human Neglect* (Armonk, NY, M. E. Sharpe, Inc., 1982), p. 52.

7. U.S. Department of Commerce, Current Population Series, P-60, *Poverty in the United States, 1987* (Washington, D.C., U.S. Government Printing Office, 1988), p. 7.

8. Michael Harrington, *The Other America: Poverty in the United States* (New York, Macmillan, 1962).

9. John Kenneth Galbraith, *The Affluent Society* (Boston, Houghton Mifflin, 1958).

10. It is doubtful if President Kennedy actually read Michael Harrington's book, *The Other America*. However the book was the subject of a long review by Dwight MacDonald in *The New Yorker*, entitled "Our Invisible Poor." This review appeared in the magazine in January, 1963, and it is probable that President Kennedy either read it or had it called to his attention.

11. Walter Heller, *New Dimensions in Political Economy* (Cambridge, MA, Harvard University Press, 1966), pp. 65 ff.

12. The impact of the Reagan Administration on the welfare state and on its spending patterns is discussed separately in chapter 4.

13. Robert D. Plotnick and Felicity Skidmore, *Progress Against Poverty: A Review of the 1964–1974 Decade* (New York, Academic Press, 1975), p. 4.

14. *Ibid.* See also the articles by Nicholas Lemann, "The Unfinished War," in *The Atlantic Monthly*, December 1988 and January 1989.

15. Nicholas Lemann, *op. cit.*

16. *Ibid.*

17. Plotnick and Skidmore, *op. cit.*, p. 66.

18. U.S. Department of Commerce, Current Population Series, *op. cit.*, p. 7. The low point in the poverty rate was attained in 1973.

19. Congress in 1988 passed the Family Support Act, but this is more properly regarded as an overhaul of AFDC (Aid to Families with Dependent Children) than as a new addition to the structure of the welfare state.

20. U.S. Department of Commerce, Current Population Series, P-60, *Receipt of Selected Noncash Benefits: 1985*, p. 2.

21. *Ibid.*

22. The Institute for Research on Poverty at the University of Wisconsin in Madison is the nation's foremost research center for the study of poverty. It was established in 1966 by a grant from the Office of Economic Opportunity. Its primary objective has been to encourage and support basic, multidisciplinary research into the nature, causes, and possible cure of poverty.

23. Robert H. Haveman, *Poverty Policy and Poverty Research: The Great Society and the Social Sciences* (Madison, WI, The University of Wisconsin Press, 1987), p. 26.

24. Sheldon H. Danziger and Daniel H. Weinberg, Editors, *Fighting Poverty: What Works and What Doesn't* (Cambridge, MA, Harvard University Press, 1986), pp. 57 ff.

25. U.S. Department of Commerce, Current Population Series, P-60, *Poverty in the United States, 1987*, p. 9.

26. *Ibid.*

27. Danziger and Weinberg, *op. cit.*, p. 52.

28. Lemann, *op. cit.*

29. *A Program for Economic Recovery* (Washington, D.C., The White House, February 18, 1981), p. 13.

30. *Ibid.*

31. Adam Smith, *An Inquiry into the Nature and Causes of the Wealth of Nations* (New York, Modern Library, 1937).

32. *Economic Report of the President* (Washington, D.C., U.S. Government Printing Office, 1989), p. 309.

33. *Ibid.*

34. *Ibid.*

35. *In kind* refers to the direct provision of a service, such as medical care or housing, rather than the direct provision of money income.

36. All governments—federal, state, and local—engage in transfer spending, but the bulk of such spending in the nation is financed by the national government. Thus, we concentrate primarily upon transfer spending at the federal level.

37. John Kenneth Galbraith, "On post Keynesian economics," *Journal of Post Keynesian Economics*, Fall, 1978.

38. David Stockman, *The Triumph of Politics: Why the Reagan Revolution Failed* (New York, Harper & Row, 1986), p. 395.

# 2 THE ANATOMY OF AMERICA'S WELFARE STATE

In the last chapter, the point was made that nearly two thirds of federal spending can be classified as *transfers*. In 1989 this amounted to $793 billion, or an average of $3187 for each man, woman, or child in the nation. Whether looked at on a total or per-person basis, this is a staggering sum. To put it another way, out of every dollar spent by Washington, 66 cents is a transfer—taxing Peter to pay Paul, so to speak. Who benefits from this federal largess? Who gets all this money? Is the federal government running, as David Stockman once suggested, a wonderful "coast-to-coast soup line," into which all of us our dipping our ladles?[1] These are critical questions to which we seek answers in this chapter.

To get answers—to lay bare the anatomy of our vast welfare state apparatus—we shall first analyze federal transfer spending in terms of the five categories outlined at the close of chapter 1. This sets the stage for getting to our more basic objective, which is to determine which people and what other entities benefit the most from the great river of funds flowing through the federal government's Byzantine structure of taxes and transfers. America's once relatively modest, New Deal-inspired welfare state has evolved into an extraordinarily complex welfare cum national security state, a state that touches nearly every citizen's life. We saw in table 1-4 that since

Table 2-1.    Federal Transfer Expenditures By Major Category as a Percentage of Total Transfer Spending: 1948–1988 (Annual Averages in Percent for Indicated Periods)

| Period | (1)<br>Transfers<br>to People | (2)<br>Grants to State<br>and Local<br>Governments | (3)<br>Net<br>Interest | (4)<br>Subsidies | (5)<br>Other [a] |
|---|---|---|---|---|---|
| 1948–1959 | 51.5 | 13.3 | 21.1 | 6.6 | 7.5 |
| 1960–1969 | 54.6 | 19.7 | 14.5 | 7.3 | 3.9 |
| 1970–1979 | 59.9 | 24.1 | 11.1 | 3.5 | 1.4 |
| 1980–1988 | 59.3 | 16.4 | 18.7 | 3.8 | 1.8 |

[a] Primarily transfers abroad (i.e., foreign economic aid).

Source: *Economic Report of the President* (Washington, D.C., U.S. Government Printing Office, 1964, 1989).

the end of World War II, approximately 90 cents out of every dollar spent at the federal level has gone either to transfers or the nourishment of the military. Until we understand this fact, it is not possible to get a clear picture of what it is that our national government really does—and more important, in this age of mounting claims on the public purse, what it *cannot* do.

## The Structure of Federal Transfer Spending

Table 2-1 gives us a percentage breakdown of total federal transfer spending by major categories for the post-World War II decades, 1948 through 1988. To restate them, these categories are 1) transfers to people; 2) grants to state and local governments; 3) net interest on the federal debt; 4) subsidies to business; and 5) a catch-all, *Other* category, consisting primarily of grants to foreign governments.

Examination of these data in detail reveals several trends. The most important is that for the first three decades of this period, transfers to people grew in relative importance, rising from an annual average of 51.5% of *all* federal transfer spending to 59.9% in the 1970s. Only in the 1980s was there a small decline in the relative importance of this category. This overall trend should not come as a surprise; transferring income to people is, after all, the ultimate *raison d'etre* of the welfare state. Later we shall dig deeper into these numbers, to discover, first, which people are benefiting from such spending: are they the rich, the poor, or the in-between? And second, how do these people-directed transfers affect the distribution of income and the poverty level in the United States? We noted in chapter 1 that transfers played a significant role in bringing down the poverty index after 1965. But progress in reducing poverty practically ended in 1973; the poverty rate actually rose in subsequent years. Yet the data in table 2-1 display a continued growth in transfers to people during the 1970s. So we have a paradox, an increase in the poverty rate alongside continued growth in transfers to people. A total explanation for this paradox must wait until chapter 3, when we analyze the overall impact of transfers and taxes on income distribution and poverty. In this chapter we will concentrate on who benefits from transfer spending.

A second important trend involves federal grants to state and local governments. Until recently these were the second most important kind of transfer outlay coming from Washington. For the first three post-World War II decades, federal *grants-in-aid to state and local governments*, (as they are formally called) rose steadily, going from 13.3% of federal transfers in the 1948–1959 period to 24.1% in the 1970s. In parallel, state and local governments came to depend more and more upon the federal government for income. In 1948, they got 10.8% of their money from Washington; by 1979 this figure had more than doubled, reaching 22.7%. As we shall note subsequently, a significant portion of federal grants to the states and localities finances the parts of the federal welfare state structure that are administered locally.

This trend in federal grants to the states and local government was reversed sharply by the Reagan Administration. In the 1980s the percent of federal grant-in-aid transfers fell to an average of 16.4%; in the same period, federal money as a source of state and local government income dropped to 15.1%. Examination of detailed data on federal grants to the states and local communities reveals that the decline in the relative importance of this category of transfers came from major reductions in federal spending in three program areas.[2] The first of these is *revenue sharing*, the program of unrestricted grants to state and local governments.[3] Revenue sharing, which totaled $6.8 billion in 1980 and was the showpiece item in the Nixon Administration's much-publicized overhaul of the federal grants-in-aid structure, was phased out entirely under Reagan. Grants under the second and third categories, *labor training and services* and *housing and community services*, were cut back significantly between 1980 and 1988, the former by 52% and the latter by 25%.[4] During the Reagan years, transfer spending for *all* purposes grew by 81.9%, but in the grant-in-aid category by only 25.6%.[5]

Of special significance are the changes in this 41 year period in transfers in the form of interest on the public debt. During the first three periods shown in table 2-1, the net interest share of federal transfers steadily declined, going from 21.1% in 1948–1959 to 11.1% in the 1970s. The primary reason for this change was a drop in the ratio of the outstanding federal debt to the gross national product (GNP), a shrinkage that came about because in these years the GNP grew more rapidly than the federal debt. In 1948, the percentage ratio of outstanding federal debt to the GNP was 96.3%; by 1979 this ratio had dropped to 33%.[6]

The 1980s—the Reagan decade—saw a sharp reversal in this trend. For 1980–1988, interest on the debt jumped to an average of 18.7% of all federal transfers, displacing grants to the states and local governments as the second largest category of transfers. In 1988, net interest on the debt was $151.4 billion as compared to total grants-in-aid of $111.4 billion. The reasons for this trend reversal are easy to understand. First, it resulted from soaring federal deficits in the 1980s, a development that pushed the federal debt–GNP ratio to 53.5% by 1988. Second, long-term interest rates on federal obligations have failed to come down to the same degree as the overall drop in inflation in the 1980s, a development that has added to the costs of servicing the debt. In the 1970s, a period noted for double-digit inflation, the yield for U.S. Treasury securities of ten years duration averaged 7.5%, but in the 1980s this average jumped by 3.33 percentage points to 10.83%, even though the yield has come down in the last few years.[7]

What is one to make of this latest development? While the long-term effects are not fully clear, by no stretch of the imagination can it be described as healthy. In *The General Theory*, Keynes spoke in a hopeful way about the possible "euthanasia of the rentier," meaning an end to conditions in which individuals were able to get rich by exploiting the scarcity value of *real* capital. Keynes also raised doubts about the social utility of interest, saying that "Interest today rewards no genuine sacrifice, any more than does the rent of land."[8] Far from being euthanized, the 1980s have seen a resurgence of the rentier class. Interest as a source of personal income in the economy now exceeds all other forms of property income—profits from proprietorships and partnerships, rental income, and dividends—and ranks second behind wages and salaries as an income source.[9] It is to say the least curious, if not ominous, to note that aside from direct work (wages and salaries), the two most important sources of income in our society are now direct income transfers to people from government and interest on the public debt, both forms of income disassociated with producing anything. Further, it does not bode well for the future of the economy when the beneficiaries of what has become the second largest category of federal transfer spending are concentrated overwhelmingly in the upper ranges of the income scale. In 1976, the most recent year for which data are available, 29.8% of all bonds (public and private) were owned by the top 1% of all persons.[10]

The last two categories of transfer spending shown in table 2-1—Subsidies and Other—declined steadily in relative importance during the post-World War II era. In the first decade after the war, these two categories accounted for 14.1% of all transfers; by the 1980s this combined percentage had dropped to 5.2%, the largest relative decline coming in the Other category. This reflects the decline in the importance of American economic assistance to foreigners over the 40-year period. Subsidies to business have also shrunk, although the figure on direct transfers to business is misleading. Increasingly in recent years, business has been subsidized through the tax code rather than directly. We will discuss this aspect of the transfer system in chapter 3. However, subsequently in this chapter we shall have a detailed look at these subsidies and at other non-people-based transfer spending by the federal government.

## Income Transfers to People

From the foregoing overview of transfer spending, we can now shift our focus to the largest single category of income transfers—those going to people. Our objective is to pin down as precisely as possible who benefits directly from these transfers. In dollar terms, such transfers totaled $481.3 billion in 1988, accounting for 43.0% of *all* federal spending, including outlays for goods and services spending as well as for transfers. As far as the transfers alone are concerned, 1988 outlays for spending included in the five categories listed in table 2-1 totaled $737 billion, including administrative expenses. Transfers to people equaled 65.3% of this figure.

To discover ultimately who is on the receiving end of this vast river of money flowing out of Washington, we must first examine the category of transfers to people in terms of the major social welfare programs that fall under this broad umbrella. This examination will set the stage for reaching our primary objective: locating the beneficiaries of people-based transfer programs within the pattern of income distribution. In the final analysis, the redistribution of income and wealth is what the welfare state is all about. So what we want to discover is the ultimate impact of transfer spending on America's class structure.

In pursuing this analysis, we shall adhere to the format developed in chapter 1, a format in which transfer spending that fits the definition of the classic welfare state is distinguished from all other forms of transfer spending, including some transfer spending that goes to people and also spending arising from non-people-based income transfer programs. The latter totaled $255.7 billion in 1988, so even for non-people-oriented programs we are not talking about small sums. It is important not to lose sight of this fundamental distinction between transfers that fit into the classic welfare state category and all other types of transfers, because a major theme of this book is the explosion of all forms of transfer spending in this society far beyond the relatively modest boundaries set down in an earlier day when America's welfare state was invented. This explosion is a fact of life in the modern-day American economy. Later we shall examine the good and the bad of it in an attempt to understand how the giant federal transfer engine affects the economy's performance, both now and in the future.

Table 2-2 provides the statistical information to accomplish the first step in this line of analysis, namely to examine in detail the major social welfare spending programs that properly belong under the rubric of transfers to people. The source of these data is the highly detailed national income and product accounts published each July in the U.S. Department of Commerce's *Survey of Current Business*. It has been necessary, however, to make some adjustments to derive the figures shown in table 2-2.

There are two major adjustments, both of which are important to getting an accurate figure on federal transfers going to people.[11] The first stems from the fact that the federal government finances a significant portion of people-based income transfers are actually made by state and local governments. Some of the money spent under the designation of Grants-in-aid to State and Local Governments in the detailed accounts in the *Survey of Current Business* fits into this qualification. Hence an adjustment has to be made in the federal figures for grants-in-aid transfers to reflect this. Federal grants-in-aid finance parts of Medicaid, AFDC (Aid to Families with Dependent Children), some unemployment compensation, children's nutrition, and other forms of public assistance. These programs are administered by the states and cities, but depend upon a combination of federal plus state and local financing. In 1988 estimated income transfers to people that were paid by the states and cities but were actually financed by federal grants-in-aid totaled $43.3 billion.[12]

The second adjustment made in table 2-2 involves estimating the portion of federal government net interest outlays paid *directly* to people. The *Survey of Current Business* national income and product accounts do not provide this information, but it can be estimated from available data on the ownership of the federal debt. The portion of the total outstanding debt held by private individuals rather than corporations, banks, and other

**Table 2-2.  Federal Transfer Expenditures to People by Major Subcategories: 1988 (in Billions of Dollars and in Percent)**

| Category of Transfers | Dollar Total | Percent of Total Transfers of People |
|---|---|---|
| *Classic welfare state programs* | | |
| Social Insurance[a] | | |
| 1.  Social Security and Disability | $213.9 | |
| 2.  Unemployment compensation | 13.1 | |
| 3.  Medicare | 86.6 | |
| Subtotal | $313.6 | 65.2% |
| *Public Assistance* | | |
| 4.  AFDC | 9.3 | |
| 5.  Supplemental Security Income (SSI) | 10.7 | |
| 6.  Food Stamps | 11.2 | |
| 7.  Medicaid | 31.5 | |
| Subtotal | $62.7 | 13.0% |
| *Total for classic welfare state* | $376.3 | 78.2% |
| *Federal retirement programs* | | |
| 8.  Civil service | 28.6 | |
| 9.  Military | 19.5 | |
| 10.  Railroad | 6.7 | |
| Subtotal | $54.8 | 11.4% |
| *Other programs* | | |
| 11.  Veterans benefits | 15.1 | |
| 12.  Black lung | 1.5 | |
| 13.  Earned-income credit | 2.7 | |
| 14.  Miscellaneous[b] | 15.7 | |
| Subtotal | $35.0 | 7.3% |
| *Total for income assistance* | $466.1 | 96.8% |
| *Interest on public debt* | | |
| 15  Payable to persons | 15.2 | 3.2% |
| *Total transfers to people* | $481.3 | 100.0% |
| *Total federal outlays* | $1,118.3 | |
| *Transfers-to-people as a percent of federal outlays* | 43.0% | |

[a] Social Insurance and other totals do not include administrative expenses as in table 1-1.

[b] Payments to nonprofit institutions, aid to students, and medical services for retired military personnel and their dependents.

Source: U.S. Department of Commerce, *Survey of Current Business*, July, 1989.

financial institutions, as well as governments, is used to get this figure.[13] This proportion is surprisingly small; in 1988, just 71.3% of the total federal debt was held privately, and of this figure the percentage held by private persons was only 10%. Thus, it is estimated that of the $151.4 billion in interest paid to private or nongovernmental entities, only $15.2 billion went directly to individuals.[14] Indirectly, of course, individuals get a much larger share of the interest payments flowing from the federal government. They get this income as either owners or creditors of the corporations, banks, insurance companies, money market funds, and other private financial entities that own the federal debt. This indirect sum is difficult to estimate; however, it does not drop out of sight in our pursuit of the ultimate beneficiaries of federal transfers. Not at all. It shows up in the figures telling us what happens to all the non-people-based transfers undertaken by the federal government (table 2-7). These we discuss subsequently.

So let us now turn to an analysis of the data in table 2-2. What do these figures tell us about how the federal government distributed nearly one-half trillion dollars ($481.3 billion in 1988) in transfer income aimed at people?

The first general conclusion that we can draw from the data in table 2-2 is that transfer spending that falls under our rubric of classic welfare state programs accounts for a major proportion of all transfers flowing directly to people. In 1988 the percentage was 78.2%. Federal retirement programs —for civil service, military, and railroad workers—accounted for the next largest percent, 11.4%, followed by other programs at 7.3%, including aid to veterans. Last came interest on the public debt at 3.2%.

Second, it is clear that both overall and specifically within the classic welfare state category, most income transfer spending stems from the Social Insurance programs, namely Social Security, Unemployment Compensation, and Medicare. These Entitlement programs take the largest share of the classic welfare state dollar. In 1988, outlays under the Social Insurance category equaled 65.2% of all federal transfers to people, and 83.3% of those transfers to people falling directly under the classic welfare state designation.

The other side of this coin is that programs directed by design at the poor—the means-tested programs—account for only a small portion of the welfare state outlays. In 1988 Public Assistance Programs accounted for only 13.0% of all people-directed transfers and 16.7% of outlays that fit into the classic welfare state designation. These programs—AFDC, Supplemental Security Income (SSI), food stamps, and Medicaid—are the programs popularly associated in the public mind with "welfare." Statistically, the figures show that only a miniscule portion of America's welfare state spending is targeted *by design* to the nation's poor. Since all programs falling under the Public Assistance classification are means tested—one has to be a low-income person or in a low-income family to qualify—these are the federal programs that aim directly at the poor. Most Americans, if they think about the matter at all, no doubt not only believe that the poor are the beneficiaries of most of the money the federal government gives away, but also that astronomically huge sums are involved. Neither belief is correct.

Although it is statistically correct that (in 1988) only 13.0% of all people-based transfer spending was targeted at the poor, it does not follow that this figure is an accurate representation of the extent to which poor or lower-income Americans benefit from federal transfer spending. This conclusion is too simplistic for two reasons. The first is that the poor, or at least some of the poor, also qualify for benefits under other federal transfer programs to people. There is no sharp line of demarcation, in other words, between Public Assistance and Social Insurance (and all other people-based transfer programs), with Public Assistance presumably going to the poor and the rest to the nonpoor. It doesn't work that way. Second, some persons and some families who *do not* fall below the poverty line get some of the public assistance money flowing out of Washington, one reason being the wide variation that exists between state programs. Eligibility and size of benefits, it should not be forgotten, are determined primarily at the state and local level. The problem at this point, then, is to determine what proportion of all federal people-based transfer spending—$481.3 billion in 1988—actually goes to persons, households, and families who fall below the poverty level.

## The 1988 Census Bureau Study

In 1988 the Bureau of the Census, a part of the U.S. Department of Commerce, published the results of the most massive study ever undertaken by the federal government to measure the effect of both transfers and taxes on the distribution of income and the prevalence of poverty in the nation.[15] This study, which is of an experimental nature, but which the Census Bureau intends to continue, covered only a single year, 1986. It was designed to show the distribution of income among households using a variety of definitions for income after taking into account both cash and in-kind transfers as well as federal plus state and local taxes. We shall draw upon the findings in this study to complete the analysis of how poverty levels are affected by the federal transfer spending documented in table 2-2, and also to examine the distribution of transfer spending in terms of America's class structure. The Census Bureau data and findings are framed primarily in terms of households (households are not the same as families), but the data can be drawn upon to forge reliable answers to both the foregoing questions, namely the impact of income transfers on poverty and their impact on America's class structure (income distribution).

We start with the data in table 2-3. This table contains distributional data for 1986 on money income for households arrayed by fifths, or quintiles, the range being from the lowest fifth of all households to the top fifth. In 1986, there were 89,479 million households in the American economy; in the same year there were 64,491 million families in the nation. By Census Bureau standards, a *household* consists of all persons who occupy a housing unit, the latter being a house, and apartment, a single room, or group of rooms intended as separate living quarters. A *family*, on the other hand, is a group of two or more persons related by birth, marriage, or adoption who reside together. There are more households than families, primarily because of one-person households. In 1986 there were on average 1.4 households per family, as compared to a ratio of 1.2 in 1967.[16] The increase in the ratio of households to families over this period reflects the growth in single-person households.

Table 2-3 contains two different kinds of distributional data. The first set of distributional data shows the percentage distribution of total money income to households for two basic categories of income. These are 1) money income *before* taxes from *all* sources, including cash transfer income from government, and 2) the total of money income received by households once government cash transfers are excluded. The latter gives us the distribution of money income that results from the free play of market forces. In the table, this distribution is labeled *market-derived income*. The second set of distributional data found in the table shows the mean, or average, income for the two foregoing income categories pertaining to each household income fifth, or quintile. Taken together, these two sets of distributional data provide an extremely clear picture of the impact that government income transfer spending has on the market-determined distribution of income to households. Transfer spending changes in a significant manner the pattern of income distribution that would prevail in the economy in the absence of income transfers.

Let us explore more fully the findings in table 2-3. Before transfers, the mean or average income of households in the top income bracket—the top fifth—was about 47 times greater than the average per household in the bottom bracket—$69,691 vs. $1493. Transfers change this significantly; after cash transfers are factored into the picture, the top bracket income average was only 12 times larger than the lower bracket figure—$70,860

**Table 2-3. Distribution of Measures of Money Income to Households by Income Quintiles: 1986**

| Types of Income | Lower Fifth | Second Fifth | Third Fifth | Fourth Fifth | Top Fifth | Index of Concentration[a] |
|---|---|---|---|---|---|---|
| 1. Money income before taxes[b] | $105.7 | $266.5 | $450.3 | $661.8 | $1,268.1 | — |
| 2. Distribution of total income | 3.8% | 9.7% | 16.4% | 24.0% | 46.1% | .420 |
| 3. Mean for total income | $5,904 | $14,890 | $25,160 | $36,981 | $70,860 | — |
| 4. Market-derived income[c] | $26.7 | $207.5 | $404.2 | $647.8 | $1,247.2 | — |
| 5. Distribution of marker-derived income | 1.1% | 8.2% | 16.0% | 25.6% | 49.2% | .473 |
| 6. Mean for market-derived income | $1,493 | $11,596 | $22,587 | $36,199 | $69,691 | — |

[a] Gini index.
[b] All money income before taxes plus cash transfers from governments, but excluding capital gains, in billions of dollars.
[c] All money income less government transfers in billions of dollars.

Source: U.S. Department of Commerce, Bureau of the Census, Consumer Income, P-60, *Measuring the Effect of Benefits and Taxes on Income and Poverty: 1986.*

compared to $5,904. Money income becomes less concentrated because of transfers. The Gini coefficient, an index which measures the degree of inequality, falls from .473 to .420 because of transfers (a fall in this index shows less inequality).[17] It is interesting to note that transfers per se did not significantly change the market-derived income shares (or averages) for the middle three fifths of households. Before transfers, the middle three fifths got 49.8% of money income, and after transfers they got 50.1%.

The picture is not quite as rosy as these statistics might suggest. They do show that the pattern of income transfer spending is relatively progressive, that is, proportionately more of transfer outlays are directed at lower-income groups than at upper-income groups. This is as it should be if welfare state spending is to succeed in its objective of eliminating want. But there is still a long way to go. Before transfers, money income in the lowest bracket averaged only 15.7% of the poverty threshold income level for households ($9531 in 1986). After transfers, this percentage increases to 61.9%. This is an improvement, but money income on the average in the lowest fifth of households still falls far short of the poverty level for households in the United States. In 1986 there were 34.5 million persons living in the 17.9 million households found in the bottom range of the quintile-based distribution scale. This means that almost all the persons living in bottom-fifth households in 1986 were below the poverty level. Census Bureau poverty statistics showed that 32.4 million persons lived below the "official" poverty threshold in 1986; for all persons, the poverty rate was 12.0% in that year.[18] In addition, consider the following. Prior to transfers, one fifth of the households got almost one half—49.2%, to be exact—of income derived from the market. After transfers, the share of the top fifth was less, but not greatly less, having fallen to 46.1%. Household income distribution is still markedly unequal in the United States.

The foregoing discussion takes us part of the way, but not the whole way, toward solving the puzzle of how much of federal people-based income transfers actually go to the poor. Other data contained in the 1986 Census Bureau study help us to reach this objective. Table 2-4 is constructed from data found in the Census Bureau study to show the portion of total money income transfers and total income transfers in kind (as calculated by the Census Bureau) going to households in each quintile. These proportions (or percentages) are then applied to the figure from table 2-2 to construct table 2-5, in which we show the distribution to households of cash transfers, in-kind transfers, and total transfers by fifths (quintiles). These data give us one of the pictures we are seeking—the distribution of federal transfer spending in terms of the percentage share of total transfers going to households in each fifth (quintile).

Table 2-4. Distribution of Cash and In-Kind Transfers to Households by Income Quintiles: 1986 (in Percent)

| Form of Transfer | Lower Fifth | Second Fifth | Third Fifth | Fourth Fifth | Top Fifth | Total |
|---|---|---|---|---|---|---|
| Cash transfers | 36.1 | 26.9 | 21.1 | 6.4 | 9.5 | 100.0 |
| In-kind transfers | 26.1 | 28.2 | 21.2 | 12.9 | 11.6 | 100.0 |

Source: U.S. Department of Commerce, Bureau of the Census, Consumer Income, P-60, *Measuring the Effect of Benefits and Taxes on Income and Poverty, 1986.*

Table 2-5. Distribution of Cash and In-Kind Transfers and Total Transfers to Households by Income Quintiles: 1986 (in Billions of Dollars and in Percent)

| Form of Transfer | Lower Fifth | Second Fifth | Third Fifth | Fourth Fifth | Top Fifth | Total |
|---|---|---|---|---|---|---|
| Cash Transfers [a] | | | | | | |
| Dollars (billions) | $97.0 | $72.3 | $56.7 | $17.2 | $25.5 | $268.8 |
| Percent | 36.1% | 26.9% | 21.1% | 6.4% | 9.5% | 100.0% |
| In-kind transfers [b] | | | | | | |
| Dollars (billions) | $33.7 | $36.5 | $27.4 | $16.7 | $15.0 | $129.3 |
| Percent | 26.1% | 28.2% | 21.2% | 12.9% | 11.6% | 100.0% |
| Total transfers [c] | | | | | | |
| Dollars (billions) | $130.7 | $108.8 | $84.1 | $33.9 | $40.5 | $398.1 |
| Percent | 32.8% | 27.3% | 21.1% | 8.5% | 10.2% | 100.0% |

[a] Includes Social Security, unemployment insurance, AFDC payments, SSI, railroad retirement, and payments to veterans.

[b] Includes Medicare, Medicaid, and food stamps.

[c] Total income transfers covered by data in this table encompass 82.7% of all federal transfers to people.

Source: U.S. Department of Commerce, Bureau of the Census, Consumer Income, P-60, *Measuring the Effect of Benefits and Taxes on Income and Poverty, 1986.*

Return for a moment to table 2-4. The table shows that slightly more than one third (36.1%) of cash transfers go to the households at the bottom of the scale. The remaining transfers are spread in a rough, progressive fashion over the other four fifths of the households, except that the top fifth gets a higher proportion of total transfers (9.5%) than the quintile immediately below (6.4% to the fourth fifth). If we tentatively consider the lower fifth of households as poor and near-poor, the middle three fifths as middle class, and the top fifth as upper class or affluent, the distribution of cash transfers roughly corresponds with the idea advanced the introduction to this book—namely, that we have in America a three-tiered welfare state. According to this breakdown, the bottom tier get 36.1% of cash transfers, the middle tier 54.4%, and the upper tier 9.5%. Roughly the same pattern prevails for in-kind transfers, save that they are less skewed toward households on the bottom. For in-kind transfers, in 1968 the bottom tier got 26.1% of the total, the middle tier 62.3%, and the upper tier 11.6%. Given the basic structure of classic welfare state spending in this country, these results are not surprising. As pointed out earlier, the overwhelming proportion of people-based transfers fall under the Social Insurance category, the beneficiaries of which are to be found predominantly outside the ranks of the poor.

Table 2-5 sums up our findings to this point, showing both the distribution in dollars (billions of dollars) and in percent to each fifth (or quintile) of households of nearly all of the $476.6 billion in transfers directed toward people, as shown in table 2-2[19]. At this point, no attempt is made to allocate to household quintiles the $48.1 billion in federal Civil Service and military retirement income or the balance of $19.9 billion under the Other Programs heading. The reason is that the precise location of the recipients of these transfers within the household array by quintiles is not known. The same may be said for the $15.2 billion falling under the Interest on the Public Debt category. Persons getting transfer income in these forms—i.e., retired civil servants, military personnel, and owners of U.S. government bonds—are most likely to be found in the upper-income ranges. Thus, if these sums had been included in table 2-5, the pattern of dollar and percentage distribution probably would have been skewed slightly more toward households at the top of the distributional scale.

In dollar volume, $130.7 billion, or 32.8% of the total, went to households in the bottom fifth of the distributional scale. Households in the middle three fifths collected $226.8 billion in benefits (56.9% of the total), while households at the top received $40.5 billion in transfers, or 10.2% of the total shown in table 2-5. Thus, the combined effect of cash and in-kind transfers follows the three-tier pattern, with some overall progression since the lower 20% of households got a larger share of transfer outlays and the upper 20% a smaller share. The middle tier (60% of households) got almost the same share of transfers (56.9%). There should be no doubt (table 2-3) that transfer spending that fits into the classic welfare state structure has played a key role in reducing poverty in this country. But there should be no doubt, either, that America's welfare state also works in a way, as columnist George Will once pointed out, that makes "the middle class purr contentedly."[20]

## Transfer Spending and Class in America

Americans do not particularly like to talk about social or economic classes, preferring mostly to think of themselves as "middle-class." Some years ago Robert Heilbroner, distinguished Professor of Economics at the New School for Social Research, wrote a significant article on this topic. In his article, "Middle-Class Myths, Middle-Class Realities," Professor Heilbroner pointed out that while surveys showed that four out of five Americans viewed themselves as belonging to the middle class, the reality is that, at best, only about 35% of the nation's population falls into this economic category.[21] In his analysis, Heilbroner arranged the population into four major classes, the poor and near-poor at the bottom (20%); the working class next up the ladder (40%), the middle class above them (35%); and finally at the top, the upper class and the truly rich (5%).

There is no precise and necessarily correct measure of economic class in America. Table 2-6 draws upon recent Census Bureau data to modify and update the picture of America's socioeconomic class structure developed by Professor Heilbroner some years earlier. In the table, which arrays families into six basic socioeconomic classes—the poor, near-poor, working class, middle class, upper middle class, and affluent and above—percentage data are given on the distribution of families and various types of income among these different classes. These data are for 1983. For reasons that are unclear, but that perhaps relate to budget stringency, the Census Bureau stopped developing this type of distributional data after 1983.

With reference to income, table 2-6 shows the distribution among these six socioeconomic classes of four types, namely, 1) wage and salary plus self-employed income; 2) income from the ownership of property; 3) income from Social Security, including railroad retirement income; and 4) income from public assistance. These data enable us to develop a reasonably clear picture of the distribution of market-based income and transfer-payment income among the six major socioeconomic classes depicted in the table. As such, the data add a further dimension to the question that we have been pursuing in this chapter, namely who are the people who benefit from the vast flood of transfer money pouring out of Washington and where are they to be found in the economic scheme of things.

Let us now return to the data in table 2-6. According to the table, 22.0%, slightly more than one fifth, of all families find themselves in the "poor" or

**Table 2-6.** Distribution by Socioeconomic Class of Families, Income, Property Income, Social Security Benefits, and Public Assistance: 1983 (in Percent)

| Income Range | All Families | Earned Income[a] | Property Income[b] | Social Security[c] | Public Assistance |
|---|---|---|---|---|---|
| 0–$9999 (Poor) | 15.9 | 1.5 | 1.5 | 15.8 | 68.8 |
| $10,000–12,499 (Near poor) | 6.1 | 1.7 | 1.4 | 10.9 | 9.0 |
| $12,500–29,999 (Working class) | 39.2 | 26.7 | 23.6 | 49.5 | 10.8 |
| $30,000–49,999 (Middle class) | 26.1 | 37.2 | 30.3 | 17.1 | |
| $50,000–74,999 (Upper middle class) | 9.1 | 20.4 | 21.3 | 5.1 | 11.4 |
| Over $75,000 (Affluent and beyond) | 3.5 | 12.5 | 21.9 | 1.6 | |
| Total | 100.0 | 100.0 | 100.0 | 100.0 | 100.0 |

[a] Includes wage and salary income and all self-employed income, farm and nonfarm.
[b] Dividends, interest, rent and royalty income, and income from trusts and estates.
[c] Including railroad retirement.

Source: U.S. Department of Commerce, Bureau of the Census, Consumer Income, P-60, *Money Income of Households, Families, and Persons in the United States*, 1983.

"near-poor" categories. But these families get only 3.2% of wage and salary plus self-employment income, and an even smaller share of property-based income, namely 2.9%. This is quite in line with the findings shown in table 2-3, wherein the lowest fifth of the nation's households got only 1.1% of market-based income in 1986. On the other hand, the two lowest income classes shown in table 2-6 received 26.7% of Social Security benefits, and an overwhelming proportion of Public Assistance, 77.8%. These figures cannot be compared directly to those in tables 2-4 or 2-5 (Distribution of Cash and In-Kind Transfers by Households), but in view of the fact that Public Assistance transfers account for only 13.0% of total transfers to people as compared to 65.2% for Social Insurance transfers (table 2-2), the findings in these tables generally reinforce one another.

The foregoing observation is underscored by the fact that the next two income classes—the working class and the middle class—represent slightly more than two thirds (65.3%) of all families, and also get about the same share of Social Security income (66.6%). In table 2-5, the middle three fifths of all households were seen to be getting 56.9% of all transfer income, both cash and in-kind. As far as market-based income is concerned, the 65.3% of families classified as either working class or middle class got a slightly smaller share of all wage, salary, and self-employed income (63.9%), and a significantly smaller share of property income (53.9%). As one would expect, property income is concentrated at the top; the 12.6% of the families falling in the upper middle class and affluent and above income classes received 43.2% of all property-based income, namely dividends, interest, rents and royalties, and income from trusts.

Let us sumarize briefly our basic findings to this point as to who benefits from federal transfer spending directed toward people in the American economy. Analysis of both household data from the 1986 Census Bureau study and family income data from earlier Census Bureau reports strongly shows that we do in fact have in America a three-tiered welfare state—one for the poor, one for the middle class, and one for the affluent and rich. With respect to direct income transfers, both cash and in-kind, the largest proportion by far goes to middle-income households and families. Household data show, for example, that the middle three fifths get 56.9% of all cash and in-kind transfers, the bottom fifth 32.8% and the top fifth 10.2% (table 2-5). Family income data give us approximately the same story, with the working and middle classes getting 59.9% of Social Security and Public Assistance income, the poor and near-poor receiving 33.8%, and the upper middle, affluent, and rich classes getting 6.3%. This, of course, is not the full picture. As we shall see in chapter 3, which deals with tax expenditures, much of the "welfare" in our society that is targeted toward the rich is generated through the tax system. Consequently, the welfare state structure overall is skewed even more strongly toward the middle and the top of the income ranges then these data on money income transfers to people indicate.

## Non-People-Based Transfer Spending

And what of the remaining transfer expenditures, those that do not go directly to people? The sums involved are not small; in 1988 they totaled $255.7 billion, which was 34.7% of all transfer spending and 22.9% of federal government outlays for all purposes.[22] Who are the beneficiaries of these transfers? A word of caution is in order here. The term *non-people-based* is to some extent a misnomer, since much of such spending eventually finds its way into the pockets of persons. But there is no easy and accurate way to identify these persons. Consequently, we have to be content largely with examining the types of programs, activities, and organizations that received the $255.7 billion spent by the federal government in 1988 under the broad rubric of non-people-based spending.

These data are found in table 2-7. Of the totals shown, it is unlikely that any but a tiny percentage reaches people in the lower income ranks. The largest share (53.3% or $136.2 billion) of non-people-based transfers goes for interest on the federal debt. Foreign holders of the federal debt got the largest part of interest outlays ($29.6 billion), followed by payments to state and local governments, commercial banks, insurance companies, corporations, and money market funds, in that order.

Grants to state and local governments, excluding grants that support people-based programs, got the second largest share of transfers shown in table 2-7. They totaled $72.2 billion in 1988, accounting for 28.2% percent of all such transfers. Within this category, the largest amount ($18.7 billion) went for income-supported welfare programs, so there is a presumption that some of this money was funneled through the state and local governments to the poor. Undoubtedly, too, administrative expenses absorbed parts of the total, but the precise amount cannot be determined. Of the Aid to Education category ($9.9 billion), approximately 68% went to elementary education, so here too, presumably, some poor children were among the beneficiaries. The second largest program under the grants category was transportation ($17.3 billion), of which 81% went for highways and 14% for mass transit.[23]

Subsidies to business (less the surplus from government enterprises) rank third in magnitude for the non-people-based transfer category. These

**Table 2-7.  Distribution of Non-People-Based Federal Transfer Expenditures by Category and Programs: 1988 (in Billions of Dollars and in Percent)**

| Category | Dollar Total | Percent of total |
|---|---|---|
| *Grants to state and local governments* | | |
| 1.  Income-supported welfare | $ 18.7 | 7.3% |
| 2.  Transportation | 17.3 | 6.8 |
| 3.  Aid to education | 9.9 | 3.9 |
| 4.  Housing and community service | 6.8 | 2.7 |
| 5.  Health and hospitals | 4.3 | 1.7 |
| 6.  Labor training | 2.8 | 1.1 |
| 7.  National defense and space | 2.5 | 1.0 |
| 8.  Natural resources | 1.6 | 0.6 |
| 9.  Government administration | 1.0 | 0.4 |
| 10.  Energy | 1.0 | 0.4 |
| 11.  Other[a] | 6.3 | 2.5 |
| Total Grants to state and local governments | $ 72.2 | 28.2% |
| *Net interest on the public debt*[b] | | |
| 1.  Commercial banks | 15.8 | 6.2 |
| 2.  Insurance companies | 9.1 | 3.6 |
| 3.  Money market funds | 1.0 | 0.4 |
| 4.  Corporations | 7.1 | 2.8 |
| 5.  State and local government | 25.6 | 10.0 |
| 6.  Foreign holders of debt | 29.6 | 11.6 |
| 7.  Other[c] | 47.9 | 18.7 |
| Total interest on the public debt | $136.2 | 53.3% |
| *Subsidies to business* | | |
| 1.  Agriculture | $ 24.2 | 9.5% |
| 2.  Housing | 12.4 | 4.8 |
| 3.  Transportation | 1.8 | 0.7 |
| 4.  Postal Service | 1.3 | 0.5 |
| Subtotal | $ 39.7 | 15.5% |
| Less: Surplus or government enterprise | 3.6 | 1.4 |
| Total subsidies to business | $ 36.1 | 14.1% |
| *International* | | |
| 1.  Foreign economic aid | $ 11.1 | 4.3% |
| *Total non-people-based transfers* | $255.7 | 100.0% |

[a] Includes civilian society, veterans aid, recreation, agriculture, and economic development.
[b] Excludes interest paid directly to persons.
[c] Includes savings and loan associations, credit unions, nonprofit institutions, mutual savings banks, and corporate pension trust funds.
Totals are rounded.

Sources: U.S. Department of Commerce, *Survey of Current Business*, July, 1989; *Economic Report of the President*, 1989.

transfers before subtracting the surplus equaled $39.7 billion in 1988, which was 15.5% of all transfers shown in table 2-2. Agriculture ($24.2 billion) and housing ($12.4 billion) got the lion's share of these transfers; their combined total is 92% of all subsidies to business. Here again, however, caution is in order. These figures by no means tell the full story of the extent to which the federal government subsidizes business. Most business subsidies work through the tax system, not by direct grants. So to complete this part of our picture, we shall have to wait until we have examined in chapter 3 the phenomenon that has come to be known as tax expenditures. Finally, foreign economic aid, a dwindling category, equaled $11.1 billion, or 4.3% of all non-people-based transfers in 1988. This was a mere 0.6% of all transfer outlays.

## Federal Transfers and the National Income

In concluding this chapter, there is yet another useful way in which we can look at how the federal government through transfer spending affects the income that people earn and ultimately get. This is by examining the relationship between total transfer spending by the national government and the national income. Why the national income? The reason is that the national income is the best single measure of the income people get from the market by virtue of their ownership of the economic resources that enter into the production of useful goods and services. These resources are the familiar economic triad of labor, land, and capital, without which production would not be possible. GNP is perhaps the best-known measure of overall economic activity, but it is a measure of the value of the national output. For our purposes, national income is better because it actually measures the income earned by persons who participate in production, either directly because they work for a living or indirectly because they own property—land and capital—that yields them an income. In short, national income is a measure of the total of wages, rents, interest income, and profits that people receive during any income period.

At this point, a caveat is in order about the matter of the ownership or resources that yield income through the market, and also about the use of the word *earned* in connection with such income. As defined above, *national income* is essentially a technical measure that simply sums up the amount of income in the forms indicated—wages, rents, interest, profits—paid out in a production period (normally a year) to those who own the resources. It does not tell us *anything* about the distribution of that ownership, save, of course, for human labor. Because we are a non-slave-owning society, labor income is distributed to those who perform the labor. But the distribution of income from land and capital depends upon those who own the land and capital; national income statistics per se cannot, and do not, tell us anything about this distribution. National income statistics merely reflect the valuation that the market places on the services contributed by capital and labor to the process of production. The income generated in this fashion goes to those who own the resources. The matter of how resource ownership is distributed, like the matter of the general distribution of wealth, is an important but different economic question than the one we are discussing here.

This brings us naturally to the word *earned* as it is commonly used in discussions about the national income and its breakdown into wages, rents, interest, and profits. In a technical, economic sense, *earned* as used above merely refers to the fact that the market will, if left to its own devices, allocate income to whoever owns a resource (capital, land, or labor) on the basis of the market's judgment of the worth of the services of that resource in production. This is simply the way that economists view the matter in the relatively simplified models they construct of how the economic system operates at this level. This market-based distributional structure *does not* in any way tell us whether a person getting income from the resources— especially property resources—that he or she owns really "deserves" that income in a deeper philosophical sense. In the practice of economic accounting at the national level, a Rockefeller, for example, may "earn" through the market millions of dollars in any one year without raising a finger in labor simply because he was fortunate enough to inherit vast amounts of property whose services are useful in the production of goods and services. It is unfortunate, perhaps, that the term *earned* is used in the context of the split of the national income figure among wages, rents, interest, and profit, because it carries the connotation that the income so obtained is thereby deserved in a more basic, philosophic sense. This is far from the truth.

The foregoing caveat aside, let us return to the matter at hand, namely how the total of federal transfer spending in relation to the national income has evolved over time. This relationship is useful because by comparing the size of the national income to transfer outlays, we get yet another way of seeing statistically the role that the federal government plays in rearranging income "earned" through private production and the market process by the mechanism of transfer spending. Early in this chapter (table 2-1), we saw that approximately two thirds of what the national government does consists of rearranging incomes. This was within the context of the government itself in terms of what it does. Now by linking transfers to the national

Table 2-8.   The National Income and Federal Transfer Expenditures: Selected Years, 1929–1989 (in Billions of Current Dollars and in Percent)

| Year | National Income | Transfer Expenditures[a] | Transfers as a Percent of National Income | Observations |
|------|-----------------|--------------------------|-------------------------------------------|--------------|
| 1929 | $ 84.7  | $ 1.2  | 1.4%  | Boom depression |
| 1933 | 39.4    | 1.8    | 4.6   | |
| 1939 | 71.2    | 3.8    | 5.3   | |
| 1945 | 181.6   | 9.9    | 5.5   | End of World War II |
| 1950 | 239.8   | 22.1   | 9.2   | Eisenhower Era |
| 1955 | 336.3   | 23.7   | 7.1   | |
| 1960 | 424.9   | 39.5   | 9.3   | Kennedy Era |
| 1965 | 585.2   | 70.9   | 12.1  | Great Society begins |
| 1970 | 832.6   | 109.0  | 13.1  | |
| 1975 | 1289.1  | 235.0  | 18.2  | Transfer explosion |
| 1980 | 2203.5  | 407.0  | 18.5  | |
| 1983 | 2719.5  | 552.4  | 20.3  | Reagan Revolution |
| 1986 | 3412.6  | 668.3  | 19.6  | |
| 1989 | 4265.0  | 792.6  | 18.5  | Bush Presidency |

[a] Includes administrative expenditures.

Source: *Economic Report of the President*, 1990; *Current Economic Indicators*, latest issues.

income, we can get some feel for the importance of these activities within the context of the economy as a whole.

The figures that tell this story are found in table 2-8. This table shows, for selected years from 1929 to 1989, the current dollar value of the national income, *all* federal transfer outlays, and the latter calculated as a percent of the former. It is the percentage figures that tell the interesting story.

In 1929, the eve of the economy's plunge into the Great Depression, transfer spending was a mere 1.4% of the national income. At this time, of course, the concept of the modern welfare state was unknown. At the depth of the depression (1933), transfers in relation to the national income jumped to 4.6%, reflecting primarily the emergency relief measures of the first year of the New Deal. During the depression years the percentage rose steadily, reaching a level of 5.3% of the national income by 1939. This happened because of the formal institutionalization of the welfare state machinery in the 1930s through Social Security and related programs. In the first two decades after the end of World War II, transfer spending grew modestly relative to the national income, reaching 9.3% of the income figure by 1960. For the most part this upward shift came about because of the broadening of the coverage of the Social Security Act and the improvement of benefits for persons covered by the legislation. In 1965 the Great Society came into the picture, which through Medicare, Medicaid, and other legislation led to the transfer explosion of the 1970s. In 1983, a year of recovery from the deep 1981–1982 recession, transfer spending reached a high watermark for the post-World War II era, equaling 20.3% of the national income. Since then and under the influence of the Reagan Revolution, the topic of chapter 4, the percentage figure has dropped back to 18.5%.

So what are we to make of these data, other than that they show a relatively steady upward trend in transfer spending calculated as a percent of the national income? What these data do is to give us a rough handle, an approximate but useful measure of the extent to which the national government involves itself in the redistribution of income that comes from production and earnings in private markets. In 1929, to illustrate, only $1.40 for every $100 was rearranged, so to speak, by deliberate action on the part of the federal government. The underlying assumption here is that the intent of transfer spending is, for better or for worse, to redistribute income. Otherwise such spending has no particular point, even with reference to subsidies to business. Look what has happened: by 1983, approximately $20 out of every $100 earned through the marketplace was subject to the redistributional reach of the national government. Here one must proceed quite cautiously; this fact is not in and of itself necessarily good, or necessarily bad, but basically represents what is going on. Moreover, the figure does mean that every transfer dollar spent involves taxing Peter and paying Paul—sometimes Peter both pays the taxes and gets the benefits. What it does show statistically is the magnitude on the stage of the national economy of the income redistribution role being played by the federal government.

## Some Summary Comments

We began this chapter by exploring statistics that tell us what the federal government does with all the money it spends annually. We discovered, first, that approximately two thirds of this spending is redistributional by nature—transfer spending, in other words. Then we followed the trail of these statistics through their impact on people, on households, on families, and on class structure in America. In this journey we were able to discover how the vast river of transfer money flowing out of Washington affects poverty and the distribution of income between the rich, the poor, and the middle classes. We saw, too, that the relatively simple schema for a welfare state put into place during the New Deal of the 1930s has evolved into an exceedingly complex structure, touching the economic life of nearly every family in America. Finally, our statistical trail brought us up against the fact that roughly one dollar out of every five earned is in some way touched by the vast redistributional machinery of the federal government.

But this is far from the whole story. What we have explored in this chapter is the spending side of the redistributional activities of our national government. There remains the other side, the taxing side. Far more than most people realize, the tax system of the federal government has become a part of this mechanism. Federal taxes are not designed simply to raise money for the national government. They are designed to do many other things, some good, some bad, but nearly all of which have a redistributional impact. So until we explore these matters, our picture of the real nature of America's welfare state and how it works is woefully incomplete. It is to this task we now turn in chapter 3.

## Notes

1. Memo by David A. Stockman and Jack Kemp to President-elect Ronald Reagan, "Avoiding a GOP Economic Dunkirk." See *The Wall Street Journal*, Friday, December 12, 1980, p. 22.

2. U.S. Department of Commerce, *Survey of Current Business*, July issues, 1989, 1984.

3. Grants-in-aid transfers directed to specific programs or objectives are called *categorical*, and state and local governments must use the funds for the designated purposes. The Nixon-inspired revenue sharing grants were not categorical; hence, they could be used for any purpose by state and local governments.

4. U.S. Department of Commerce, *Survey of Current Business*, *op. cit.*

5. *Ibid.*

6. *Economic Report of the President* (Washington, D.C., U.S. Government Printing Office, 1989), pp. 342, 397.

7. *Ibid.*, p. 390.

8. John Maynard Keynes, *The General Theory of Employment, Interest, and Money* (New York, Harcourt, Brace & World, 1962), p. 376.

9. *Economic Report of the President* (Washington, D.C., U.S. Government Printing Office, 1990), p. 323.

10. *Statistical Abstract of the United States* (Washington, D.C., U.S. Government Printing Office, 1983), p. 481.

11. The adjustments are made by using data from the Social Security Administration's *Statistical Supplement* to the *Social Security Bulletin*, which shows the proportion of AFDC and other forms of public assistance paid by the states and the proportion paid by the federal government.

12. U.S. Department of Commerce, *Survey of Current Business*, July, 1989, pp. 62, 64.

13. *Economic Report of the President*, 1990, *op. cit.*, p. 394.

14. *Ibid.*

15. U.S. Department of Commerce, Bureau of the Census, *Measuring the Effect of Benefits and Taxes on Income and Poverty: 1986* (Washington, D.C., U.S. Government Printing Office, 1988).

16. U.S. Department of Commerce, Bureau of the Census, Current Population Reports, P-60, *Money Income of Households, Families, and Persons in the United States: 1987* (Washington D.C., U.S. Government Printing Office, 1988), pp. 3, 10.

17. The Gini coefficient or index is a statistical measure of income inequality. Its value ranges from 1 to 0; an *increase* in its value—a move in the index toward 1—indicates an increase in income inequality.

18. U.S. Department of Commerce, Bureau of the Census, Current Population Reports, P-60, *Poverty in the United States: 1987*, (Washington, D.C., U.S. Government Printing Office, 1988), p. 7.

19. The data in table 2–5 account for 83.5% of all federal transfers to people.

20. George Will, *Washington Post*, September 24, 1989, p. 37. Mr. Will is a member of the *Washington Post* Writer's Group.

21. Robert L. Heilbroner, "Middle-Class Myths, Middle-Class Realities," *The Atlantic monthly*, October, 1976, Vol. 238, No. 4, pp. 37–42.

22. The totals pertain to all on-budget outlays in the National Income and Product Accounts framework.

23. U.S. Department of Commerce, *Survey of Current Business*, July, 1987, p. 64.

# 3  TAX EXPENDITURES: THE HIDDEN TRANSFERS

The picture being drawn of the redistributional role of the national government will not be complete until we have described and analyzed the phenomenon of *tax expenditures*, aptly described as *hidden transfers*. This strange-sounding phrase and the concept that lies behind it was developed by the late Stanley S. Surrey, former Assistant Secretary of the Treasury, in the waning days of Lyndon Johnson's administration. Even though tax expenditures are a concept not fully or uncritically accepted by economists and fiscal experts, the concept is now enshrined in the law. Through it we obtain further insight into the extent to which governmental power is being used to determine who gets what in the way of money income in our society. Thus, to paint the full picture of America's welfare state and how it works, we need to examine tax expenditures and their impact on the distribution of income.

Even though the notion of a tax expenditure appears to be an oxymoron, there is a basic logic to the concept. Moreover, the concept is not difficult to understand. As we saw in the last chapter, the federal government is deeply involved in providing income directly or indirectly (in cash or in kind) to persons, business firms, nonprofit institutions, and even other governments in our society. It does this through the mechanism of transfer payments. We

57

must also recognize, however, that the way in which people and business firms are treated for tax purposes gives the national government enormous power over the amount of money income that people finally get and keep. Paying taxes leaves all persons and business firms with less money in their pockets—less take-home money, as is sometimes said. This elementary fact would be of no great consequence if in its taxing policies the federal government treated everyone equally. In this context, *equally* does not mean that every person pays the same amount of taxes. It means something quite different, namely that after people and business firms pay their taxes, they are left in the same economic position *relative* to each other as they were before paying taxes. If such were the case, the tax system would be neutral as far as the distribution of income is concerned.[1] Sometimes this idea is described as the principle of equal treatment for persons in like circumstances, a principle easy to state but hard to implement.

The foregoing discussion begins to tell us what tax expenditures are all about. Basically, they bear on the fact that the tax system is not neutral, that people in like circumstances are not treated equally in the way they are taxed. Tax expenditures concern the extent to which the tax system is used as a deliberate instrument to change the distribution of money income that would prevail if taxes truly were neutral. The concept should not be confused with the fact that tax revenue is used to finance transfer spending that alters money income distribution; it is more subtle and more far-reaching than that. Tax expenditures concern the fact that *after* paying taxes, persons or business firms who were in like circumstances before paying taxes find their economic situation changed relative to one another. This is a different matter than the fact that some of the taxes we pay may go to finance transfer spending.

Unlike transfer spending, for which there is no official definition in the statutes, tax expenditures are defined by law. In the 1974 Congressional Budget Act, tax expenditures are identified as "....those revenue losses attributable to provisions of the federal tax laws which allow a special exclusion, exemption, or deduction from gross income, or which provide a special credit, a preferential rate of tax, or a deferral of tax liability."[2] In plain English, this means that some people get breaks in determining either their income for tax purposes or their taxes that other people do not get. To take an extreme but simple example, we have, on the one hand, a senior citizen with $10,000 in income from Social Security and $10,000 in interest income from municipal or state bonds, and on the other, a worker with a $20,000 income from a factory job. They are in like circumstances economically speaking, because both have a total income of $20,000. But all the income received by the senior citizen is exempt from federal income taxation, whereas at least a part of the worker's income after allowable deductions and adjustments may be taxable. Tax revenue is lost to the federal government because of the special treatment accorded the kind of income the senior citizen gets as compared to the kind the worker gets. To be precise, tax expenditures equal the tax revenue that the federal government *does not get* because special or selective tax relief is extended to some persons and business firms.

Why are these losses called expenditures? Literally, they are not expenditures—that is, outlays of money by the government—but their economic effect is similar to payments actually made by the government. If the federal government pays out money to someone through transfer spending, that person's income is increased. In similar fashion, if the federal government exempts some or all of a person's income from taxation, that individual's usable or spendable income is greater than what it would have been in the absence of any favored tax treatment. The income position of the individual or business is changed in either case, but when tax expenditures are involved, the change comes about through a reduction in liabilities rather than through an increase in transfer payments.

What lies behind this concept is the assumption that the "normal" objective of the tax system is to raise revenue for the government. Whenever an individual, a group of individuals, or some business firms get special treatment so that their taxes are less than they would have been in the absence of the special treatment, we have a tax expenditure. In its primer on tax expenditures, the U.S. General Accounting Office (GAO) summarized the concept as follows:

> The tax expenditure concept is based upon the idea that an income tax system can be divided into two parts. One part contains just the rules that are necessary to carry out the revenue-raising function of a tax on income; rules prescribing how net income is to be measured, what the tax unit is, what tax rates apply, and so forth. The other part contains exceptions to these rules that reduce some people's incomes, but not others'. *These exceptions have the same effect as Government payments to favored taxpayers.* By identifying these provisions as tax expenditures, officials are better able to determine the total amount of government effort or influence in a program area.[3]

Not only are tax expenditures defined by law, but the 1974 Budget Act also required that both the President and the Congressional Budget Office prepare each year a list of tax expenditures with estimates of their costs to the federal government in revenue lost. Further, the Joint Committee on

Taxation now publishes annually five-year projections of tax expenditures for use by the two major revenue committees of the Congress.[4] In making this report, the Joint Committee on Taxation (JCT) adheres to the GAO structure described in the previous paragraph, namely distinguishing between the "normal" and "exceptional" features of the income tax system.

Aside from the basic fact that the economic effect of tax expenditures differs little from transfer payments, there are two other important reasons why it is desirable to have a full accounting of this side of the fiscal actions by the federal government. Prior to the 1974 Budget Act, tax benefits that significantly affected the income position of particular groups often originated in administrative rulings by the Internal Revenue Service, rulings that were not necessarily mandated directly or indirectly by the Congress. Thus, they escaped scrutiny by the Congress, something that might not have happened if they were line items in the budget. If, however, they are built into the budget and viewed like expenditures, even though cast in the language of the tax system, they should become a part of the expenditure control that is a normal part of the congressional budgetary process. Such is the theory. It is by no means clear, however, that the existence of a tax expenditure budget always results in closer congressional control and scrutiny over the tax expenditure side of the federal government's ledger.

A second important reason for the construction of a tax expenditure budget is that by means of such a budget it is possible, in principle, at least to determine whether or not a particular social or economic objective might not be achieved more efficiently and more equitably through a direct transfer payment rather than by special or favored tax treatment for some persons, groups, or business firms. Politically, the advantage of tax expenditures is that their income distribution effects are hidden from view, which is not normally the case with transfer outlays. Using the federal tax system to attain social or economic objectives that many people deem "good" —home ownership, for example—is an old story in the United States. It is not necessarily wrong that the tax system is used for social engineering, but in a democracy it is healthy and desirable that citizens know the extent to which this is being done. A tax expenditure budget supplies this information. Aside from some major changes in tax expenditures as a result of the Tax Reform Act of 1986 (discussed subsequently), there is no strong evidence that through the tax expenditure budget the Congress is continually examining whether or not some of the objectives sought through tax relief could be attained more fairly and efficiently through transfer spending. The Congress should do this, but until the public is much more aware than it now is of the existence of tax expenditures and demands such action, it is unlikely to happen.[5]

## A Short History of Tax Expenditures

Even though the concept of tax expenditures was developed relatively recently, the use of the tax code to subsidize particular activities is as old as the first income tax law enacted after adoption of the Sixteenth Amendment to the Constitution. The 1913 income tax law allowed deductions for mortgage interest and state and local taxes on homes owned by taxpayers, as well as deductions for some nonbusiness state and local taxes. These deductions have remained essentially unchanged ever since, resisting all efforts to eliminate or modify them. Charitable contributions, another major tax expenditure for individuals, were made a deductible item by the 1917 Revenue Act. The notion of accelerated depreciation was introduced into the tax code in 1946.

From 1967, when the first comprehensive listing was compiled, until 1986, tax expenditures grew steadily both in absolute amount and as a percentage of the GNP. The first break in this trend came in the 1987 fiscal year, when the effects of the Tax Reform Act of 1986 began to be felt. This Act and its impact on tax expenditures are discussed in the next section. In 1967, the first year for which detailed data are available, tax expenditures for corporations and individuals combined totaled $36.6 billion, a figure equal to 4.5% of the 1967 GNP and 23.9% of all federal revenues. There were 50 different types of tax expenditures then.

Table 3-1 traces the growth of tax expenditures as a percent both of the GNP and of total federal revenues since 1967. These percentages peaked in fiscal years 1986 and 1987. In 1986, tax expenditures totaled $424.5 billion, reaching 10.0% of the GNP and 52.1% of federal revenues. In 1987 the percentages were 10.0% and 50.2%, more than double what they were in 1967. Thereafter, they dropped sharply because of the elimination of some major types of tax expenditures in the Tax Reform Act of 1986. As the discussion in the next section will show, changes in the corporation income tax account for the greater proportion of the decline shown. Figures 3-1 and 3-2 traces these changes graphically. The dramatic nature of the changes wrought in tax expenditures by the 1986 law is also evident in these charts.

A close look at figure 3-1 shows that from 1967 to 1979 (13 years), tax expenditures measured as a percent of all federal revenues grew from 23.9% of federal revenues to 30.5% in 1979. Table 3-2 shows a similar pattern for tax expenditures relative to the GNP. As compared to the years from 1980 through 1988, this growth was relatively moderate. For the whole of the 13-year period (1967–1979) tax expenditures averaged 27.1% of federal revenues and 5.2% of the nation's GNP. The onset of the 1980s saw, however, a sharp increase in tax expenditures, both as a percent of federal

Table 3-1.    Tax Expenditures in Dollars and as a Percent of GNP and Federal Revenues: 1967–1990 (in Billions of Dollars and in Percent)

| Year[a] | Dollar Amounts | Percent of GNP | Percent of Federal Revenues |
|---|---|---|---|
| 1967 | $ 36.6 | 4.5% | 23.9% |
| 1968 | 44.1 | 4.9 | 24.9 |
| 1969 | 46.6 | 4.8 | 23.3 |
| 1970 | 43.9 | 4.3 | 22.5 |
| 1971 | 51.7 | 4.7 | 25.5 |
| 1972 | 59.8 | 4.9 | 25.8 |
| 1973 | 65.4 | 4.8 | 24.8 |
| 1974 | 82.0 | 5.6 | 29.6 |
| 1975 | 92.9 | 5.8 | 31.9 |
| 1976 | 97.4 | 5.5 | 30.2 |
| 1977 | 113.5 | 5.7 | 30.3 |
| 1978 | 123.5 | 5.5 | 29.1 |
| 1979 | 149.8 | 6.0 | 30.5 |
| 1980 | 181.5 | 6.6 | 33.7 |
| 1981 | 228.6 | 7.5 | 36.7 |
| 1982 | 253.5 | 8.0 | 39.4 |
| 1983 | 295.3 | 8.7 | 45.7 |
| 1984 | 322.0 | 8.5 | 45.2 |
| 1985 | 365.1 | 9.1 | 47.0 |
| 1986 | 424.5 | 10.0 | 52.1 |
| 1987 | 450.5 | 10.0 | 50.2 |
| 1988 | 321.1 | 6.6 | 33.5 |
| 1989 | 292.7 | 5.7 | 28.0 |
| 1990 | 312.1 (est.) | N.A. | N.A. |

[a]1967 to 1973, calendar years; 1974 to 1990, fiscal years.

Source: Congressional Budget Office, *Annual Report on Tax Expenditures*, September, 1981, for years 1976 through 1981. For years 1982 through 1990, tax expenditure totals are from the Joint Committee on Taxation, *Estimates of Federal Tax Expenditures*, Annual Reports for 1982–1989. *Economic Report of the President*, 1989, is the source for GNP and total federal revenue data.

revenues and as a percent of the GNP. For the years 1980 through 1987 (eight years), tax expenditures averaged 43.8% of federal revenues and 8.6% of GNP.

The reason for this relatively explosive growth in tax expenditures during these years was not because their rate of growth jumped significantly above the growth rate for the earlier period. From 1967 through 1979, the average

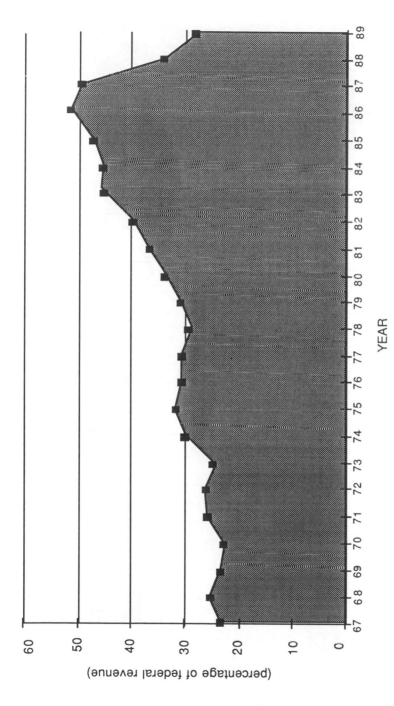

Figure 3-1  Tax expenditures as a percent of federal revenue: 1967-1989

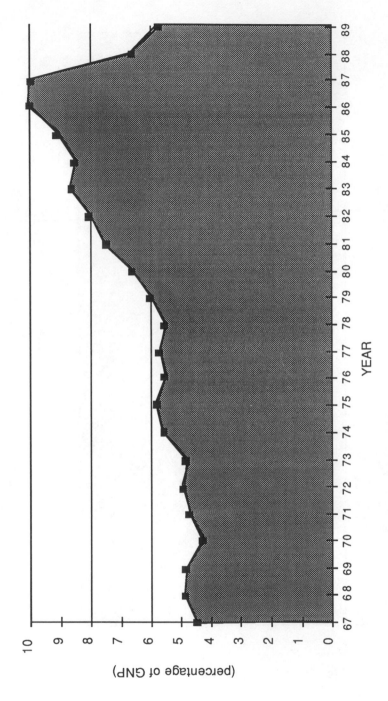

Figure 3-2 Tax expenditures as a percent of GNP: 1967–1989

annual rate of growth for tax expenditures was 12.2%. In the later period, 1980–1987, this average increased to 14.9%. The more important reason is that the Economic Recovery Tax Act of 1981, labeled a "Christmas Tree" bill by its critics, added 11 new tax expenditures (there were 92 in 1980) and expanded 21 existing ones.[6] After 1987, tax expenditures as a share of both federal revenues and the GNP dropped dramatically, falling to 28.0% of federal revenues and 5.7% of the GNP by 1989.

Besides the marked upward jump in tax expenditures between 1980 and 1987, there was a slight upward bulge in their magnitude between 1973 and 1975. After 1975, the ratio of tax expenditures to federal revenues dropped slightly before it began to shoot upward in the 1980s. The reason for these changes was the 1974–1975 recession, the most severe downturn since the Great Depression until the 1982–1983 collapse. In a recession, direct money transfers like Social Security benefits or unemployment compensation increase significantly. Since such transfers are exempt in whole or part from the personal income tax, their expansion automatically entails a rise in tax expenditures. In a recession, the federal government loses in two ways: 1) it pays out more income in the form of transfers, and 2) if such transfer income is not taxable, there is an automatic increase in tax expenditures. To illustrate, consider the following: In the two years prior to the 1974–1975 recession, federal transfer payments to people increased by 13.3% per year. In the two recession years, 1973 and 1974, transfers jumped by 33% per year. But in the two postrecession recovery years of 1976 and 1977, the rate of increase in transfer spending per year dropped to 7.6%.[7]

Our next question involves the breakdown of tax expenditures between those directed at individuals and those designed to benefit corporations. Related to this is the question of the ratio of corporate and individual tax expenditures to corporate and individual tax revenues. Data pertaining to these matters are found in tables 3-2 and 3-3. These data are for fiscal years 1980 through 1990.

In 1980, corporate tax expenditures totaled 24.3% of all tax expenditures. This percentage ratio rose slightly to a peak figure of 28.2% in 1986, and steadily declined thereafter, falling to an estimated 12.4% by fiscal 1990. For the entire 11-year period, corporate tax expenditures averaged 19.3% of the total, while the average of individual tax expenditures was 80.7%. It is clear that, overwhelmingly, most tax expenditures in the economy have been directed toward persons.

The data in table 3-3 show a different and somewhat more erratic picture, especially for corporate tax expenditures. From 1980 through 1986, the percentage ratio of corporation tax expenditures to tax revenues from corporations rose rapidly, reaching a peak of 147.8% in 1986. In the latter

Table 3-2.  Corporate, Individual, and Total Tax Expenditures: 1980–1990 (in Billions of Dollars and in Percent)

| Fiscal Year | Total Tax Expenditures | Corporate Tax Expenditures | Percent of Total | Individual Tax Expenditures | Percent of Total |
|---|---|---|---|---|---|
| 1980 | $181.5 | $ 44.1 | 24.3% | $137.4 | 75.7% |
| 1981 | 228.6 | 48.8 | 21.3 | 179.8 | 78.7 |
| 1982 | 253.5 | 55.1 | 27.7 | 198.4 | 72.3 |
| 1983 | 295.3 | 56.2 | 19.0 | 239.1 | 81.0 |
| 1984 | 322.0 | 75.2 | 23.4 | 246.8 | 76.6 |
| 1985 | 365.1 | 94.9 | 26.0 | 270.2 | 74.0 |
| 1986 | 424.5 | 119.9 | 28.2 | 304.6 | 71.8 |
| 1987 | 450.5 | 97.1 | 21.6 | 353.4 | 78.4 |
| 1988 | 321.1 | 62.0 | 19.3 | 259.1 | 80.7 |
| 1989 | 292.7 | 37.3 | 12.7 | 255.4 | 87.3 |
| 1990 | 312.1 (est.) | 38.7 | 12.4 | 273.4 | 87.6 |

Sources: 1980–1982 data, Congressional Budget Office, *Annual Reports on Tax Expenditures*; 1983–1990 data, Joint Committee on Taxation, *Annual Reports on Tax Expenditures*.

year, in other words, the amount of potential revenue lost to the federal government through tax expenditures was almost one-and-one-half times greater than the tax revenue actually collected from corporations. This resulted primarily from opening the tax expenditure gates by the Economic Recovery Tax Act of 1981. After 1986 this percentage ratio dropped even more rapidly than it rose in the early years of the decade. By 1990 the percentage ratio of corporate tax expenditures to corporate tax revenue had fallen to 27.5%, a decline primarily resulting from the closing of some major corporate loopholes by the Tax Reform Act of 1986.

Personal tax expenditures in relation to revenue from the personal income tax follow a similar pattern, although not as extreme as the corporate data. In 1980 the percentage ratio of personal tax expenditures to revenue from the personal income tax was 54.8%. This percentage ratio reached a peak of 88.3% in 1987, and then declined to the estimated percentage ratio of 58.1% for 1990. The reasons for this pattern are essentially the same as for corporate tax expenditures: opening the gates in the 1981 Act and closing them somewhat with the 1986 Act.

What are the major sources of tax expenditures? Tables 3-4 and 3-5 address this question for persons and for corporations. For individuals, exclusions from income, deductions from income, and tax credits were the

Table 3-3. Corporate and Individual Tax Expenditures and Federal Corporate and Individual Income Tax Revenues: 1980–1990 (in Billions of Dollars and in Percent)

| Fiscal Year | Corporate Tax Expenditures | Corporate Tax Revenue | Percentage Ratio: Corporate Tax Expenditures To Corporate Taxes | Individual Tax Expenditures | Personal Income Tax Revenue | Percentage Ratio: Individual Tax Expenditure To Personal Income Taxes |
|---|---|---|---|---|---|---|
| 1980 | $ 44.1 | $ 70.2 | 62.8% | $137.4 | $250.7 | 54.8% |
| 1981 | 48.8 | 69.4 | 70.3 | 179.8 | 289.6 | 62.1 |
| 1982 | 55.1 | 52.1 | 105.8 | 198.4 | 310.0 | 64.0 |
| 1983 | 56.2 | 55.7 | 100.9 | 239.1 | 292.5 | 81.7 |
| 1984 | 75.2 | 75.3 | 99.9 | 246.8 | 362.5 | 68.1 |
| 1985 | 94.9 | 74.6 | 127.2 | 270.2 | 340.4 | 79.4 |
| 1986 | 119.9 | 81.1 | 147.8 | 304.6 | 357.0 | 85.3 |
| 1987 | 97.1 | 97.7 | 99.4 | 353.4 | 401.2 | 88.3 |
| 1988 | 62.0 | 108.3 | 57.2 | 259.1 | 408.0 | 63.5 |
| 1989 | 37.3 | 118.5 (est.) | 31.5 | 255.4 | 436.8 (est.) | 58.5 |
| 1990 | 38.7 | 140.7 (est.) | 27.5 | 273.4 | 470.5 (est.) | 58.1 |

Sources: 1980–1982 data, Congressional Budget Office, *Annual Reports on Tax Expenditures*; 1983–1990 data, Joint Committee on Taxation, *Annual Reports on Tax Expenditures*. Corporate and personal income tax revenues are from the *Economic Reports of the President*, 1989.

**Table 3-4. Major Sources of Tax Expenditures for Individuals: 1989[a] (in Billions of Dollars and in Percent)**

| Sources of Tax Expenditures | Dollars | Percent |
|---|---|---|
| *Exclusions from income* | | |
| 1.  Interest income | | |
|    a.  From state and local government bonds | $ 17.1 | |
|    b.  From life insurance and annuity savings | 5.2 | |
|       Subtotal | $ 22.3 | 8.7% |
| 2.  Capital gains | | |
|    a. From deferral on home sales | 9.8 | |
|    b. From home sales for persons over 65 | 3.3 | |
|    c. Exclusion at death | 4.5 | |
|       Subtotal | $ 17.6 | 6.9 |
| 3.  Employee benefits | | |
|    a. Armed Forces personnel | 1.7 | |
|    b. Miscellaneous fringe benefits | 5.5 | |
|       Subtotal | $  7.2 | 2.8 |
| 4.  Health | | |
|    a. Contributions by employers and self-employed to medical insurance premiums and care | 27.6 | |
|    b. Untaxed Medicare benefits | 6.5 | |
|       Subtotal | $ 34.1 | 13.4 |
| 5.  Income and Social Security | | |
|    a. Contributions to pension plans | $ 55.8 | |
|    b. Social Security and RR retirement | 18.4 | |
|    c. Workmen's compensation | 2.9 | |
|       Subtotal | $ 77.1 | 30.2 |
| 6.  Veterans' benefits | $  1.5 | |
|    Subtotal | $  1.5 | 0.6 |
|    Total for exclusions from income | $159.8 | 62.6% |
| *Deductions from income* | | |
| 1.  Mortgage interest on owner-occupied homes | 30.8 | |
| 2.  Property taxes on owner-occupied homes | 8.0 | |
| 3.  Personal interest | 5.7 | |
| 4.  Charitable contributions | 11.9 | |
| 5.  Nonbusiness state and local government income and property taxes | 16.5 | |
| 6.  Medical expenses | 2.5 | |
|    Total for deductions from income | $ 75.4 | 29.5% |
| *Tax credits* | | |
| 1.  Child care and dependent care expenses | 4.0 | |
| 2.  Earned income credit | 1.2 | |
|    Total for tax credits | $  5.2 | 2.0% |
|    Total for individual exclusion, deductions, and tax credits | $240.4 | 94.1% |

[a] Fiscal year.

Source: Congress of the United States, Congressional Budget Office, *The Effects of Tax Reform on Tax Expenditures* (Washington, D.C., March, 1989).

Table 3-5. Major Sources of Tax Expenditures For Corporations: 1989[a] (in Billions of Dollars and in Percent)

| Sources of Tax Expenditures | Dollars | Percent |
|---|---|---|
| 1. Exclusions from income | $14.1 | 37.8% |
| 2. Deductions from income | 18.6 | 49.9 |
| 3. Tax credits | 4.6 | 12.3 |
| Total | $37.3 | 100.0% |

[a] Fiscal year.

Source: Congress of the United States, Congressional Budget Office, *The Effects of Tax Reform on Tax Expenditures* (Washington, D C., March, 1986).

sources of 94.1% of all tax expenditures. The balance came from a variety of relatively minor business expenses applicable to proprietorships and partnerships but not directly to persons. For corporations, these three categories were the source for 100% of tax expenditure. In 1989, exclusions from income were the major source of tax expenditures for individuals, totaling $159.8 billion or 62.6% of all individual tax expenditures. Deductions from income were second in importance, adding up to $75.4 billion, or 29.5% of tax expenditures benefiting persons. Tax credits to individuals were relatively small, amounting to only $5.2 billion, or 2.0% of the total. As for corporations (table 3-5), deductions from income are the most important source of tax expenditures, amounting to $18.6 billion, or 49.9% of the total, in 1989. Exclusions from income in the amount of $14.1 billion (37.8% of the total) were next, followed by tax credits of $4.6 billion (12.3% of the total).

Having examined the major sources of tax expenditures for both persons and corporations, we now turn to another matter. What are the more significant, specific activities subsidized by tax expenditures? Table 3-6 answers this question. The data in table 3-6 come from the Joint Committee on Taxation and are the Committee's estimates for the fiscal year 1990; these data reflect as fully as possible the impact of the 1986 Tax Reform Act on tax expenditures.

As can be seen from the data in the table, retirement is the activity supported most by tax expenditures. Included under "retirement" are major exemptions from taxable income, such as employer contributions to pension funds, Social Security income, and life insurance benefits. Support for retirement accounts for 27.9% of estimated tax expenditures in fiscal 1990 of $312.3 billion.

**Table 3-6.   Major Activities Subsidized by Tax Expenditures: 1990[a] (in Billions of Current Dollars and in Percent)**

| Activity | Dollar Value | Percent of Total |
|---|---|---|
| 1.  *Retirement* | | |
| Contributions to pensions | $ 59.8 | |
| Social Security | 21.0 | |
| Life insurance | 6.2 | 27.9% |
| Subtotal | $ 87.0 | 27.9% |
| 2.  *Home ownership* | | |
| Mortgage interest | 25.4 | |
| Property Taxes | 8.1 | |
| Capital gains treatment | 13.7 | 15.1% |
| Subtotal | $ 47.2 | 15.1% |
| 3.  *Health and health insurance* | | |
| Employer contributions to health insurance | 32.6 | |
| Medical expenses | 2.8 | |
| Untaxed Medicare benefits | 9.0 | |
| Subtotal | $ 44.4 | 14.2% |
| 4.  *Municipal bond interest* | $ 20.7 | 6.6% |
| 5.  *Investments* | | |
| Depreciation | 14.6 | |
| Investment credits | 3.8 | |
| Subtotal | $ 18.4 | 5.9% |
| 6.  *State and local taxes* | $ 19.2 | 6.1% |
| 7.  *Charitable contributions* | $ 10.5 | 3.4% |
| 8.  *Capital gains at death* | $  5.4 | 1.7% |
| Total: Items 1–8 | $252.8 | 80.9% |
| 9.  *Other* | 59.5 | 19.1% |
| Total: All tax expenditures | $312.3 | 100.0 |

[a] Fiscal year.

Source: Congress of the United States, Joint Committee on Taxation, *Estimates of Federal Tax Expenditures for Fiscal Years 1990–1994*, February 28, 1989.

Home ownership is the second most prominent activity supported by tax expenditures, equal to $47.2 billion or 15.1% of all tax expenditures in this fiscal year. The home ownership total covers the deductibility of mortgage interest, property taxes on homes, and the exclusion of capital gains resulting from the sale of homes.

Next in significance is support for health and health insurance, only slightly less than home ownership, Tax expenditures bolstering this activity totaled $44.4 billion, or 14.2% of the total. The exemption of employer contributions to health insurance and Medicare benefits from taxable income plus the deductibility of medical expenses are the primary tax expenditures found in the health and health insurance category. Next comes encouragement for local borrowing by exemption of income on municipal bonds from federal taxation. This activity totaled $20.7 billion in fiscal 1990, representing 6.6% of all tax expenditures. Indirect federal support for state and local governments comes by allowing state and local income and property taxes as a deductible item on the federal income tax. These tax expenditures equaled $19.2 billion, accounting for 6.1% of the total.

Investment activity is encouraged by favorable treatment for depreciation and through investment tax credits. Tax expenditures for these purposes were $18.4 billion, or 5.9% of the total. Charitable activities are encouraged by including charitable contributions as a deductible item on income taxes. The tax expenditure amount for this purpose in fiscal 1990 was $10.5 billion, or 3.4% of all tax expenditures. Finally, capital gains at death are excluded from taxable income, the amount here being $5.4 billion, or 1.7% of the total in fiscal 1990. The social rationale for this is by no means clear, although this particular tax expenditure obviously encourages the building of private fortunes.

A different kind of comparison is shown in table 3-7. Here we classify both tax expenditures and transfers by 16 major functional categories that are typically used for the detailed breakdown of federal spending in the national income and product accounts. In this table these data on transfer spending are for the 1988 calendar year and these data on tax expenditures are for fiscal 1989. In examining these figures, it is important to keep in mind that *both* tax expenditures and transfers are ways of subsidizing different activities. Almost any activity can be supported by one or the other or both. The rationale, however, for focusing on one subsidy technique rather than the other is by no means always clear.

Several things should be noted about these data. First, transfers are much larger than tax expenditures—2.5 times greater for the years shown in table 3-7. Second, the greatest disparity is in the functional area of commerce and housing. This area accounts for 35.4% of tax expenditures, but a mere 2.8% of transfer spending. What does this signify? It shows that the way in which business activity is subsidized is primarily through the tax system—exclusions and deductions from income plus tax credits—rather than by direct outlays. If we combine both tax expenditures and transfers for these different functional categories. we find that support for commerce and housing ranks third in significance (12.1%) behind Social Security,

**Table 3-7.   Tax Expenditures and Transfer Expenditures by Functional Budget Categories: 1988, 1989[a] (in Billions of Dollars and in Percent)**

| Budget Category | Dollar Value of Tax Expenditures | Percent of Total | Dollar Value of Transfer Spending | Percent of Total |
|---|---|---|---|---|
| 1.  National Defense | $1.8 | 0.6% | $   2.0 | 0.3% |
| 2.  International Affairs | 4.6 | 1.6 | 11.1 | 1.5 |
| 3.  Space and Technology | 1.7 | 0.6 | — | |
| 4.  Energy | 0.8 | 0.3 | −1.8 | −0.2 |
| 5.  Natural Resources | 1.8 | 0.6 | 1.6 | 0.2 |
| 6.  Agriculture | 0.3 | 0.1 | 25.2 | 3.4 |
| 7.  Commerce and Housing[b] | 103.7 | 35.4 | 20.8 | 2.8 |
| 8.  Transportation | 0.1 | — | 19.0 | 2.6 |
| 9.  Community and Regional Development | 0.7 | 0.2 | 0.5 | 0.1 |
| 10.  Education, Training, Employment, and Social Services[c] | 23.9 | 8.2 | 105.2 | 14.3 |
| 11.  Health | 33.6 | 11.5 | 5.1 | 0.7 |
| 12.  Medicare | 6.5 | 2.2 | 86.6 | 11.8 |
| 13.  Income Security | 64.1 | 21.9 | 72.6 | 9.9 |
| 14.  Social Security | 18.0 | 6.1 | 215.2 | 29.2 |
| 15.  Veterans | 1.8 | 0.6 | 19.8 | 2.7 |
| 16.  General Purpose Fiscal Assistance | 29.3 | 10.0 | 153.3 | 20.8 |
| Total | $292.7 | 100.0% | $736.1 | 100.0% |

[a] 1988 data for transfer spending, calendar year; 1989 data for tax expenditures, fiscal year.

[b] Transfer spending includes subsidies to Postal Service.

[c] Transfer spending includes Medicaid payments and federal support for public assistance payments.

Sources: U.S. Congress, Congressional Budget Office, *The Effects of Tax Reform on Tax Expenditures* (Washington D.C., Congressional Budget Office, March, 1988); U.S. Department of Commerce, *Survey of Current Business*, July, 1989.

which is first with 22.7%, and fiscal assistance to state and local governments, which is second with 17.7% of the combined total for *all* transfers and tax expenditures.

Social Security accounts for the largest share of transfers (29.2%), but ranks sixth (6.1%) in its share of tax expenditures. The subsidy of Social Security income through tax expenditures comes about because of the exemption of most of such income from personal income taxation. Here we have an instance of how tax expenditures and transfers may interact to increase the extent to which any activity is subsidized. Income is increased through a transfer payment, and then some or all of that income is exempt from taxation.

The functional category "health" is another area where there is a large difference between tax expenditures and transfers. Health ranks third among tax expenditures, accounting for 11.5% of the tax expenditure total, but on the transfer side it was responsible for a mere 0.7% of all transfer spending in 1988. On the tax expenditure side, most of the $33.6 billion total for health shown in table 3-7 comes from the exclusion from taxable income of employer contributions for medical insurance premiums and the deductibility of medical expenses.

Examination of the contrasting data in table 3-7 for the 16 functional federal budget categories shown in the table raises this question: Is there any general principle at work that explains the government's preference for tax expenditures in some instances and for transfers in others? Not really. As the Congressional Budget Office says in its primer on tax expenditures, "Policymakers have seldom confronted the choice between funding a Government program through the tax system and funding it by the authorization and appropriation process...tax expenditures have been enacted as a simple decision to reduce someone's taxes, normally with no thought given to enacting a direct spending program instead."[8] Two factors that favor tax expenditures over transfers are 1) it is usually more popular to cut taxes than to increase spending, and 2) tax expenditures are often quite simple to administer, requiring little more than a few added entries on a tax return.

## Tax Expenditures and the Tax Reform Act of 1986

As we saw in table 3-1 and figures 3-1 and 3-2, tax expenditures grew steadily from 1967 (when the government first began to report them in detail) until 1987, when they reached a peak of $450.5 billion. After that they dropped off sharply, primarily because of the impact of the Tax Reform Act of 1986, one of the most far-reaching pieces of tax legislation in the post-World War II period.

The best-known and most highly publicized consequences of this Act were the reductions in tax rates for both corporations and individuals. For corporations the rate was reduced from 46% to 34%, and for individuals the number of income brackets was reduced from 14, with a top marginal rate of 50%, to basically two brackets, with rates of 15% and 28%. For persons, both the standard deduction and personal exemptions were raised.

Less well understood is that the Act also broadened significantly the federal tax base, and in so doing shifted some of the tax burden from individuals to corporations.[9] Base-broadening was achieved primarily by a reduction in tax expenditures. If tax expenditures are eliminated or reduced, there is an automatic enlargement of the tax base. This is because income that heretofore had not been taxed, or had been only partially taxed, is now taxed more fully. The economic effect is the same as if more revenue sources had been brought into the revenue code.

Tax expenditures were reduced by the 1986 legislation in essentially three ways. The first was outright elimination, which was rare. However, where it did happen, as with capital gains and the investment tax credit, the benefits were big. The Congressional Budget Office, for example, estimated that in fiscal year 1991 the tax savings on these two items alone would equal $93.1 billion.[10] Second, a number of major tax expenditures were modified, including elimination of sales taxes from the deductibility of state and local taxes, and changes in accelerated depreciation for equipment and structures, IRA contributions, and interest earning. Table 3-8 shows a comparison of projected changes in the 21 largest tax expenditures for fiscal year 1991, before and after the effects of the 1986 Act are taken into account. These estimates were prepared by the Congressional Budget Office and the Joint Committee on Taxation.

The third way in which tax expenditures were modified by the 1986 legislation was through introduction of the concept of *passive* income (or passive business activity) into the tax code. This is a new idea. Passive income results from trade or business activities in which a taxpayer does not materially participate, or from *any* rental real estate activity, *regardless* of whether the taxpayer materially participates.[11] Under the Tax Reform Act, losses from passive activities can only be deducted from gains from similar activities. For example, capital losses can only be deducted from capital gains, or interest deductions on property purchased as an investment can be deducted only from net investment income.

In the law, "material" participation means that the individual is involved in the business on a "regular, continuous, and substantial basis."[12] The primary impact of this part of the Act was to curtail tax losses (tax expenditures) to the government that arose out of a variety of tax shelters based upon limited partnership investments by individuals. "Limited" partners in a partnership have only limited liability for the losses of the business (unlike full partners), but they are also prohibited from participating in the operations of the business. The 1986 Act implicitly treats involvement in a

Table 3-8.  Projected Revenue Losses from the Largest Tax Expenditures Under Prior Law: Fiscal Year 1991 (in Billions of Dollars)

| Tax Expenditure | Status After TRA[a] | Projected Revenue Losses for Fiscal Year 1991 | |
|---|---|---|---|
| | | Before TRA | After TRA |
| 1. Net exclusion from income of pension contributions and earnings | Modified | 71.7 | 53.6 |
| 2. Capital gains deduction | Repealed | 56.1 | 0.0 |
| 3. Investment tax credit | Repealed | 38.6 | 1.6 |
| 4. Deductibility of mortgage interest on owner-occupied homes | Modified | 43.6 | 35.8 |
| 5. Deductibility of state and local income and sales taxes | Sales tax Repealed | 36.1 | 18.4 |
| 6. Exclusion of employer contributions for medical insurance and health care | Unchanged | 42.0 | 37.7 |
| 7. Exclusion of Social Security benefits | Unchanged | 23.8 | 20.3 |
| 8. Accelerated depreciation: Equipment | Modified | 23.9 | 16.5 |
| 9. Exemption of income on private-purpose tax-exempt bonds | Modified | 19.6 | 10.2 |
| 10. Exclusion of IRA contributions and interest earnings | Modified | 19.2 | 9.0 |
| 11. Deductibility of charitable contributions | Unchanged | 19.9 | 13.9 |
| 12. Exclusion of interest on general-purpose state and local bonds | Unchanged | 17.4 | 10.9 |
| 13. Accelerated depreciation: Nonresidential structures | Modified | 12.9 | 6.9 |
| 14. Nonmortgage consumer interest deductions | Phased out | 14.7 | 0.9 |
| 15. Deductibility of real estate taxes | Unchanged | 12.4 | 8.9 |
| 16. Progressive corporate tax rates | Modified | 10.2 | 5.5 |
| 17. Deduction fo two-earner married couples | Repealed | 9.4 | 0.0 |
| 18. Exclusion of untaxed Medicare benefits | Unchanged | 9.1 | 8.0 |
| 19. Deferral of capital gains on home sales | Unchanged | 13.0 | 11.6 |
| 20. Exclusion of capital gains at death | Unchanged | 6.5 | 5.1 |
| 21. Exclusion of capital gains on home sales for people 55 or over | Unchanged | 4.3 | 3.9 |

[a] TRA = Tax Reform Act of 1986.

Notes: The year 1991 was chosen for comparison of projected tax expenditures because virtually all the provisions of TRA will then be fully in effect. The estimates under both prior law (before TRA) and current law (after TRA) are based on the same economic assumptions. These are from CBO's January 1988 forecast, which included projected changes in investment activity brought about by TRA.

Source: Congressional Budget Office *The Effects of Tax Reform on Tax Expenditures* (Washington, D.C., March, 1988).

business as a limited partner as intrinsically passive. It was expected that the new rules regarding passive income, coupled with changes in the tax rules involving depreciation and capital gains, would bring a shift in personal financial investment away from tax-motivated investments and thereby would reduce revenue losses from tax shelters.[13]

The overall impact of the Tax Reform Act of 1986 on tax expenditures, both individual and corporate, is shown in table 3-9, in which estimates for tax expenditures for 1989 *after* the Tax Reform Act are compared with estimates of what they would have been in the same fiscal year if the Act had not been passed. The before-TRA estimates for 1989 were prepared by the Joint Committee on Taxation in the spring of 1988, before the reform bill was hammered into a law.[14] As the figures in the table show, the percentage reduction in tax expenditures was greatest for corporations. These expenditures were cut by 65.3%, going from an estimated $107.5 billion before the Tax Reform Act to $37.3 billion after the Act. Individual tax expenditures dropped by 39.5%, from $422.1 billion before the Act to $255.4 billion afterwards. For corporations, the largest dollar volume was in the functional area of commerce and housing. As pointed out earlier, business is subsidized much more heavily in the economy by the tax expenditure process than by direct payments. Thus, a 65.3% reduction in corporate tax expenditures represents a major reduction in business subsidies. For individuals, the largest dollar change ($77.8 billion) also came under the commerce and housing classification. This change results primarily from the elimination of the favored treatment of income from capital gains, and from modifications in the deductibility of mortgage interest on owner-occupied homes.

## Some Problems with Tax Expenditures

Although the tax expenditure concept is a highly useful one for understanding and analyzing what the federal government does and how it affects the economy, the concept is not free from limitations and problems. It is appropriate to look at some of these.

Strictly speaking, tax expenditures are not additive in the same way as, say, transfers. This does not mean that we cannot make direct comparisons between tax expenditure and transfer outlays for similar programs, as is done in table 3-7. But it does means that the arithmetic totals that include *all* tax expenditures have important limitations because of the interdependence of different types of tax expenditures. In other words, the total for all tax expenditures does not measure precisely the revenue that the federal

**Table 3-9.  Tax Expenditures in 1989 and the Tax Reform Act of 1986 (in Billions of Dollars)**

| Budget Category | Individual Tax Expenditures Before 1986 TRA[a] | After 1986 TRA | Net Change | Corporate Tax Expenditures Before 1986 TRA | After 1986 TRA | Net Change |
|---|---|---|---|---|---|---|
| 1. National Defense | $4.7 | $1.8 | $-2.9 | — | — | — |
| 2. International Affairs | | 1.5 | 1.5 | $1.8 | $ 3.1 | $1.3 |
| 3. Space and Technology | 0.2 | — | -0.2 | 3.4 | 1.7 | -1.7 |
| 4. Energy | 2.2 | 1.2 | -1.0 | 2.5 | -0.4 | -2.9 |
| 5. Natural Resources | 5.4 | 1.5 | -3.9 | 1.0 | 0.3 | -0.7 |
| 6. Agriculture | 0.9 | -0.1 | -1.0 | 2.8 | 0.4 | -2.4 |
| 7. Commerce and Housing | 155.2 | 77.4 | -77.8 | 87.5 | 26.3 | -61.2 |
| 8. Transportation | — | — | — | 0.1 | 0.1 | — |
| 9. Community and Regional Development | 1.5 | 0.7 | -0.8 | 0.3 | | -0.3 |
| 10. Education, Training, Employment, and Social Service | 34.4 | 22.5 | -11.9 | 2.3 | 1.4 | -0.9 |
| 11. Health | 41.1 | 33.4 | -7.7 | 0.5 | 0.2 | -0.3 |
| 12. Medicare | 8.6 | 6.5 | -2.1 | — | — | — |
| 13. Income Security | 104.6 | 64.1 | -40.5 | — | — | — |
| 14. Social Security | 21.0 | 18.0 | -3.0 | — | — | — |
| 15. Veterans Benefits | 2.5 | 1.7 | -0.8 | 0.1 | 0.1 | — |
| 16. General Purpose Fiscal Assistance | 39.8 | 25.2 | -14.6 | 5.2 | 4.1 | -1.1 |
| Total | $422.1 | $255.4 | $-166.7 | $107.5 | $ 37.3 | $-70.2 |

[a] TRA = Tax Reform Act of 1986.

Source: Joint Committee on Taxation, *Estimates of Federal Tax Expenditures for Fiscal Years 1987-1993* (Washington, D.S., U.S. Government Printing Office, March 8, 1988); Congressional Budget Office, *The Effects of Tax Reform on Tax Expenditures* (Washington, D.C., March, 1988).

government would gain if *all* the tax expenditures were eliminated. This fact can be explained by considering as an example two types of tax expenditures: tax-free interest on state and municipal bonds, and income from capital gains. For the purpose of clarification, assume that capital gains are still taxed at a lower rate than ordinary income, even though the Tax Reform Act of 1986 eliminated such favored treatment for income from capital gains. Now suppose that both types of tax expenditures were eliminated simultaneously, meaning that income from both sources became fully taxable at ordinary rates. This change would push many people into higher income ranges, and the government would see its revenues increased. But suppose, on the other hand, that only the tax expenditures relating to interest on state and municipal bonds were eliminated. In this case, there would again be an increase in people in the upper income ranges, but not such a large increase as in the first example. Further, since the tax expenditure relating to income from capital gains is not changed, the increase in federal revenue would not be as great. The point is that the effect on government revenue of eliminating several tax expenditures simultaneously may be greater (or lesser) than the effect would be from eliminating them on a one-by-one basis. This does not mean that we cannot make use of tax expenditures totals as we have done in most of the tables in this chapter. Rather, we need simply to guard against the simplistic belief that these totals necessarily represent the revenue the government could actually gain if tax expenditures were eliminated in one fell swoop.[15]

A second problem stems from the fact that, unlike revenue estimates and *actual* budget outlays, tax expenditure estimates remain just that—estimates. They do not become "real" or measurable in an ex post sense, as do tax receipts and budget outlays. This is not to say that they could not be revised as time passes, but it would be a formidable statistical task, given the fact that the estimates made in each year rest upon economic and demographic assumptions peculiar to that year.[16]

Further, what the Congressional Budget Act (1974) requires is that the Congressional Budget Office—now the Joint Committee on Taxation—make an annual report that *projects* tax expenditures for each of the next five fiscal years. So tax expenditures budgets are entirely ex ante, looking ahead to what may be, not looking back to what was. The difficulties involved in making these projections are reflected in the figures shown in table 3-10. Some of these estimates were made before the Tax Reform Act of 1986 made itself felt, but they still can be used to illustrate an important point. In general, it appears that the closer the fiscal year is to the year in which the estimate is made, the lower—and perhaps more accurate—is the estimate. For example, the Joint Committee on Taxation estimate of tax

Table 3-10. Estimates of Total Tax Expenditures: Fiscal Years 1989–1994 (in Billions of Dollars)

| Joint Committee on Taxation Report | Fiscal Years | | | | | |
|---|---|---|---|---|---|---|
| | 1989 | 1990 | 1991 | 1992 | 1993 | 1994 |
| November 9, 1984[a] | 513.8 | | | | | |
| April 12, 1985[a] | 546.1 | 597.9 | | | | |
| March 1, 1986[a] | 592.8 | 578.3 | 631.5 | | | |
| February 27, 1987 | 315.2 | 335.7 | 355.6 | 377.8 | | |
| March 8, 1988 | 292.7 | 319.4 | 340.3 | 363.5 | 388.7 | |
| February 28, 1989 | | 312.1 | 322.5 | 353.0 | 379.0 | 406.2 |

[a] Estimates made prior to the Tax Reform Act of 1986.

Sources: Joint Committee on Taxation, *Estimates of Federal Tax Expenditures For Fiscal Years*, 1983–1994.

expenditures for fiscal 1990 made in February of 1987 was $335.7 billion. Two years later, in February 1989, the estimate for the same fiscal year was $312.1 billion, a difference of $23.6 billion. In all instances except one—the 1985 estimate compared to the 1984 estimate for fiscal 1989—the estimates declined as the estimating year got closer to the year for which the estimate was being made. This is perhaps as it should be, for the closer one is to the future data for which an estimate is to be made, the more likely it is that the assumptions about economic and other factors that underlie the estimates will be accurate. The importance of this is that care must be used in making comparisons of tax expenditure totals over time.

The figures for tax expenditures presented up to this point reflect the way in which the Congressional Budget Office and the Joint Committee on Taxation calculate them. Technically, data presented in this way are called *revenue loss estimates*, indicating that they measure revenue lost to the U.S. Treasury because of provisions in the tax law permitting exclusions, deductions, and credits. There is, however, an alternative way to measure tax expenditures. This is the *outlay equivalent* approach, which estimates the expenditure outlays that would be necessary to provide the same after-tax incentive for a program or activity *if* the program or activity were supported by a direct outlay rather than indirectly through the tax system.

There is merit to the outlay equivalent approach to tax expenditures, even though neither the Congressional Budget Office or the Joint Committee on Taxation has accepted this alternative for estimating tax expenditures. The merit lies in viewing tax expenditures as subsidies, and thinking of subsidies as involving the expenditures of public funds. From this perspective, the outlay equivalent can be compared directly to transfer spending. Transfer spending and outlay equivalents are, in effect, on the same side of the budget ledger—the spending side. Hence it is easy to make a direct comparison. Tax expenditures estimated as revenue losses are, however, on the other side of the budget ledger—the revenue side—so direct comparisons are not quite as simple.

There are also problems with the outlay equivalent approach. One such problem is that in many instances the outlay equivalent figure will be significantly higher than the revenue loss figure. This is because obtaining the same economic incentive effect for a particular activity may require a higher direct outlay, because one will have to take into account the effect of taxation on the outlay. This presumes that the income associated with the activity is taxable, and thus, it is after-tax income that ultimately counts as far as subsidizing a particular activity is concerned. If the income associated with the activity in question is not taxable, then the problem does not apply.

To illustrate the problem, assume a family is in the 28% tax bracket with $10,000 deductible mortgage interest on its home. This family saves in taxes by deducting the $2800 mortgage interest from their income before calculating their tax. The family's $2800 in tax saving is the revenue lost to the government because of this particular type of tax expenditure. Presumably, this mortgage interest "subsidy" exists to promote the socially desirable activity of home ownership. Now if the deductibility of mortgage interest, a tax expenditure, were replaced by a direct money subsidy to the home-owner, how big would the outlay have to be to achieve the same effect, namely $2800 more of income to the family than if the subsidy did not exist? The outlay equivalent approach seeks to answer this question. For the family in this example to be as well off under a direct subsidy that is taxable, the grant to the family would have to be $3889. In the 28% bracket, taxes paid on this amount would be $1089, leaving the family with $2800 of after-tax income, exactly the amount they would save under a mortgage deduction system. However, the subsidy would in this instance cost the government $3889. The story does not end here, however. Although the government initially pays out more in a direct subsidy than it loses through the deductibility route, it eventually gets some of the money back in the form of taxes paid on the additional income received as a grant or direct subsidy. In the simple example used to illustrate this problem, the government would eventually get back in taxes an amount just equal to the added cost of the direct subsidy, namely $1089. But that is because of the oversimplified assumption that *all* the household income in this instance is being taxed at the 28% rate. Reality is more complex.

Another difficulty with the outlay equivalent approach, one cited by the late Stanley S. Surrey, the inventor of the tax expenditure concept, is that this approach presumes that Congress would be willing to replace each tax expenditure program with direct outlays having the same benefits. Mr. Surrey argued that this is not likely to happen, first, because generally the initial costs of direct outlays are higher than existing revenue losses, and, second, the unequal distributional pattern for direct outlay equivalents would be more obvious than the unequal distributional pattern for revenue losses from tax expenditure programs, a topic we shall examine in the next section.[17]

Even though both the Congressional Budget Office and the Joint Committee on Taxation continue to compile their tax expenditure budget estimates on a revenue-loss basis, data reflecting the other approach are available. They are compiled by the Office of Management and Budget (OMB) and presented annually in a Special Analysis G for Tax Expenditures in the government's budget document for each fiscal year. Table 3-11 contains a comparison for both corporate and individual tax expenditures for these two approaches, the revenue loss and the outlay equivalent approaches. Data in the table are estimates for fiscal 1990. The figures shown for the outlay equivalent approach reflect the point discussed earlier, namely that in many instances these figures will be higher than the comparable revenue loss technique. No attempt is made in the outlay equivalent data to adjust them for possible increases in tax revenues flowing from higher incomes linked to higher direct outlays. This is probably impossible.

## Tax Expenditures and the Distribution of Income

Unfortunately, detailed and complete figures on the distribution of tax expenditures by income class do not exist. Evidence and data that are available, fragmentary though they may be, indicate that the distribution of tax expenditures by income class is heavily weighted toward persons and families in the upper ranges of the income scale. The late Stanley S. Surrey and his co-author, in their definitive book *Tax Expenditures*, refer to the distribution of tax expenditures as being "upside down," meaning that the "overwhelming majority of tax expenditure programs disproportionately benefit the upper-income groups."[18] In 1982 the Treasury Department, at the request of Representative Henry Ruess, then Chairman to the Joint Economic Committee, prepared a set of comprehensive estimates of the distribution of tax expenditures by income class. Their estimates were for income in 1981. One set was based upon the allocation of selected tax expenditures to adjusted gross income classes on the basis of tax data, and the second was an allocation of a different group of tax expenditures on the basis of sources

Table 3-11. A Comparison of Revenue Loss and Outlay Equivalent Approaches to Tax Expenditures for Fiscal Year 1989 (in Billions of Dollars)

| Budget Category | Revenue Loss | | | Outlay Equivalent | | |
|---|---|---|---|---|---|---|
| | Corporations | Individuals | Total | Corporations | Individuals | Total |
| 1. National Defense | | $1.9 | $1.9 | | $2.2 | $2.2 |
| 2. International Affairs | $3.5 | 1.3 | 4.8 | $5.2 | 1.8 | 7.0 |
| 3. Space and Technology | 2.1 | | 2.1 | 2.5 | | 2.5 |
| 4. Energy | | 1.0 | 1.0 | 2.5 | 1.1 | 3.6 |
| 5. Natural Resources | 2.1 | 0.4 | 2.5 | 2.8 | 0.4 | 3.2 |
| 6. Agriculture | 0.1 | 0.7 | 0.8 | 0.2 | 1.3 | 1.5 |
| 7. Commerce and Housing | 38.6 | 84.1 | 122.7 | 57.3 | 98.4 | 155.7 |
| 8. Transportation | 0.1 | | 0.1 | 0.3 | | 0.3 |
| 9. Community and Regional Development | 0.8 | 0.4 | 1.2 | 1.2 | 0.6 | 1.8 |
| 10. Education, Training, Employment, and Social Security | 1.5 | 17.0 | 18.5 | 3.7 | 26.5 | 30.2 |
| 11. Health[a] | 0.4 | 38.9 | 39.3 | 3.4 | 44.0 | 47.4 |
| 12. Income Security | 0.2 | 65.6 | 65.8 | 0.3 | 84.6 | 84.9 |
| 13. Social Security | | 17.4 | 17.4 | | 17.4 | 17.4 |
| 14. Veterans Benefits | | 1.8 | 1.8 | | 1.9 | 1.9 |
| 15. General Purpose Fiscal Assistance | 3.8 | 26.6 | 30.4 | 5.3 | 31.1 | 36.4 |
| Total | $53.2 | $257.1 | $310.3 | $84.7 | $311.3 | $396.0 |

[a] Includes Medicare

Source: U.S. Treasury, *Special Analysis G, Budget of the U.S. Government*, Fiscal Year 1990.

other than tax returns. The Treasury regarded the latter distribution as less reliable than the one based directly on tax returns. Table 3-12 contains distribution based on tax returns and table 3-13 the distribution derived from nontax sources.[19]

Table 3-12 contains 13 different categories of tax expenditures , of which only one, assistance to the elderly, can be described as targeted primarily toward the poor. Most of the others in the table are aimed at the middle and upper-income classes. The tax expenditures included in the table ($81.3 billion) account for 45.2% of all tax expenditures going to individuals in 1981 ($179.8 billion).

What the data in table 3-12 show is that these particular tax expenditures are heavily skewed toward the top of the income scale. Less than 1% of all persons filing tax returns in 1981—0.7%, to be exact—received 18.8% of the tax expenditures shown in the table. These are taxpayers found in the $100,000 and above income ranges. At the bottom, where we find taxpayers in the $10,000 adjusted gross income class and below, the number of persons and families filing returns was 36.7% of total returns filed, but this group received only 2.0% of all tax expenditures. The three top income groups—those with $50,000 of adjusted gross income or above—represented but 4.3% of those who filed tax returns, but received 43.1% of all tax expenditures in the categories included in the tables. It should be noted that the number of persons or families filing tax returns is not the same as the number actually paying income taxes. In 1981, according to the Treasury, 85.8% of the returns filed represented taxable income. But the number filing is a good indication of the number of persons or families in the various income classes shown in the table.

Table 3-13 contains the second set of distributional data compiled by the Treasury, a set based upon non-tax-return sources and covering a different set of tax expenditures. The total of tax expenditures shown in this table ($74.4 billion) is equal to 41.4% of all personal tax expenditures for 1981. At least three of the tax expenditures contained in this table are relatively favorable to persons and families in the lower income ranges. These are the exclusion of employer contributions for premiums on group medical insurance, the exclusion of Social Security and Railroad Retirement income, and the exclusion of workmen's compensation and unemployment benefits. Overall, these tax expenditures are less regressive in their distribution than those included in table 3-12.

For the nine tax expenditures shown in table 3-13, the above-$100,000 income classes (0.7% of the total) received 8.0% of the tax expenditure total, a smaller share than for the 13 items shown in table 1-12. At the other end of the income scale, the 36.7% of taxpayers who filed returns and who

Table 3-12. Distribution of Selected Tax Expenditures by Adjusted Gross Income Class: 1981 (in Millions of Dollars and in Percent)

| Tax Expenditure | Less than $10,000 | $10,000– 15,000 | $15,000– 20,000 | $20,000– 30,000 | $30,000– 50,000 | $50,000– 100,000 | $100,000– 200,000 | Over $200,000 | Total |
|---|---|---|---|---|---|---|---|---|---|
| 1. Excluded income earned abroad | $4 | $14 | $21 | $53 | $158 | $385 | $221 | $74 | $930 |
| 2. Investment credits | 75 | 199 | 249 | 557 | 744 | 745 | 414 | 454 | 3,437 |
| 3. Capital gains | 428 | 384 | 308 | 1,140 | 2,564 | 3,179 | 2,148 | 3,081 | 13,232 |
| 4. Residential energy credits | 45 | 45 | 67 | 167 | 198 | 73 | 15 | 4 | 614 |
| 5. Dividend and investment exclusion | 24 | 28 | 30 | 87 | 170 | 128 | 33 | 8 | 508 |
| 6. Mortgage interest | 220 | 343 | 892 | 3,633 | 8,639 | 4,672 | 979 | 225 | 19,603 |
| 7. Home property taxes | 109 | 198 | 374 | 1,429 | 3,257 | 2,291 | 725 | 302 | 8,685 |
| 8. Charitable contributions | 36 | 129 | 249 | 985 | 2,550 | 2,109 | 1,126 | 1,652 | 8,836 |
| 9. Child care | 92 | 218 | 188 | 382 | 364 | 62 | 7 | 1 | 1,314 |
| 10. Medical expenses | 85 | 190 | 299 | 827 | 1,201 | 614 | 150 | 56 | 3,422 |
| 11. Elderly (added exemption) | 406 | 407 | 260 | 360 | 374 | 225 | 76 | 23 | 2,131 |
| 12. Causality losses | 8 | 21 | 41 | 109 | 249 | 178 | 52 | 37 | 695 |
| 13. State and local taxes | 118 | 230 | 497 | 2,276 | 6,209 | 550 | 2,032 | 1,352 | 17,844 |
| Total | $1,650 | $2,406 | $3,475 | $12,005 | $26,757 | $19,711 | $7,978 | $7,269 | $81,251 |
| Percent distribution | 2.0% | 2.9% | 4.3% | 14.8% | 32.9% | 24.3% | 9.8% | 9.0% | 100.0% |
| Cumulative percent of tax expenditures | 2.0% | 4.9% | 9.2% | 24.0% | 56.9% | 81.2% | 91.0% | 99.0% | 100.0% |
| Commulative percent of taxable returns | 36.7% | 51.1% | 62.8% | 81.2% | 95.7% | 99.3% | 99.8% | 99.9% | 100.0% |

Source: Congressional Budget Office, Tax Expenditures: Budget Control Options and Five-Year Budget Projections for Fiscal Years 1983–1987, November, 1982.

Table 3-13.  Distribution of Selected Tax Expenditures by Adjusted Gross Income Classes on the Basis of Data Other Than Tax Returns: 1981 (in Millions of Dollars and in Percent)

| Tax Expenditure | Less than $10,000 | $10,000– 15,000 | $15,000– 20,000 | $20,000– 30,000 | $30,000– 50,000 | $50,000– 100,000 | $100,000– 200,000 | Over $200,000 | Total |
|---|---|---|---|---|---|---|---|---|---|
| 1. Exclusion of benefits to military and veterans | $858 | $520 | $482 | $815 | $504 | $176 | $37 | $8 | $3,400 |
| 2. Exclusion of interest on state and local funds | 4 | 5 | 7 | 25 | 230 | 2,019 | 1,441 | 868 | 4,599 |
| 3. Deductibility of consumer credit interest | 9 | 98 | 332 | 1,566 | 3,606 | 1,888 | 549 | 199 | 8,246 |
| 4. Capital gains on home sales | 11 | 5 | 61 | 225 | 524 | 354 | 120 | 49 | 1,349 |
| 5. Exclusion of employee contributions to medical insurance premiums | 888 | 1,191 | 1,464 | 3,851 | 4,470 | 1,450 | 252 | 53 | 13,619 |
| 6. Exclusion of SS and RR Retirement Benefits | 5,029 | 1,787 | 1,254 | 1,822 | 1,278 | 731 | 209 | 55 | 12,165 |
| 7. Exclusion of workmen's compensation and unemployment benefits | 1,859 | 1,004 | 519 | 936 | 354 | 93 | 20 | 8 | 4,793 |
| 8. Exclusion of contributions to pension plans | 964 | 1,371 | 1,893 | 5,495 | 8,306 | 4,345 | 1,463 | 513 | 24,350 |
| 9. Exclusion of insurance premiums | 83 | 112 | 163 | 444 | 642 | 282 | 84 | 36 | 1,851 |
| Total | $ 9,705 | $ 6,093 | $ 6,175 | $15,179 | $19,914 | $11,338 | $ 4,180 | $ 1,789 | $74,372 |
| Percent distribution | 13.0% | 8.2% | 8.3% | 20.4% | 26.8% | 15.2% | 5.6% | 2.4% | 100.0% |

Source: Congressional Budget Office, *Tax Expenditures: Budget Control Options and Five-Year Budget Projections for Fiscal Years 1983–1987*, November, 1982.

**Table 3-14.   Distribution of Tax Expenditures by Income Class for Combined Totals from Tables 3-12 and 3-13: 1981 (in Millions of Dollars and in Percent)**

| Income Class | Total Tax Expenditures | Percent Distributions | Number of Returns[a] | Percent Distributions |
|---|---|---|---|---|
| Below $10,000 | $ 11,355 | 7.3% | 34,666 | 36.7% |
| 10,000–15,000 | 8,499 | 5.5 | 13,457 | 14.4 |
| $15,000–20,000 | 9,650 | 6.2 | 10.936 | 11.7 |
| $20,000–30,000 | 27,184 | 17.5 | 17,254 | 18.4 |
| $30,000–50,000 | 46,671 | 30.0 | 13,538 | 14.5 |
| $50,000–100,000 | 31,049 | 20.0 | 3,384 | 3.6 |
| $100,000–200,000 | 12,158 | 7.8 | 549 | 0.6 |
| Over $200,000 | 9,258 | 5.8 | 116 | 0.1 |
| Total | $155,624 | 100.0% | 93,600 | 100.0% |

[a] In thousands.

Source: Congressional Budget Office, *Tax Expenditures: Budget Control Options and Five-Year Budget Projections for Fiscal Years 1983–1987*, November, 1982.

fell in the less-than-$10,000 income class got 13.0 % of the total tax expenditure outlays shown in this table. The bulk of these particular tax expenditures went to the middle-income ranges, those between $20,000 and $100,000. Here are found a little more than one third of the returns filed (36.5%), but these income classes received 62.4% of tax expenditures. Income classes below $20,000, which accounted for 62.8% of all returns, got 29.5% of the total.

We get a better overall picture of the distribution of tax expenditures in 1981 if we combine the data from tables 3-12 and 3-13 into a single table. This is done in table 3-14, which shows the combined total of tax expenditures for the eight income classes shown in the other two tables. The observation made earlier about the overall regressiveness of tax expenditures is not changed by combining these data. For 1981, the combined totals shown in table 3-14 account for 86.5% of tax expenditures in that year ($179.8 billion). The distribution of the combined total is still skewed heavily toward the upper income groups. The data in table 3-14 show that the top 0.7% of persons and families filing tax returns got 13.6% of total tax expenditures in that year, whereas the 36.7 in the lowest income bracket (below $10,000) received but 7.3% of the total. The middle income range brackets (from $20,000 to $100,000, representing 36.5% of the returns) received 67.5% of the 17 types of tax expenditures included in the totals.

Persons and families with incomes of less than $20,000 (62.8%) got 19.0 % of the tax expenditure total.

Since the 1982 Treasury study of the distribution of tax expenditures, the Joint Committee on Taxation has continued include distributional data in its annual estimates of tax expenditures, but on a much more limited basis than the Treasury study. In its 1989 report, the Joint Committee on Taxation analyzed the distribution by income class for eight major types of tax expenditures.[20] These figures are shown in table 3-15 and represent estimates for 1990.

The total for tax expenditures shown in the table is $77.0 billion, which is equal to 28.2% of the total of tax expenditures estimated by the Committee for that year ($273.4 billion). These figures are for individuals, not corporations. The coverage by the Committee is much smaller than the Treasury study, but is still useful for a more up-to-date judgment about the distribution of tax expenditure subsidies. Since 1983, when the Committee took over from the Congressional Budget Office, the items included in the Committee's selective list of tax expenditures have remained fairly constant. The more recent figures do not include capital gains, which have been phased out (except as related to owner-occupied houses), while the 1986 and 1987 reports included distributional data on home mortgages, an omission from the most recent tabulation.

In table 3-15, three of the eight items are targeted generally toward persons and families at the lower end of the income distribution scale. These are the earned income credit, untaxed Social Security benefits, and additional deductions for the elderly and the blind. In spite of the inclusion of these three types of tax expenditures in the total, the overall pattern of distribution remaims regressive. The top three income brackets (incomes over $75,000) account for only 5.7% of all estimated returns in 1990 but benefit from 38.5% of total tax expenditures shown in the table. At the lowest end of the scale, we find 22.4% of all returns, but these persons and families will get only 3.0% of the tax expenditures. The middle range, from $30,000 through $75,000, includes 30.4% of tax returns filed, and receives 33.2% of the tax expenditure total. Persons and families with less than $30,000 in income account for 63.9% of tax returns and get 28.3% of the tax expenditures contained in the table. This distribution seems on the surface slightly less unequal than the distribution shown in table 3-14, but too much should not be made of this because of the limited number of tax expenditure items contained in table 3-15.

It is interesting to examine the distribution for some of the better-known tax expenditures. The deductibility of interest on home mortgages is a case in point. When elimination of this tax expenditure was proposed during the

**Table 3-15. Distribution of Selected Tax Expenditures by Adjusted Gross Income Class: 1990 (in Millions of Dollars and in Percent)**

| Tax Expenditure | Income Class | | | | | | | | | Total |
|---|---|---|---|---|---|---|---|---|---|---|
| | Less than $10,000 | $10,000– 20,000 | $20,000– 30,000 | $30,000– 40,000 | $40,000– 50,000 | $50,000– 75,000 | $75,000– 100,000 | $100,000– 200,000 | Over $200,000 | |
| 1. Medical expenses | $14 | $229 | $354 | $710 | $328 | $474 | $243 | $373 | $149 | $2,874 |
| 2. Real estate deductions | 3 | 87 | 358 | 670 | 645 | 2,264 | 1,210 | 1,884 | 1,208 | 8,329 |
| 3. State and local tax deductions | 3 | 92 | 434 | 1,017 | 995 | 3,675 | 2,150 | 4,743 | 6,703 | 19,812 |
| 4. Charitable contributions | 1 | 62 | 307 | 826 | 705 | 2,041 | 1,099 | 2,408 | 5,627 | 13,076 |
| 5. Child care | 57 | 577 | 1,012 | 848 | 548 | 652 | 184 | 106 | 30 | 4,014 |
| 6. Earned income credit | 1,466 | 3,804 | 593 | 58 | 8 | 7 | | | | 5,936 |
| 7. Untaxed Social Security benefits | 781 | 4,846 | 5,971 | 6,753 | | 1,619 | 1,141 | | 287 | 21,388 |
| 8. Elderly and disabled deduction | | 252 | 506 | 574 | | 201 | 67 | | 6 | 1,606 |
| Total | $2,325 | $9,949 | $9,535 | $14,685 | | $10,933 | $15,598 | | $14,010 | $ 77,035 |
| Percent distribution | 3.0% | 12.9% | 12.4% | 19.1% | | 14.2% | 20.3% | | 18.2% | 100.0% |
| Number of returns | 27,312 | 28,311 | 22,275 | 16,535 | 9,123 | 11,428 | 3,034 | 2,873 | 986 | 121,877 |
| Percent distribution | 22.4% | 23.2% | 18.3% | 13.6% | 7.5% | 9.4% | 2.5% | 2.4% | 0.8% | 100.0% |

a In thousands.

Source: Joint Committee on Taxation, *Estimates of Federal Tax Expenditures for Fiscal Years 1990–1994*, February 28, 1989.

debate and discussion leading up to the Tax Reform Act of 1986, there was such a firestorm of protest that the idea was dropped like a hot potato. Data on the distribution of the home mortgage deduction for 1988 are found in the 1988 Joint Committee on Taxation Report. The value of this particular tax expenditure in 1988 was $27.7 billion, which was equal to 10.7% of the tax expenditure total in the same year of $259.1 billion (for individuals). How was this particular item allocated? Persons and families with incomes of over $100,000 got 22.1% of this benefit. On the other hand, families and persons with incomes below $30,000 received but 10.1% of the total. The number of persons and families filing returns in the income ranges *below* $30,000 equaled 70.5% of returns filed, whereas persons and families in the over $100,000 range were but 2.0% of the total. The purpose of the home ownership interest deduction is to encourage home ownership by Americans, but doing this through the tax expenditure route results in large subsidies to a relatively small segment of the population. If legislation were proposed in the Congress saying, in effect, that the nation will provide quite small direct subsidies to encourage home ownership to the roughly 70% of the population with incomes below $30,000, and that these subsidies would increase rapidly as family income increases above this level, would such legislation pass? The question answers itself, yet this is the way the majority of tax expenditures work.

The upside-down or regressive distribution of tax expenditures helps explain an important puzzle. It was pointed out in the last chapter that we had an explosion in transfer spending in this country in the 1970s. Yet in that same period, as throughout the post-World War II era until the 1980s, the distribution of money income remained remarkably stable. How, one is entitled to ask, could this happen when transfers were expanding with great rapidity? Since Presumably most transfer or welfare state spending is thought to be directed toward persons at the lower end of the income scale—the unemployed, the disabled, and the poor—why would not this explosion, in conjunction with progression in the tax system, tilt the distribution of income in the direction of greater equality? We know that this did not happen. The explanation apparently lies with the equally explosive growth in tax expenditures—the hidden transfers in this period. As we have seen, the distribution of tax expenditures is highly skewed toward the upper-income groups. So it seems reasonable to conclude that the two trends just about offset one another, at least until the start of the 1980s. Transfers and a progressive tax system were offset by tax expenditures, which tipped more and more after-tax income toward those at the top of the income scale, effectively undercutting the progressiveness of the federal income tax system. This was true even though on paper a system with 14 brackets and a top marginal rate of 50% looks progressive.

Table 3-16.   The National Income and Tax Expenditures: Selected Years, 1967–1989 (in Billions of Current Dollars and in Percent)

| Year | National Income[a] | Tax Expenditures[b] | Tax Expenditures as a Percent of National Income |
|------|--------------------|---------------------|--------------------------------------------------|
| 1967 | $677.7             | $ 36.6              | 5.4%                                             |
| 1970 | 832.6              | 43.9                | 5.3                                              |
| 1975 | 1,289.1            | 92.9                | 7.2                                              |
| 1980 | 2,203.5            | 181.5               | 8.2                                              |
| 1985 | 3,234.0            | 365.1               | 11.3                                             |
| 1987 | 3,665.4            | 450.5               | 12.3                                             |
| 1988 | 3,072.6            | 321.1               | 8.1                                              |
| 1989 | 4,217.4[b]         | 292.7               | 6.9                                              |

[a] Calendar year basis.
[b] Fiscal year basis.

Sources: Congressional Budget Office, *Annual Reports on Tax Expenditures*, selected years, and Joint Committee on Taxation, *Estimates of Federal Tax Expenditures*, Annual Reports for selected years. *Economic Report of the President*, 1989.

## Some Concluding Comments

As we wind up our discussion in this chapter, some additional remarks are in order. In the next-to-last section of chapter 2, a comparison was made for selected years between transfer expenditures and the national income, the purpose being to get a rough idea of how much of every dollar of income "earned" through involvement in production was affected by transfer spending. The statistics on this relationship are shown in table 2-8. In 1983, transfer spending reached a post-1929 peak of 20.3% of the national income, which meant that approximately 20 cents out of every dollar of income earned was being re-arranged by the transfer machinery of the national government.

It would seem appropriate to make the same kind of comparison for tax expenditures, keeping in mind the caveat about their additive nature. Then by combining the data on *both* transfer and tax expenditures for selected years, we shall have an even better picture of the scope of income redistributional activity carried on by the federal government. The first such comparison—tax expenditures in relation to the national income—is found in table 3-16. These data are on a fiscal year basis, and are for selected years since 1967, the year for which the Congressional Budget office developed the first systematic and detailed data on tax-based subsidies. Tax expen-

Table 3-17. The National Income and the Combined Total of Transfers and Tax Expenditure for Selected Years, 1967–1989 (in Billions of Dollars and in Percent)

| Year | National Income [a] | Tax Expenditures [b] | Transfer Expenditures [a] | Total for Transfers and Tax Expenditures | Transfers and Tax Expenditures as a Percent of National Income |
|------|------|------|------|------|------|
| 1967 | $ 677.7 | $ 36.6 | $ 73.1 | $109.7 | 16.2% |
| 1970 | 832.5 | 43.9 | 109.0 | 152.9 | 18.4 |
| 1975 | 1,289.1 | 92.9 | 235.0 | 327.9 | 25.4 |
| 1980 | 2,203.5 | 181.5 | 407.0 | 588.5 | 26.7 |
| 1985 | 3,234.0 | 365.1 | 630.4 | 995.5 | 30.8 |
| 1987 | 3,665 4 | 450.5 | 691.2 | 1,141.7 | 38.7 |
| 1988 | 3,972.6 | 321.1 | 737.0 | 1,058.1 | 26.6 |
| 1989 | 4,217.4 | 292.7 | 788.7 | 1,081.4 | 25.6 |

[a] Calendar year basis.
[b] Fiscal year basis.

Sources: Congressional Budget Office, *Annual Reports on Tax Expenditures*, selected years, and Joint Committee on Taxation, *Estimates of Federal Tax Expenditures*, Annual Reports for selected years. *Economic Report of the President*, 1989.

ditures as a proportion of the national income grew steadily from 1967 through 1987, the year in which they reached their peak. After 1987 and under the influence of the Tax Reform Act of 1986, they declined, falling to 6.9% in fiscal 1989.

Table 3-17 combines transfer spending data with figures on tax expenditures as discussed in this chapter. The table covers the same selected years as table 3-16. Between 1967 and 1987, the combined total of transfers and tax expenditures computed as a percent of the national income than doubled, rising from 16.2% in 1967 to 38.7% in 1987, the peak year for the combined figure. By 1987, one could say that because of the federal government's massive transfer and tax system, more than one third of income "earned" in the productive process—the national income—was being "rearranged." Since 1987, this combined percentage has fallen sharply, primarily because of tax reforms enacted in 1986. The percentage is now down to 25.6%. These figures, of course, do not and cannot tell us whether or not this change is good or bad. They only give us an indication of the magnitude of the situation. The extent to which the federal government should be involved in income redistribution, and the ways in which it should do this, are issues that go beyond the matter of measurement. They involve fundamental questions about the nature and evolutionary direction of America's contemporary welfare state, questions that will confront the nation well into the next century. Two such questions, both of great importance, concern the coming impact of the Baby Boomers on the Social Security system, and the matter of adequate health insurance for all Americans. These are issues we shall address in the final chapter in this book.

## Notes

1. Even though in principle a tax system might be neutral, it is unlikely in reality to be so. The mere fact of taxation is likely to affect different people differently, even though they apparently are equally situated before taxation. Thus, there is likely to be *some* redistributional effect from any tax structure, even if it is not designed to bring about a redistribution.

2. Congress of the United States, Joint Committee on Taxation, *Estimates of Federal Tax Expenditures for Fiscal Years 1990–1994*, February 28, 1989, p. 3.

3. U.S. General Accounting Office, *Tax Expenditures: A Primer*, PAD 80-26, 1979, p. i.

4. The Congressional Budget Office no longer prepares this list, the task having been taken over by the Joint Committee on Taxation. The Joint Committee on Taxation consists of the two revenue committees of the Congress, namely, the House Ways and Means Committee and the Senate Finance Committee.

5. This will not be easy to accomplish, since there is little public understanding of transfer spending per se, let alone of tax expenditures.

6. Congress of the United States, Congressional Budget Office, *Tax Expenditures: Budget*

*Control Options and Five-Year Budget Projections for Fiscal Years 1983–1987*, November, 1982, p. 5.

7. *Economic Report of the President*, (Washington, D.C., U.S. Government Printing Office, 1990) p. 389.

8. U.S. General Accounting Office, *op. cit.*, p. 19.

9. Congress of the United States, Congressional Budget Office, *The Effects of Tax Reform on Tax Expenditures*, p. 19.

10. *Ibid.*, p. ix.

11. *Ibid.*, p. vii.

12. *Ibid.*, p. 16 (see also Joint Committee on Taxation, *General Explanation of the Tax Reform Act of 1986*, May 4, 1987, p. 218).

13. *Ibid.*, *The Effects of Tax Reform*, p. 17.

14. Joint Committee on Taxation, *Estimates of Federal Tax Expenditures for Fiscal Years 1989–1993*, March, 1988.

15. The same argument may be applied to transfers. See Stanley S. Surrey and Paul R. McDaniel, *Tax Expenditures* (Cambridge, MA, Harvard University Press, 1985), p. 231.

16. Congress of the United States, Congressional Budget Office, *Tax Expenditures: Current Issues and Five-Year Budget Projections for Fiscal Years 1982–1986*, September, 1981, p. 9.

17. Stanley S. Surrey, *op. cit.*, p. 232.

18. *Ibid.*, p. 72.

19. Congress of the United States, Congressional Budget Office, *Tax Expenditures: Budget Control Options and Five-Year Projections for Fiscal Years 1983–1987*, November, 1982, pp. 95 ff.

20. Joint Committee on Taxation, *Estimates of Federal Tax Expenditures for Fiscal Years 1990–1994*, February 28, 1989, pp. 20 ff. y.

# 4 THE WELFARE STATE UNDER ASSAULT: THE REAGAN REVOLUTION

When Ronald Reagan took the presidential oath in early 1981, the change in leadership represented much more than the usual post-World War II swing from a mildly liberal Democratic administration to a mildly conservative Republican administration. Unlike the earlier Nixon and Ford Administrations, President Reagan and his new administration set out in their first year to overthrow the basic consensus that had set the bounds for policy since the war. This consensus involved, first acceptance of the broad contours of America's welfare state as it had evolved since the 1930s, and, second, a belief in active demand management to promote economic stability and growth within this framework. The Reagan Administration was determined to dismantle this consensus and to bring about thereby a radical shift in the economic role played by the federal government.

This is what we shall examine in this chapter, beginning with an explanation of Mr. Reagan's basic strategy, showing how this grand objective was to be accomplished. To explain the strategy and how it originated, we shall have a look at the ideas and the influence that came from the key architects of this strategy. The prime movers behind the Reagan program were David A. Stockman, Director of the Office of Management and Budget (OMB) in the first Reagan Administration, and supply-side true believers like Jude

Wanniski and Congressman Jack Kemp. We shall also briefly look at the Reagan plan and its origins from the perspective of the overall economy, examining what the Administration expected to happen in comparison with what actually happened. This will give us the necessary background for the main business of this chapter which is, first, to examine critically the impact of the Reagan counter revolution on America's welfare state within the context given to that concept in this book and second to show what effect the Reagan years have had on the distribution of income in the United States. We then will have set the stage for the final chapter, in which we shall sketch out the boundries of the welfare state as it now exists, including an analysis of current problems and future prospects.

## The Reagan Program for Economic Recovery

President Reagan went before the Congress on the evening of February 18, 1981 to spell-out, in his first major address to the Congress, the essential details of the Administration's plan for "economic recovery."[1] In his historic speech, the President outlined a plan involving a four fold strategy that would, he said, "reverse the debilitating combination of sustained inflation and economic distress which continues to face the American economy."[2] The first step in the recovery plan involved a substantial reduction in the rate of growth of federal spending, the objective being to scale back sharply the *relative* size of the federal government. Americans have forgotten, the President went on to say, that "government spending has become so extensive that it contributes to the economic problems it was designed to cure. More government intervention in the economy cannot possibly be a solution to our economic problems."[3] Federal spending would fall, the President asserted, from the current 23% of the gross national product (GNP) to 19% by 1986.

The second major element in the Reagan program was a 10% reduction per year in personal income tax rates for three years as well as substantial tax relief for business by accelerating business depreciation. The expectation was that the latter would stimulate investment in new plant and equipment, thereby promoting substantial job growth. The personal income tax cuts were originally the brainchild of Senator William V. Roth and Representative Jack Kemp, both Republicans and converts to the new doctrine of supply-side economics. After briefly flirting with the idea of seeking the Republican nomination in 1980, Kemp backed off and then joined Ronald Reagan's campaign as chief policy theoretician. During the early months of 1980, Kemp successfully converted Ronald Reagan to supply-side economics and its major policy idea, a tax cut as originally proposed by Kemp–Roth.[4]

The third element in the President's Program was regulatory relief. This sprang from the President's own strong personal conviction, as well as the long-standing view of most conservatives, that excessive federal regulation had both retarded economic growth and contributed to inflationary pressures. To implement this phase of the recovery program, the President told the Congress that in its first month in office the Administration already had established a Task Force on Regulatory Relief, chaired by Vice President Bush, abolished the Council on Wage and Price Stability, postponed the effective date for all pending regulations, and accelerated the decontrol of domestic oil.

The final plank in the economic recovery plan was a pledge to cooperate with the Board of Governors of the Federal Reserve System in the development of policies that would "restore a stable currency and healthy financial markets."[5] Specifically, the President called for a steady reduction in the rate of growth for money and credit from the 1980 levels—the broadly-based money supply M2 grew by 8.9% in 1980—to one half those levels by 1986. At this time, apparently neither the President nor his closest advisers noted the irony of the situation, namely that in the realm of monetary policy the President's program called for restricting the monetary spigot, but in the realm of fiscal policy, the thrust was clearly expansionary. The contradictory effects of these two policy recommendations would not become known until some months later.

The statistical story of the Program for Economic Recovery is told in table 4-1. A brief explanation for the figures in the table and their arrangements is in order. Line 1 is essentially a forecast of expenditures that would have taken place under the Carter Administration's lame-duck budget *plus* the added defense outlays that the Reagan Administration thought to be necessary over those already programmed by Carter. These are the estimated figures from which the Reagan Administration was to derive all its budget "savings" on the expenditures side.

Line 2 contains the budget ceilings projected by the Reagan Administration, including the planned increases in military spending. Line 3, which is the difference between lines 1 and 2, represents, therefore, the targeted budget savings, which add up to $471.3 billion. It is important not to forget that this figure, and all the figures in the economic recovery program, were not real when the President presented them to the Congress early in February, 1981. They were projections—that is, estimates, good or bad —about what the future would entail. Line 4, labeled the "asterisk" savings, turned out to be of crucial political and strategic significance in the

Table 4-1.  The Reagan Economic Program: 1981–1986 (in Billions of Dollars and in Percent)

| Program Item | Years[a] | | | | | | Total |
|---|---|---|---|---|---|---|---|
| | 1981 | 1982 | 1983 | 1984 | 1985 | 1986 | |
| 1. Carter budget with added defense outlays | $ 659.1 | $ 736.9 | $ 812.8 | $876.0 | $ 961.6 | $1035.9 | $5082.3 |
| 2. Reagan's budget ceiling (including defense) | 654.7 | 695.5 | 733.1 | 771.6 | 844.0 | 912.1 | 4611.0 |
| 3. Targeted budget savings | 4.4 | 41.4 | 79.7 | 104.4 | 117.6 | 123.8 | 471.3 |
| 4. The "asterisk" savings[b] | — | — | 21.2 | 30.7 | 31.0 | 28.0 | 110.9 |
| 5. Projected receipts under Carter budget | 609.0 | 702.4 | 807.6 | 917.2 | 1033.2 | 1159.8 | 5229.2 |
| 6. Reagan budget receipts | 600.2 | 650.5 | 710.2 | 772.1 | 850.9 | 942.0 | 4525.9 |
| 7. "Lost" tax revenues (line 5 minus line 6) | 8.8 | 51.9 | 97.4 | 145.1 | 182.3 | 217.8 | 703.3 |
| 8. Targeted budget deficit (−) or surplus (+) | −54.5 | −45.0 | −22.9 | +0.5 | +6.9 | +29.9 | −85.1 |
| 9. Outlays as a percent of GNP | 23.0% | 21.8% | 20.4% | 19.3% | 19.2% | 19.0% | — |
| 10. Receipts as a percent of GNP | 21.1% | 20.4% | 19.7% | 19.3% | 19.3% | 19.6% | — |

[a] Fiscal years.
[b] Savings to be determined later.

Source: The White House, *A Program For Economic Recovery*, February 18, 1981.

implementation of the President's program during the rest of 1981. It totaled $110.9 billion, and represented potential savings that David Stockman and his co-workers at OMB could not identify in terms of specifics when they were putting the President's program together in the hurried and hectic atmosphere that prevailed before the President went before the Congress. These amounts were identified by an asterisk in the strategy sessions. Howard Baker, then a Senator, had dubbed them the "magic asterisk," for it was blithely assumed that they would be taken care of at a later date.

In line 5 are found the revenues that presumably would have accrued to the government under the lame-duck budget of the Carter Administration. These were based upon tax rates and policies in effect at the time the Reagan Administration came into office. Next, in line 6, we find the projected budget receipts under the Reagan budget, taking into account the effect of Reagan's 10-10-10 reduction in personal income tax rates, depreciation changes aimed at stimulating business investment, and some relatively minor increases in user fees as a revenue source. Also underlying these projections are the assumptions about the economy's performance over the period, assumptions shown in table 4-2 which reflect the expected impact of supply-side economics on that performance. We shall discuss these when we turn to comment on the data in table 4-2.

Line 7 is a crucial line. It gives us the "lost" tax revenues or personal "savings" to taxpayers, depending upon one's preferred viewpoint, resulting from the difference between the projected revenues under Carter and the projected revenues under Reagan. These lost revenues or tax savings total $703.1 billion, a staggering figure.

Finally, we come to the bottom line—what does all this add up to in terms of the budget deficit? Here on line 8 we find the magic number. By 1984 the Reagan program promised a modest budget *surplus* of $0.5 billion, which, if it had materialized would have been the first time since 1969 that the federal government had operated in the black. After 1984, the surplus was expected to grow, reaching a targeted $29.9 billion two years later.

Lines 9 and 10, the last two lines, round out the numbers for the program. They show, first, projected outlays as a percent of the GNP over the period, and, second, the same percentage figure for receipts. When President Reagan presented his program, federal spending (1980) was 22.5% of the GNP, and federal revenues were 20.3%.

Before we turn to our analysis of the figures in table 4-1 and show how they were supposed to interact and bring about a successful conclusion to the President's revolution, we need to take a quick look at the key assumptions behind these numbers. The key to the success of the program lay in how the economy would actually perform over the six-year period shown in

Table 4-2.  Projected and Actual Values for Real GNP Growth, Inflation and Unemployment Rates 1981–1986 (in Percent)

| Economic Variable | Years | | | | | |
|---|---|---|---|---|---|---|
| | 1981 | 1982 | 1983 | 1984 | 1985 | 1986 |
| *Projected Values* | | | | | | |
| 1.  Real GNP[a] | 1.1 | 4.2 | 5.0 | 4.5 | 4.2 | 4.2 |
| 2.  Consumer Prices[b] | 11.1 | 8.3 | 6.2 | 5.5 | 4.7 | 4.2 |
| 3.  Unemployment | 7.8 | 7.2 | 6.6 | 6.4 | 6.0 | 5.6 |
| *Actual Values* | | | | | | |
| 4.  Real GNP[c] | 1.9 | −2.5 | 3.6 | 6.8 | 3.4 | 2.7 |
| 5.  Consumer Prices[d] | 8.8 | 3.8 | 3.8 | 3.9 | 3.8 | 1.1 |
| 6.  Unemployment | 7.6 | 9.7 | 9.6 | 7.5 | 7.2 | 6.2 |

[a] In 1972 dollars.
[b] 1967 = 100.
[c] In 1982 dollars.
[d] 1982–1984 = 100.

Sources: The White House, *A Program for Economic Recovery, February, 18, 1981. Economic Report of the President*, 1989.

table 4-1. The Reagan assumptions for the crucial economic numbers are shown in table 4-2. These numbers are for real GNP, the inflation rate, and the unemployment rate. There were others, but these three were the most critical.[6] Basically, the forecasts for GNP growth and the decline in inflation embodied two crucial supply-side assumptions. The first is that the economy would respond magnificiently to the cut in tax rates, and, second, that once the financial and business community understood clearly that an anti-inflationary policy was in place *to stay*, inflationary expectations would vanish almost immediately, thereby bringing down the inflation rate without the wrenching pain of putting the economy through the wringer of a recession. As David Stockman explains in his book, *The Triumph of Politics: Why the Reagan Revolution Failed*, "The heart of the supply-side synthesis rested upon the notion of a 'push-pull' economic dynamic. Hard money policies would 'pull down' the rate of inflation and nominal GNP growth. The tax cut and the whole range of supply-side economic policy changes would 'push up' the rate of real output and employment expansion. Both effects would occur in a simultaneous time frame."[7]

The perceptive reader cannot help but notice that the forecasts for real growth between 1982 and 1986 were unusually high, well above actual experience at *any* time during the post-World War II period. Specifically, and beyond the broad generalities of supply-side economics, where did they come from? According to Stockman, they emerged from a fractious debate that absorbed nearly all of the energies of the forecasting team during the whole of January and early February in 1981. Three, not one, economic doctrines contended for supremacy at this time namely, monetarism, reflected in the views of Beryl Sprinkel, who became Undersecretary of the Treasury for Monetary Affairs in the first Reagan administration; supply-side economics, led by Paul Craig Roberts, who also entered the Treasury and is now a columnist for *Business Week* magazine; and the eclectic viewpoint, represented by Murray Weidenbaum, newly appointed Chairman of the Council of Economic Advisers and a long-time professor at Washington University in St. Louis: Stockman said his own position was a combination of the supply-side and monetarist viewpoints.[8]

The primary problem was the basic incompatibility between what the supply-siders and the monetarists wanted. The former wanted the highest real growth rate possible, and the latter the lowest possible rate of growth for *money* GNP. As Stockman points out in his account of how the Reagan Revolution was forged, Murray Weidenbaum joined the forecasting team late in the game, by which time the first forecasts had been made. Unhappily, the arithmetic of the 5% growth rate for real GNP for the supply-siders and the 7% growth rate for money GNP for the monetarists added up to a 2% inflation rate by the third or fourth year of the program. This figure Weidenbaum simply would not buy. "Nobody," Stockman reports Weidenbaum as saying "is going to predict a two percent inflation on *my* watch. We'll be the laughing stock of the world."[9] Further, the numbers did not add up in a much more important way, for within a year after the tax cut the deficit soared to a wholly unacceptable $150 billion!

All this took place a scant three weeks before date scheduled for the President to go before the Congress with his blueprint for economic recovery. The forecasting team, Stockman recalls, "went into a white heat of pressure."[10] What finally emerged in time for the President's appearance were the crucial numbers shown in the upper half of table 4-2. They eventually came to be known as the *Rosy Scenario*, but these forecasts were crucial to the success of the economic revolution planned by Mr. Reagan and reflected in table 4-1. Murray Weidenbaum, Stockman reports, wrote the final numbers, but its underlying architecture, the push-pull hypothesis, was the work of a "small band of ideologues," namely the supply-siders.[11] The actual numbers for the three critical variables are found in the lower half of table 4-2. The inflation rate came down much faster than planned, primarily because of the unexpected severity of the 1981–1982 recession, but real growth fell seriously short of what was predicted and, one might add, necessary for the success of the Reagan Revolution.

Before we turn to a more in-depth discussion of the architects of the economic recovery program, we need to return to the numbers in table 4-1 and examine more fully just how everything was supposed to work out. In its bedrock essentials, the President's program called for a massive reduction in revenues (over $700 billion) in combination with a sizable increase in military outlays, and a balanced federal budget within three years. Earlier, when still contending against Mr. Reagan for the Republican 1980 presidential nomination, George Bush called the combination of lowered taxes, more military spending, and a balanced budget "voodoo economics." John Anderson, a now all-but-forgotten independent candidate for president in 1980, said it could only be done with "smoke and mirrors."

So how was it to be done? The best way to answer question is to look at the totals for the entire period, not the figures for any individual year. The success of the entire program hinged upon two developments. The first was that the economy would grow at a rate sufficient to generate the projected revenues shown on line 6 in table 4-1. Supply-side economics had to come through if this was to happen. Second, David Stockman and the OMB had to succed in persuading the President and the President had to succeed in persuading the Congress to make the targeted budget cuts shown in line 3. If these two things happened, then over the period (1981–1986) the total revenue shortfall would be only $85.1 billion, a figure with which the economy could easily live, and one that would permit a balanced budget to be reached by 1984. Just as the tight-money pull-down scenario had to mesh in a simultaneous time frame with the supply-side pull-up scenario if the underlying assumptions of the recovery program were to be realized, so also the planned budget reductions would have to mesh with the anticipated revenue gains for the final goals of the Reagan Revolution to be reached —a balanced budget within the frame of a smaller, leaner federal government. These things did not happen. After a look at the architects of the Program for Economic Recovery, we will turn to the question of what went wrong.

## The Architects of the Reagan Revolution

Supply-side economics provided the underlying theoretical rationale for the Reagan counterrevolution, while David Stockman was the impresario who pushed first an eager Reagan and second a reluctant Congress in this direction. As is well known by now, supply-side economics is the brainchild of

Arthur Laffer, formerly an economics professor at the University of Southern California. The story, apocryphal or not, is that Laffer first sketched out the fundamental idea of what has come to be known as supply-side economics on a napkin in a Washington, D.C. restaurant.[12] The idea is that the real key to economic growth, to a rising level of productivity, and to productivity generally is the *level* of taxation. When taxes are too high, incentives to produce, to save, and to invest are seriously impaired. The cure, therefore, is to reduce taxes. Laffer formalized this idea by sketching out what has become known as the Laffer Curve. There are two levels of taxation, he argued, at which government revenues would be zero. The first would happen if the rate of taxation was zero, for then a government would not collect any taxation. Revenues would also be zero if the tax rate was 100%, for then there would be a complete collapse of production and hence the government could not collect any taxes. But in between there is a wide range of rates that will produce varying amounts of revenue. Somewhere within this range there is a tax rate that will produce the maximum revenue for the state. At tax rates above this optimum tax rate, revenues will fall, and at tax rates below the optimum, they will also fall. Laffer allegedly illustrated his idea by drawing a rough curve connecting on one axis the 100% and zero tax rates and showing on the other axis the tax revenue associated with each particular tax rate. His curve was purely hypothetical —no empirical Laffer Curve exists.

What is truly important about Laffer Curve in the context of the Reagan Revolution is not whether an empirical curve really exists. Rather, it is that Laffer was convinced, as were his more zealous converts, that the economy in the late 1970s was riding on the upside of the of curve, which is to say that tax rates had gone *above* the optimum point that would produce the maximum revenue for the government. The logic then is to cut taxes and in so doing to *increase* the amount of revenue flowing into the coffers of the government. If Laffer's basic premise is granted, namely that there exists *some* rate of taxation beyond which incentives to produce will be so badly hurt that tax revenues *must* fall, then the logic of his conclusions is irrefutable. The basic trouble with this, of course, is that there is no empirical evidence telling us where the optimum rate of taxation is to be found. In the American economy, for example, taxes for all levels of government (federal, state, and local) were equal to 31.1% of the GNP.[13] In Scandinavian countries, this ratio has been above 50% for years, but production has not fallen. So where is the appropriate level? We simply don't know. Laffer's second point, namely that the economy is on the upside of the curve and therefore a tax cut is in order, has to be taken on faith. There is no way empirically to determine this.

One of the strongest and most enthusiastic early supporters of Laffer's argument was Jude Wanniski, at the time an editorial writer for the *Wall Street Journal* and later founder of his own economic consulting firm. Through Wanniski, the *Journal* and Jack Kemp, a rising star in the Republican Party, were converted to the supply-side ideology. Others who played a leading role as supply-siders in shaping the Reagan program were Paul Craig Roberts, mentioned earlier, and Norman Ture, a Washington, D.C. economic consultant before joining the Treasury under Reagan.

Although the tax cut was the centerpiece of the supply-side argument, it was not the whole story. The most avid of the supply-siders, especially Congressman Kemp and Jude Wanniski, wanted a return to the gold standard, believing that leaving the gold standard ended any check on the power of the government to create money. Rampant inflation was the consequence.[14] For Wanniski, according to Stockman, "gold was like the True Cross."[15] The supply-siders did not succeed, however, in getting their ideas about a return to gold into either the 1980 Republican platform or the *Program for Economic Recovery* that the President took before the Congress in 1981. Finally, there is the matter of the budget deficit, something that orthodox Republicans had nearly always viewed with loathing. But the supply-siders and the then new breed of Republican politicians, like Jack Kemp, were indifferent to the deficits, believing, as Laffer and Wanniski argued, that real growth stimulated by the tax cuts would produce enough new revenue so that the deficits would take care of themselves.

David Stockman's role as an architect of the Reagan Revolution was far more comprehensive and complex than providing a theoretical rationale for what the President wanted to do. Although he accepted in general the supply-side premise that high taxes were a barrier to growth and improved productivity, he did not uncritically accept the argument that the tax cut would generate enough new revenues so that budget deficits would cease to be a worry. "The Reagan Revolution," he said, "...required a frontal assault on the American welfare state. That was the only way to pay for the massive Kemp–Roth tax cut."[16] In his image-shattering interview with William Greider in the December 1981 issue of *The Atlantic Monthly*, Stockman was even more brutally frank, saying that "...Kemp–Roth was always a Trojan horse to bring down the top rates."[17] Stockman's candid remarks earned him a trip to a symbolic woodshed with the President, but did not cost him his job.

To understand fully Stockman's true beliefs about supply-side economics, one must go back to an article he published in 1975 in *The Public Interest* entitled "The Social Pork Barrel." At that time he was on the staff of Congressman John Anderson, and thinking about running for Congress in 1976. He did and he won, a victory that a Michigan newspaper said made Stockman a "...new political powerhouse in Southern Michigan."[18] David Stockman's article in *The Public Interest* was the product of a lengthy intellectual journey. This journey took him from conservative Republican roots nourished by his boyhood on a Michigan farm, through neo-Marxism and the antiwar movement while a student at Michigan State University in the 1960s, then into a brief flirtation with the ministry at the Harvard Divinity School, and finally back to the Republican fold as a neoconservative on the legislative staff of John Anderson. By then he had become firmly convinced that the "good society"—the ideal of which Walter Lippmann wrote—was "...best served by a smaller, less activist state and by a more dynamic, productive and fluid marketplace. Social progress was as much a matter of unshackling the powers of the latter as it was of extending the reach of the former."[19]

The basic problem, he wrote in his 1975 article, is that worthy social programs, even though they begin at relatively modest levels, develop a "built-in momentum" that eventually makes them "uncontrollable," a situation that he thought characterized three fourths of federal outlays (1975). What might have been "...the bright promise of the Great Society has been transformed into a flabby hodge-podge...that increasingly looks like a great social pork barrel".[20] The "built-in momentum," of indiscriminate social spending not only outpaces current revenues, but absorbs the growth-induced "fiscal dividend" several years into the future. The tragic consequence of this is that the society cannot finance either an adequate system of national health insurance or a decent nationwide income guarantee program, social objectives that Stockman strongly supports.[21]

The basic principle that undergirds this development is the tendency to distribute the benefits from social welfare spending widely, rather than to concentrate them on those in genuine need. Politicians, Stockman argues, have distorted Bentham's greatest good for the greatest number into "the greatest goodies for the greatest number," leading to a distorted welfare state in which the haves as well as the have-nots are being subsidized. What we have is a system that increasingly shunts middle-class taxes through the public sector and back to middle-class beneficiaries.[22]

So what is to be done? The answer, Stockman then says, does not lie in the conventional liberal wisdom of a reordering of government priorities— that is, less military and more social spending—or in a sweeping tax reform. The only real cure for the pork-barrel approach to social spending is a frontal assault on the welfare state. Using all of his formidable persuasive skills and deeply detailed knowledge of the budget numbers, Stockman set out in the late winter and through the spring of 1981 to persuade an eager

President and a reluctant Congress to go down this road. He came close, but did not succeed, for reasons we shall discuss in the next section.

## What Went Wrong?

As noted earlier, Stockman accepted the basic theory of supply-side economics, but he did not buy the idea that the tax cuts would stimulate sufficient growth to generate the revenues needed to balance the budget by 1984. "The Reagan Revolution," as he defined it, "required a frontal assault on the American welfare state. That was the only way to pay for the massive Kemp–Roth tax cuts."[23] In a paper he and Congressman Jack Kemp prepared for President-elect Reagan in late December 1980 ("Avoiding a GOP Economic Dunkirk"), the federal budget was described as having become an "automatic 'coast-to-coast' soup line that dispenses remedial aid with almost reckless abandon...."[24] In this paper Stockman and Kemp did not resort to the usual campaign rhetoric promising that through elimination of "waste and fraud" the budget could be balanced. Though the language of the "Dunkirk" memo was circumspect, it was clear that the "frontal assault on the American welfare state" required reductions in entitlement spending. Though they used the more innocent-sounding term "revision" in their memo, it was clear that such revisions could go in only one direction— down.

The problem was how to accomplish this. In the lame-duck budget that the Reagan Administration took over from President Carter, transfers to people took 48 cents of every dollar of federal spending, military spending 25 cents, and interest on the debt another 10 cents. That left only 17 cents for all other federal programs. Clearly, neither defense nor social spending could be exempted if the Administration was to come up with the $41.4 billion in savings for fiscal 1982 that Reagan Revolution required. To achieve this, Stockmam derived a three-pronged strategy. First, he drew upon what he admittedly described as an "amateur's knowledge' of rational-expectations economic theory to come up with a *fiscal expectations* theory. Once the financial world of Wall Street saw that the new administration consisted neither of fiscal con men nor of practitioners of "voodoo economics," the nation's capital markets would respond positively. The bond and stock markets would soar, capital would flow into new, long-term investments, and the Federal Reserve would have a margin, admittedly narrow, within which it could curtail money growth without triggering a recession.[25] The second prong involved what Stockman called the "cats and dogs" saving proposals, namely the savings to be gained from a "comprehensive scrub" of the lame-duck Carter budget for fiscal 1982. At best this prong would produce about $10 billion in saving.[26] The real savings would come form Stockman's third prong, which he basically described as his "Grand Doctrine." It would entail a "...sweeping reform of the big middle class entitlement programs: Social Security, Medicare, and federal retirement pensions." His Grand Doctrine, Stockman explained in *The Triumph of Politics*, was "...basically hostile to the prevailing 'social insurance' premise upon which these giant programs rested. Stripping out the 'unearned' benefits and the welfare components from the retirement programs and *means-testing* Medicare would result in huge cost reductions."[27] The third prong also involved either elimination or reduction of some of the better-known tax expenditures, including oil-depletion allowances and tax-free interest on industrial development bonds, and putting a cap on the tax deductibility of home mortgage interest for upper-income taxpayers.[28]

The details of the third prong of Stockman's Grand Doctrine were not spelled out in the 1981 document, *A Program for Economic Recovery*. The specifics by federal department and agency shown in the February 18 document were, for all practical purposes, a wish list of planned budgetary cuts, for as David Stockman freely admits in his book, he never believed they could review the "...entire $740 billion budget (fiscal 1982) before February 18."[29] The *real* budget-cut packages were to be transmitted later—in March and April—to the Congress. What the February 18 message did was to reveal the framework of Reagan's fiscal plan. "But," Stockman explained, "the thing that would ultimately make it add up—sweeping curtailment of middle-class entitlements— would remain shrouded in mystery, at least temporarily. The *false* impression that you could have huge tax cuts and a big defense increase without storming the twin citadels of the welfare state— Social Security and Medicare—could easily be conveyed."[30]

So what went wrong? First, the bull market that Stockman hoped would give the Federal Reserve the needed margin to clamp down on money growth without precipitating a recession did not arrive in time. In 1982 both the Dow Jones and the Standard and Poor indices were down, 5.2% for the Dow and 6.5% for the Standard and Poor index.[31] The tight money policy the Federal Reserve pursued in 1981 and the first half of 1982 led to a recession, not real growth in an atmosphere of stable prices. Much more important, however, practically all of the third prong in Stockman's strategy was rejected, both by the Administration and by the Congress.

Stockman's first defeat came on defense. As he points out in his book, cutting defense had never been on his "...real ideological agenda," but he recognized that at least some cuts had to be made in the Pentagon's projected spending as a "political lubricant" for other cuts.[32] His problem was compounded by two things. First, there was the celebrated "error" made in January when the defense increases were being made, an error which neither the President nor Defense Secretary Caspar Weinberger apparently fully understood. In the 1980 presidential campaign, Reagan had demanded a 7% increase in real defense spending through 1986. This 7% increase, which Weinberger reluctantly accepted, was to be built upon President Carter's 1980 defense budget of $142 billion. What was missed in the frenzied budget calculations made by Stockman's forecasting team in January of 1981 was that the fiscal 1981 budget inherited from the Carter Administration already contained a defense fund figure with a 9% *rate of real growth* built into it! As a result of the fiasco in the desert for the ill-fated rescue attempt of the hostages in Iran, the Congress had raised Carter's request for defense funds. So they added Reagan's 7% increase to a budget total already raised, and by doing this ended up with a real growth rate for the defense budget of more than 10%. By February 18, the figures were already out, and, as Stockman said, "...they were squealing with delight throughout the military-industrial complex."[33]

Stockman's second problem with defense turned out to be Caspar Weinberger, Reagan's newly named Secretary of Defense. Weinberger had been Director of OMB in the Ford Administration, where he had been such a zealous budget-cutter that he earned the nickname of "Cap the Knife." So Stockman naturally assumed that Weinberger, while strongly committed to rebuilding the nation's defenses, would be prudent with military spending. He could not have been more wrong. Not only did Weinberger refuse to recognize that the January "error" resulted in inflated numbers for the defense buildup, he was wholly intransigent on anything but the most minuscule cuts in the planned defense budget. Defense became effectively off-limits for any serious budget savings.

Next came Social Security and Medicare. Stockman planned to find major savings here through a variety of avenues. These included reducing the welfare element (so-called unearned benefits) in Social Security outlays—many workers get back in benefits far more than they paid in taxes—reducing dependents' benefits and tightening up on the rules for disability benefits, sharply increasing the penalties for early retirement, correcting the error made in the 1970s that stemmed from the indexing of wage records, and putting a cap on Medicare payments. By May 1981, Stockman and the OMB had put together the Social Security package, which, at a meeting on May 11, presumably got the President's endorsement. But the White House backed off, insisting that the plan be announced to the public by Richard Schweiker, Secretary of Health and Human Services (HHS). After Schweiker's press conference of May 12, a political storm hit with gale force. A few days later, the Senate voted 96 to 0 for a resolution denouncing Stockman's plan in its entirety. Social Security and Medicare were now off-limits to any serious budget cuts. As Stockman notes ruefully in his book, "...Social Security, the heart of the U.S. welfare state, was now safely back in the world of actuaries who had kept its massive expansion quiet over the decades. The centerpiece of the American welfare state had now been overwhelmingly ratified and affirmed in the white heat of political confrontation."[34]

The tax expenditure component of Stockman's third prong was short-lived, being shot down even before the February 18 document was completed. At a meeting with the President on Wednesday, February 11, the matter of the oil depletion allowances came up. The President, Stockman reported in his book, came to life and launched a short lecture saying how the whole idea of tax expenditures was a "liberal myth." "The idea implies," Stockman reports the President as saying, "that government owns all your income and has the right to decide what you can keep. Well, we're not going to have any of that kind of thinking around here."[35] Another source of budget savings went off-limits.

Stockman's last hope was the tax bill. He did not early on abandon his faith in supply-side economics, but in view of the losses on the budget-cutting side, he wanted to modify the tax cut. The rate reduction for the first year of Kemp–Roth was changed from 10% to 5%, and its implementation was delayed until late in the year (1981). As William Greider reported in his article in *The Atlantic Monthly* what Stockman also sought was a compromise on the tax cut with Representative Dan Rostenkowski, Chairman of the House Ways and Means Committee, which would not only moderate the size of the tax cut, but avoid a "bidding war."[36] This plan did not work. The negotiations fell apart. Kemp–Roth degenerated into a bidding war between the Democrats and the Republicans, the cost of which was $268 billion added on to the expected revenue losses from the modified Kemp–Roth (5-10-10) of $383 for 1982–1986.[37] Table 4-3 shows Stockman's own tabulation of the costs of the 1981 tax reduction bill through fiscal year 1990.

By November of 1981 it was clear to Stockman, though not to other members of the Administration nor to the President himself, that the Reagan Revolution as originally conceived had failed. As early as June, Stockman realized, the limit had been reached with respect to the willingness of the Congress to reduce spending. "The borders of the American welfare state had been redefined, but they had been only slightly and symbolically shrunken from where they had stood before," was how he described what had happened to the "revolution" on the spending side.[38]

Table 4-3.  David Stockman's Estimates of the Revenue Lost From the 1981 Tax Reduction Bill: 1982–1990[a] (in Billions of Dollars)

| Year | Kemp-Roth[b] | Business Coalition Bill[c] | Politician's Tax Ornaments | Total Cost | Percentage of GNP |
|------|------|------|------|------|------|
| 1982 | $25 | $10 | $6 | $41 | 1.3% |
| 1983 | 58 | 18 | 17 | 93 | 2.9 |
| 1984 | 87 | 26 | 24 | 137 | 3.8 |
| 1985 | 100 | 36 | 33 | 169 | 4.4 |
| 1986 | 113 | 50 | 48 | 211 | 5.0 |
| 1987 | 127 | 61 | 63 | 251 | 5.5 |
| 1988 | 142 | 65 | 76 | 283 | 5.8 |
| 1989 | 158 | 66 | 92 | 316 | 6.0 |
| 1990 | 173 | 70 | 109 | 352 | 6.2 |
| Total | $983 | $402 | $468 | $1853 | — |

[a] Fiscal years.

[b] As modified to 5–10–10.

[c] Liberalized depreciation which allowed business to write off buildings in ten years, machinery in five years, and vehicles in three years. Known as a 10-5-3 tax cut.

Source: David A. Stockman, *The Triumph of Politics* (New York, Harper & Row, 1986), p. 268.

By October it was equally clear to Stockman, if not to his colleagues in the Administration, that the tax reduction and the bidding war was leading the nation into an era of staggering and unprecedented deficits. The Rosy Scenario had disappeared.

Stockman's ultimate verdict on the Reagan experiment is devasting. In the final pages of his book, *The Triumph of Politics*, he has this to say:

> "Looking back, the only thing that can be said to have been innocent about the Reagan Revolution was its objective of improving upon what we inherited. The inflation-battered American economy of 1980 was no more sustainable or viable than is the deficit-burdened economy of 1986....
>
> But the Reagan Revolution's abortive effort to rectify these inherited conditions cannot be simply exonerated as a good try that failed.... In fact, it was the basic assumptions and fiscal architecture of the Reagan Revolution itself which first introduced the folly that now envelops our economic governance.
>
> The Reagan Revolution was radical, imprudent, and arrogant. It defied the settled consensus of professional politicians and economists on its two central assumptions. It mistakenly presumed that a handful of ideologues were right and

all the politicians were wrong about what the American people wanted from government. And it erroneously assumed that the damaged, disabled, inflation-swollen U.S. economy inherited from the Carter administration could be instantly healed when history and most of the professional economists said it couldn't be done."[39]

## What did the Reagan Revolution Accomplish?

The foregoing is David Stockman's verdict. We now need to go beyond the generality of his view and examine with greater precision the impact of the Reagan years on America's welfare state. Specifically, we shall answer two basic questions in this section. First, how did Reagan Revolution affect the structure of federal transfer spending? This question is directed not to classic welfare state spending alone, but to *all* transfers, including those to people, as well as to non-people-based programs. The second question concerns taxation and income distribution. As should be apparent from the discussion up to this point, America's welfare state is shaped not just by how the federal government spends money for transfer purposes, but also by the form and manner in which taxes are levied to pay federal financing. To the extent that data permit, we shall analyze how the tax cuts (and increases) of the Reagan era have affected the distribution of income in the American economy. Answers to these two basic questions will provide a overview of the contours of America's contemporary welfare state. Such an overview gives us the necessary backdrop for examination of the major problems confronting the welfare state's structure as the nation moves toward the twenty-first century.

Let us first look at what happened in the 1980s with transfers to people. Current dollar data for these figures are shown in table 4-4. They largely confirm David Stockman's conclusion that during the Reagan era the borders of the welfare state shrunk only slightly. Any overall shrinking in transfer spending directed to people was primarily relative. From 1980 through 1988, total transfers to people grew by 69.9%, while government spending in total grew by 81.8%. This reflects a shift in federal priorities during the Reagan years, not an absolute decline in transfer outlays. Increased military spending largely accounts for this. In this same period, the GNP in current dollars grew by 78.6%.[40] Thus, the size of government, at least as measured by its spending totals, grew rather than declined in the Reagan era.

If we look at the composition of these totals, there are no startling surprises to be found. There was no shrinkage whatsoever in the *relative*

**Table 4-4. Federal Transfer Expenditures by Major Categories to People: 1980, 1984, 1988 (in Billions of Current Dollars and in Percent)**

| Category of Transfers | 1980 Dollar Volume | 1980 Percent Distribution | 1984 Dollar Volume | 1984 Percent Distribution | 1988 Dollar Volume | 1988 Percent Distribution |
|---|---|---|---|---|---|---|
| *Classic welfare state expenditures* | | | | | | |
| *Social Insurance* | | | | | | |
| 1. Social Security and Disability | $119.4 | 42.3% | $173.0 | 44.7% | $ 213.9 | 44.4% |
| 2. Unemployment compensation | 20.3 | 7.2 | 16.0 | 4.1 | 13.1 | 2.7 |
| 3. Medicare | 35.6 | 12.6 | 62.6 | 16.2 | 86.6 | 18.0 |
| Subtotal | $175.3 | 62.1% | $251.6 | 65.0% | $ 313.6 | 65.2% |
| *Public Assistance* | | | | | | |
| 4. AFDC | 7.3 | 2.6 | 8.3 | 2.1 | 9.3 | 1.9 |
| 5. Supplemental Security Income (SSI) | 5.9 | 2.1 | 8.3 | 2.1 | 10.7 | 2.2 |
| 6. Food stamps | 8.2 | 2.9 | 10.7 | 2.8 | 11.2 | 2.3 |
| 7. Medicaid | 14.3 | 5.1 | 20.6 | 5.3 | 31.5 | 6.5 |
| Subtotal | $ 35.7 | 12.6% | $ 47.9 | 12.4% | $ 62.7 | 13.0% |
| *Total for classic welfare state programs* | $ 211.0 | 74.7% | $299.5 | 77.4% | $ 376.3 | 78.2% |

Federal retirement programs

| | $ | % | $ | % | $ | % |
|---|---|---|---|---|---|---|
| 8. Civil Service | $ 15.2 | 5.4 | $ 22.1 | 5.7 | $ 28.6 | 5.9 |
| 9. Military | 12.5 | 4.4 | 15.3 | 4.0 | 19.5 | 4.1 |
| 10. Railroad | 4.8 | 1.7 | 6.1 | 1.6 | 6.7 | 1.4 |
| Subtotal | $ 32.5 | 11.5% | $ 43.5 | 11.7% | $ 54.8 | 11.4% |
| *Other programs* | | | | | | |
| 11. Veterans benefits | $ 13.8 | 4.9 | $ 14.8 | 3.8 | $ 15.1 | 3.1 |
| 12. Black lung | 1.8 | 0.6 | 1.6 | 0.4 | 1.5 | 0.3 |
| 13. Earned income credit | 1.3 | 0.5 | 1.2 | 0.3 | 2.7 | 0.6 |
| 14. Miscellaneous[a] | 12.7 | 4.5 | 12.4 | 3.2 | 15.7 | 3.3 |
| Subtotal | $ 29.6 | 10.5% | $ 30.0 | 7.8% | $ 35.0 | 7.3% |
| *Total For Income Assistance* | $273.1 | 96.4% | $373.0 | 96.4% | $ 446.1 | 96.8% |
| Interest on public debt | | | | | | |
| 15. Payments to persons | $ 10.1 | 3.6% | $ 13.8 | 3.6% | $ 15.2 | 3.2% |
| *Total transfers to people* | $283.2 | 100.0% | $386.8 | 100.0% | $ 481.3 | 100.0% |
| *Total federal outlays* | $615.1 | — | $895.6 | — | $1,118.3 | — |
| *Total transfers to people as a percent of federal outlays* | 44.9% | — | 43.2% | — | 43.0% | — |

[a] Largely payments to nonprofit institutions, aid to students, and payments for medical services for retired military personnel and their dependents at nonmilitary facilities.
All figures rounded.

Sources: U.S. Department of Commerce, *Survey of Current Business*, July issues. 1984, 1989.

size of spending for classic welfare state purposes. As a matter of fact, the relative share of classic welfare spending within the context of total transfers to people rose, both for social insurance and public assistance. The share of the former increased more, from 61.9% in 1980 to 65.2% in 1988, while the share of the latter rose only from 12.6% to 13.0%. The percentage increase for social insurance spending was 78.9%, greater than the overall gain of 69.9% in transfers to people during the period. Public assistance spending grew by 75.6% in these years. A minuscule amount of relative shrinkage took place in federal retirement programs, their share of the transfers-to-people dollar dropping from 11.5% percent in 1980 to 11.4% in 1988. Normal attrition rather than policy changes probably accounts for this. The most shrinkage took place in the Other programs category, for here spending dropped from 10.5% of total people-based transfers in 1980 to 7.3% in 1988. Few programs in this category experienced any absolute spending cutbacks—the black lung program being the exception—but their growth generally was slower than other people-based spending.

We get a slightly different perspective if we look at transfers to people in constant, inflation-adjusted dollars. These data are found in table 4-5, in which the current dollar figures have been deflated by using the consumer price index. Within the categories under the classic welfare state designation, three kinds of transfers declined. These were unemployment compensation, which dropped by 54.9%; AFDC which declined by 11.2%; and food stamps, which were cut by 5.0%. The sharp cut in unemployment spending—the only cut in the social insurance category—resulted obviously from the recovery from the 1980–1982 recession. The two other cuts came in programs specifically directed toward the poor, namely AFDC and food stamps, the effect of which was to tilt the redistributional machinery of the federal government even more heavily in favor of the middle class. It is not without significance that parallel to the decline in real spending for AFDC and food stamps, the poverty index—the percentage of families falling below the poverty level—grew 11.5% in 1980 to 13.9% in 1984, and then dropped back to 12.1% by 1987. The poverty rate for families headed by a woman with no male present jumped from 36.7% in 1980 to a peak of 40.6% in 1982, before falling back to 38.3% in 1987.[41] Other significant real cuts came in the Other programs category; overall real spending here dropped by 17.5% during the Reagan years. In total, transfers to people in constant dollars increased by 18.7% as compared to a real increase for all federal outlays of 26.6%. This shows, as do the figures in table 4-4, the *relative* shift of spending during the Reagan Administration away from people-oriented programs to other activities, especially military spending. In real terms, the GNP rose by 26.3% from 1980 through 1988. Real military spending increased by 52.7%.[42]

Table 4-5.  Federal Transfer Expenditures To People By Major Categories In 1982–1984 Dollars: 1980, 1984 and 1988[a]

| Category of Transfers | 1980 | 1984 | 1988 | Percent Change 1980–1988 |
|---|---|---|---|---|
| Classic welfare state expenditures | | | | |
| Social Insurance | | | | |
| 1.  Social Security and Disability | $144.9 | $166.5 | $180.8 | 24.8% |
| 2.  Unemployment compensation | 24.6 | 15.4 | 11.1 | −54.9 |
| 3.  Medicare | 43.2 | 60.3 | 73.2 | 69.4 |
| Subtotal | $212.8 | $242.2 | $265.1 | 24.6% |
| *Public Assistance* | | | | |
| 4.  AFDC | $  8.9 | 8.0 | 7.9 | −11.2 |
| 5.  Supplemental Security Income | 7.2 | 8.0 | 9.0 | 25.0 |
| 6.  Food stamps | 10.0 | 10.3 | 9.5 | −5.0 |
| 7.  Medicaid | 17.4 | 19.8 | 26.6 | 52.9 |
| Subtotal | $ 43.3 | $ 46.1 | $ 53.0 | 23.1% |
| *Total for classic welfare state programs* | $256.1 | $288.3 | $318.1 | 24.2% |
| *Federal retirement programs* | | | | |
| 8.  Civil Service | $ 18.4 | $ 21.3 | $ 24.2 | 31.5% |
| 9.  Military | 15.2 | 14.7 | 16.5 | 8.6 |
| 10.  Railroad | 5.7 | 5.9 | $  5.7 | — |
| Subtotal | $ 39.4 | $ 41.9 | $ 46.3 | 17.5% |
| *Other programs* | | | | |
| 11.  Veterans benefits | $ 16.7 | $ 14.2 | $ 12.8 | −23.4 |
| 12.  Black lung | 2.2 | 1.5 | 1.3 | −40.9 |
| 13.  Earned income credit | 1.6 | 1.2 | 2.3 | 43.8 |
| 14.  Misc.[b] | 15.4 | 11.9 | 13.3 | −13.6 |
| Subtotal | $ 35.9 | $ 28.9 | $ 29.6 | −17.5% |
| *Total For Income Assistance* | $331.4 | $359.0 | $394.0 | 18.9% |
| *Interest on public debt* | | | | |
| 15.  Payments to persons | $ 12.3 | $ 13.3 | $ 12.8 | 4.1% |
| *Total transfers to people* | $343.7 | $372.3 | $406.8 | 18.4% |
| *Total federal outlays* | $746.5 | $862.2 | $945.3 | 26.6% |

[a] Current dollar figures deflated by the Consumer Price Index.

[b] Largely payments to nonprofit institutions, aid to students, and payments for medical services for retired military personnel and their dependents at nonmilitary facilities.

Totals are rounded.

Sources: U.S. Department of Commerce, *Survey of Current Business*, July issues, 1984, 1989.

The story is different when we turn to non-people-based transfer spending. The appropriate data for transfer spending under this rubric are found in tables 4-6 and 4-8. Within the broad non-people-based classification, there are four spending categories. They include 1) grants-in-aid to state and local governments; 2) interest on the public debt other than interest received by individuals; 3) subsidies to business; and 4) transfers to foreigners, which consists essentially of foreign economic aid. As was done with transfers to people, we shall look first at current dollar expenditures in these categories, and then at their changes when measured in constant dollars.

The figures in table 4-6 show some very large changes during the Reagan era in the *relative* distribution of spending between the four categories mentioned above. In current dollars, spending in all four categories increased, but as we shall see shortly, this was not true for real or inflation-adjusted spending. Relatively speaking, transfer spending in the grants-in-aid category dropped sharply, going from 51.7% of total non-people-based transfer spending in 1980 to 28.3% in 1980. This was primarily the result of the elimination of the Comprehensive Employment and Training Act (CETA) in the early months of the Reagan Administration, and the phasing out entirely of revenue sharing, one of the Nixon Administration's proudest accomplishment. Federal grants-in-aid for education, housing, health and hospitals, and income support and welfare also declined in their relative importance. Since many of these programs provided indirect benefits to lower-income persons, these changes helped tilt the overall picture of transfer spending in the United States further away from the poor.

The story is different with respect to interest on the debt and subsidies to business. Interest payments on the debt other than to individuals rose from 35.5% of all non-people-based transfers in 1980 to 53.3% in 1988. The reason for this *relative* shift is clear: privately held debt rose from $616.4 billion in 1980 to $1852.8 billion in 1988, a 200.6% increase! During this same period, both short- and long-term rates on federal obligations dropped, the three-month Treasury bill rate going from 11.5% in 1980 to 6.7% in 1982, and the rate for ten-year bonds declining from 11.5% in 1980 to 8.9% in 1988.[43] Servicing the enormous debt acquired in the 1980s eats up a growing proportion of federal transfer spending, a situation not likely to change in the near future. Transfers in the form of subsidies to business also grew in relative importance in the 1980s, although the change here was not as dramatic as either the relative decline in grants-in-aid or the relative growth in debt service. Agriculture by far gained the most, relatively speaking. Its share of total non-people-based transfer spending jumped from 2.9% in 1980 to 9.5% in 1988. The severity of the agricultural depression in

**Table 4-6. Distribution of Non-People-Based Federal Transfer Expenditures By Category and Programs: 1980, 1984, 1988 (in Billions of Current Dollars and in Percent)**

| Category | 1980 Dollar Total | 1980 Percent Distribution | 1984 Dollar Total | 1984 Percent Distribution | 1988 Dollar Total | 1988 Percent Distribution |
|---|---|---|---|---|---|---|
| *Grants to state and local governments* | | | | | | |
| 1. Income-supported welfare | $ 12.4 | 10.2% | $ 19.7 | 9.9% | $ 18.7 | 7.3% |
| 2. Transportation | 12.1 | 9.9 | 14.9 | 7.5 | 17.3 | 6.8 |
| 3. Aid to education | 7.9 | 6.5 | 7.8 | 3.9 | 9.9 | 3.9 |
| 4. Housing and community service | 8.8 | 7.2 | 7.1 | 3.6 | 6.8 | 2.7 |
| 5. Health and hospitals | 3.3 | 2.7 | 3.3 | 1.7 | 4.3 | 1.7 |
| 6. Labor training | 7.4 | 6.1 | 2.7 | 1.4 | 2.8 | 1.1 |
| 7. National defense and space | 1.1 | 0.9 | 1.3 | 0.7 | 2.5 | 1.0 |
| 8. Natural resources | 1.0 | 0.8 | 1.4 | 0.7 | 1.6 | 0.6 |
| 9. Government administration | 0.5 | 0.4 | 0.6 | 0.3 | 1.0 | 0.4 |
| 10. Energy | 1.0 | 0.8 | 0.8 | 0.4 | 1.0 | 0.4 |
| 11. Revenue sharing | 6.8 | 5.6 | 4.6 | 2.3 | — | — |
| 12. Other | 0.7 | 0.6 | 2.0 | 1.0 | 6.3 | 2.5 |
| Total grants to state and local governments | $ 63.0 | 51.7% | $ 66.2 | 33.4% | $ 72.2 | 28.3% |

**Table 4-6.** (Continued)

| Category | 1980 Dollar Total | 1980 Percent Distribution | 1984 Dollar Total | 1984 Percent Distribution | 1988 Dollar Total | 1988 Percent Distribution |
|---|---|---|---|---|---|---|
| *Net interest on the privately held public debt* | | | | | | |
| 1. Commercial banks | $ 9.7 | 8.0% | $ 17.7 | 8.9% | $ 15.8 | 6.2% |
| 2. Insurance companies | 2.1 | 1.7 | 6.1 | 3.1 | 9.1 | 3.6 |
| 3. Money market funds | 0.3 | 0.2 | 2.4 | 1.2 | 1.0 | 0.4 |
| 4. Corporations | 1.7 | 1.4 | 4.8 | 2.4 | 7.1 | 2.8 |
| 5. State and local governments | 7.6 | 6.2 | 16.5 | 8.3 | 25.6 | 10.0 |
| 6. Foreign holders of debt | 11.3 | 9.3 | 18.3 | 9.2 | 29.6 | 11.6 |
| 7. Other | 10.7 | 8.8 | 35.8 | 18.1 | 47.9 | 18.7 |
| Total interest on the public debt | $ 43.3 | 35.5% | $101.8 | 51.3% | $ 136.2 | 53.3% |

| | (1) $ | (1) % | (2) $ | (2) % | (3) $ | (3) % |
|---|---|---|---|---|---|---|
| *Subsidies to business* | | | | | | |
| 1. Agriculture | $ 3.5 | 2.9 | $ 12.6 | 6.3% | $ 24.2 | 9.5% |
| 2. Housing | 5.2 | 4.3 | 9.7 | 4.9 | 12.4 | 4.8 |
| 3. Transportation | 2.6 | 2.1 | 1.9 | 1.0 | 1.8 | 0.7 |
| 4. Postal services | 2.3 | 1.9 | 1.6 | 0.8 | 1.3 | 0.5 |
| Subtotal | 13.6 | 11.2% | $ 25.8 | 13.0% | $ 39.7 | 15.5% |
| Less: Subsidies to business | 2.0 | 1.6 | 4.7 | 2.4 | 3.6 | 1.4 |
| Total subsidies to business | $ 11.6 | 9.5% | $ 21.1 | 10.6% | $ 36.1 | 14.1% |
| *International* | | | | | | |
| 1. Foreign economic aid | $ 4.0 | 3.3% | $ 9.2 | 4.6% | $ 11.1 | 4.3% |
| *Total non-people-based transfers* | $121.9 | 100.0% | $198.3 | 100.0% | $ 255.7 | 100.0% |
| *Total federal outlays* | $615.1 | — | $895.6 | — | $1,118.3 | — |
| *Total non-people transfers as a percent of federal outlays* | | 19.8% | | 22.1% | | 22.9% |

Sources: U.S. Department of Commerce, *Survey of Current Business*, July issues. 1984, 1989.
Totals are rounded.

Table 4-7.  Total Federal Transfer Expenditures to People and to Non-People-Based Programs: 1980, 1984, 1988 (in Billions of Current Dollars and in Percent)

| Category of Transfers | 1980 | 1984 | 1988 |
|---|---|---|---|
| 1.  Total transfers to people | $ 283.2 | $ 386.8 | $ 481.3 |
| 2.  Percent of total federal outlays | 44.9% | 43.2% | 43.0% |
| 3.  Non-people–based transfers | $ 121.9 | $ 198.3 | $ 255.7 |
| 4.  Percent of total federal outlays | 19.8% | 22.1% | 22.9% |
| 5.  Total of transfers | $ 405.1 | $ 585.1 | $ 737.0 |
| 6.  Percent of total federal outlays | 65.9% | 65.3% | 65.9% |
| 7.  Total federal outlays | $ 615.1 | $ 895.6 | $1,118.3 |
| 8.  GNP | $2,732.0 | $3,772.2 | $4,880.6 |
| 9.  Federal transfers as a percent of GNP | 14.8% | 15.5% | 15.1% |

Source: Tables 4-5 and 4-6, *Economic Report of the President*, 1990.

the mid-1980s brought large increases in federal payments to the farm economy, increasing thereby the relative share of agriculture in its part of transfer spending. Subsidies for housing increased somewhat in relative importance, from 4.3% in 1980 to 4.8% in 1983, but the other two major categories for direct business subsidies, transportation and the postal service, recorded relative declines. Foreign economic aid also grew slightly in relative importance, as its share of non-people-based transfers rose from 3.3% in 1980 to 4.3 in 1988. Overall, the *relative* importance of non-people-based transfers rose form 19.8% of all federal spending in 1980 to 22.9% in 1980.

Table 4-7 combines some of the key total figures (in current dollar amounts and in percents ) from tables 4-5 and 4-6 and thereby gives us an overall picture of what happened to transfer spending during the 1980s. It shows, first, that there was *no* significant change in the proportion of federal outlays going for transfer purposes during the eight years of the Reagan regime. Transfers continued to absorb about two thirds of all federal spending, just as they had since the end of the 1960s. If the intent of the Reagan Revolution was to roll back the boundaries of Americas's welfare state as defined by the ratio of transfer to total federal spending, the revolution failed to come off. In 1980 transfers consumed 65.9% of federal spending; eight years later, this percentage figure remained at an identical 65.9%.

As detailed above, however, there was a change in the composition of transfers. People-based transfer spending declined from 44.9% of all transfer spending in 1980 to 43.0% in 1990. The counterpart of this, of course, is an increase in the *relative* share of transfers going to non-people-based programs. This change was from 19.8% of the transfer total in 1980 to 22.9% in 1988. This shift, as has been stressed, further tilted the broad incidence of transfer spending away from the lowest income groups, the reason being that many of the beneficiaries of the shift—holders of the federal debt, large farmers, etc.—are in the upper ranges of the income distribution scale.

Table 4-8 shows in constant 1982–1984 dollars what happened to non-people-based transfer spending during the 1980s. These data, too, show the drastic change in *relative* spending within this general category during the 1980s. Grants-in-aid to state and local governments measured in constant dollars dropped by 20% during the period, reflecting their decline in relative importance during the Reagan era. Net interest on the public debt had the greatest growth, 119.0%, followed by subsidies to business, 117.0%, and foreign economic aid, 91.8%. Overall, constant dollar transfers in the non-people-based category grew by 46.1% in the period.

Table 4-9 gives a combined picture of the change in people- and non-people-based transfers as measured in constant dollars for the 1980s. These data reflect, as did the data shown earlier in table 4-7, the relative shifts that took place in transfer spending during the Reagan era, even though overall there was no change in the proportion of federal spending going to transfers. All transfers when measured in constant dollars grew by almost the exact same amount as did total federal outlays when measured in constant dollars, namely 26.7% for transfers and 26.6% for total federal outlays. Since both military spending and non-people-based transfer spending grew faster in constant dollars than did total federal outlays, it obviously follows that both types of spending grew at the expense of transfers to people.[44]

So what are we to conclude at this point? At least on the spending side, David Stockman was right: there was no Reagan Revolution. The borders of America's welfare state had been slightly redefined, but they had not shrunk. In constant dollars, federal transfer spending, total federal outlays, and real GNP grew at an almost identical pace during the 1980s (table 4-9), while the ratio of transfer spending to both total federal spending and the GNP remained practically constant in the same period (table 4-7). What did increase in the Reagan years was the ratio of total federal spending to the GNP—from 22.5% in 1980 to 22.9% in 1988. This is accounted for almost wholly by the rise in military spending relative to the GNP, from 5.2% in 1980 to 6.1% in 1988.[45] Further, the redefining of the borders of the welfare state came almost entirely at the expense of direct transfers to

Table 4-8.  Non-People-Based Federal Transfer Expenditures in 1982–1984 Dollars: 1980, 1984, 1988[a]

| Category of Transfers | 1980 | 1984 | 1988 | Percent Change 1980–1988 |
|---|---|---|---|---|
| *Grants to state and local governments* | | | | |
| 1. Income-supported welfare | $15.0 | $18.9 | $15.8 | 5.3% |
| 2. Transportation | 14.7 | 14.3 | 14.6 | −0.7 |
| 3. Aid to education | 9.6 | 7.5 | 8.4 | −12.5 |
| 4. Housing and community service | 10.7 | 6.8 | 5.7 | −46.3 |
| 5. Health and hospitals | 4.0 | 3.2 | 3.6 | −10.0 |
| 6. Labor training | 9.0 | 2.6 | 2.4 | −73.3 |
| 7. National defense and space | 1.3 | 1.3 | 2.1 | 61.5 |
| 8. Natural resources | 1.2 | 1.3 | 1.4 | 16.7 |
| 9. Government administration | 0.6 | 0.6 | 0.8 | 33.3 |
| 10. Energy | 1.2 | 0.8 | 0.8 | −33.4 |
| 11. Revenue sharing | 8.3 | 4.4 | — | −100.0 |
| 12. Other[b] | 0.8 | 1.9 | 5.5 | 507.5 |
| Total grants-in-aid to state and local government | $ 76.5 | $ 63.7 | $ 61.2 | −20.0% |
| *Net interest on public debt* | | | | |
| 1. Commercial banks | $ 11.8 | $ 17.0 | 13.4 | 13.6% |
| 2. Insurance companies | 2.5 | 5.9 | 7.7 | 208.0 |
| 3. Money market funds | 0.4 | 2.3 | 0.8 | 100.0 |
| 4. Corporations | 2.1 | 4.6 | 6.0 | 185.7 |
| 5. State and local governments | 9.2 | 15.9 | 21.6 | 134.8 |
| 6. Foreign holders of debt | 13.7 | 17.6 | 25.0 | 81.8 |
| 7. Other | 13.0 | 34.5 | 40.5 | 211.5 |
| Total interest on public debt | $ 52.5 | $ 98.0 | $115.0 | 119.0% |
| *Subsidies to business* | | | | |
| 1. Agriculture | $ 4.2 | $ 12.1 | $ 20.5 | 388.1% |
| 2. Housing | 6.3 | 9.3 | 10.5 | 66.7 |
| 3. Transportation | 3.1 | 1.8 | 1.5 | −51.6 |
| 4. Postal services | 2.8 | 1.5 | 1.1 | −60.7 |
| Subtotal | $ 16.5 | $ 24.8 | $ 33.6 | 103.6% |
| Less: subsidies to business | 2.4 | 4.5 | 3.0 | 25.0 |
| Total subsidies to business | $ 14.1 | $ 20.3 | $ 30.6 | 117.0% |
| *International* | | | | |
| 1. Foreign economic aid | $ 4.9 | $ 8.9 | $ 9.4 | 91.8% |
| *Total non-people-based transfers* | $147.9 | $190.9 | $216.1 | 46.1% |

[a] Current dollar figures deflated with the consumer price index.

[b] Includes federal support for welfare and social services, civilian safety, veterans aid, recreation, agriculture, and economic development.

Totals are rounded.

Sources: U.S. Department of Commerce, *Survey of Current Business*, July Issues, 1984, 1989.

Table 4-9. Total Federal Transfer Expenditures to People and to Non-People-Based Programs in Constant 1982–1984 Dollars: 1980, 1984, 1988[a]

| Category of Transfers | 1980 | 1984 | 1988 | Percent Change 1980–1988 |
|---|---|---|---|---|
| 1. Transfers to people | $ 343.7 | $ 372.3 | $ 406.9 | 18.4% |
| 2. Non-people-based transfer programs | 147.9 | 190.9 | 216.1 | 46.1% |
| 3. Total transfers | $ 491.6 | $ 563.2 | $ 623.0 | 26.7% |
| 4. Total federal outlays | $ 746.5 | $ 862.0 | $ 945.3 | 26.6% |
| 5. Real GNP | $3,187.1 | $3,501.4 | $4,024.4 | 26.3% |

Source: Tables 4-5 and 4-8, *Economic Report of the President*, 1990.

people or to non-people-based transfer programs whose ultimate beneficiaries generally were lower-income persons and families, as is the case with programs for housing, aid to education, labor training, and some revenue sharing.

If, however, the overall structure of America's welfare state was not changed significantly on the spending side during the Reagan era, the same cannot be said if we look at it from the perspective of taxes, both total taxes and taxes whose purprose is to finance portions of the classic welfare state. It is to this that we now turn.

## Tax Changes and America's Welfare State in the 1980s

There were three major changes in federal tax laws in the 1980s which had an impact upon the welfare state. Of these, only one, the Economic Recovery Tax Act of 1981 (ERTA), was strictly a part of the Reagan Revolution. The other two major changes were tax amendments to the Social Security Act in 1983 and the Tax Reform Act 1986, both of which were bipartisan in nature. A brief comment on each of these is in order before we examine their impact on America's welfare state.

As stressed earlier in this chapter, the Economic Recovery Tax Act of 1981 was the vehicle by which the Kemp–Roth tax cuts got enacted into law. Overall, the cut in the rates on individual incomes was 23%. As we have seen, ERTA did far more than simply cut individual tax rates. It became ultimately a "Christmas Tree" bill that also brought about significant changes in the tax burden on corporations. The Social Security tax amendments of 1983 were a bipartisan undertaking, one that stemmed from, first, the emergence a sizable deficit in the Social Security Trust Funds in 1982 and in 1983, and, second, a growing public fear about the ability of the system to finance the hordes of "baby boomers" expected to reach retirement in the early part of the twenty-first century. A bipartisan Congressional coalition led primarily by Senator Daniel Patrick Moynihan of New York pushed through reforms involving increases in both the rate applied to the payroll tax and the maximum of annual earnings subject to the payroll tax. The combined rate for employer and employee was scheduled to increase to 15.3% by 1990, and the maximum annual income from wages and salaries subject to the tax was raised to $49,500.[46] The Tax Reform Act of 1986, also a bipartisan effort, changed the individual income tax primarily by replacing the existing multibracketed system with two basic brackets, 15% and 28%, and lowered the maximum rate to 28%.[47] The threshold for the tax-exempt level of income was supposed to be raised to 120% of the poverty level for a married couple with two children, primarily by increasing the personal exemption and the earned-income credit. The latter was also indexed. As pointed out earlier in chapter 3, the 1986 law eliminated or modified a number of tax expenditures applicable to corporations, the purpose being to increase corporate tax revenues as a percent of total revenues.

Two basic questions need to be answered with respect to the tax changes enacted during the 1980s. First, how did they affect the general structure of federal tax revenues? We shall examine this question first. Second, and far more important for the purposes of this book, how did these tax changes affect the distribution of income in America? Until we find an answer to this question, our analysis of the evolution of America's welfare state up to the present will be incomplete.

Table 4-10 tells us some important things about what happened to the general structure of federal taxes in the 1980s as the result of the three major tax law changes enacted during the decade. This table shows for 1980 through 1989 the three major federal taxes—the personal income tax, payroll or Social Security taxes, and the corporation income tax—as a percent of total federal revenues for each year in this period. Several trends are apparent. First, the personal income tax continues to supply the largest portion of federal revenue, although its share declined during the decade, from 48.4% in 1980 to 44.0% in 1989. Second, the share of revenue supplied by payroll taxes has grown steadily from 1980 through 1989. Payroll taxes are now almost as large as the personal income tax as a source of federal revenue. The relative share of corporate income taxes declined during the decade, although the extent of this decline was reversed slightly after 1982. Overall, and contrary to popular opinion, taxes were not reduced during the

Table 4-10.   The Structure of Federal Tax Receipts: 1980–1989 (in Percent)

| | | Specific Tax[a] | | |
| Year | Federal Tax Revenue As A Percent of GNP | Personal Income Taxes | Payroll Taxes | Corporate Income Taxes |
|---|---|---|---|---|
| 1980 | 19.5 | 48.4 | 35.0 | 13.2 |
| 1981 | 20.9 | 46.7 | 34.2 | 10.3 |
| 1982 | 20.0 | 47.9 | 36.8 | 7.7 |
| 1983 | 19.4 | 42.3 | 38.3 | 9.2 |
| 1984 | 19.2 | 42.7 | 39.2 | 10.4 |
| 1985 | 19.6 | 43.9 | 39.4 | 9.7 |
| 1986 | 19.6 | 43.7 | 40.1 | 10.1 |
| 1987 | 20.1 | 44.5 | 38.5 | 11.1 |
| 1988 | 19.9 | 42.5 | 40.2 | 11.5 |
| 1989 | 20.0 | 44.0 | 40.3 | 10.0 |

[a] As a percent of total federal revenues.

Source: *Economic Report of the President*, 1990.

decade, at least if this controversial question is measured by federal taxes as a percent of the GNP. From 1980 through 1989 this percentage rose slightly from 19.5% in 1980 to 20.0% in 1989. In general, and because of the changes in the rate structure of the personal income tax and the growing importance of payroll taxes in the federal government's tax structure, it is a fair conclusion that taxes at the federal level became significantly less progressive during the 1980s. Only in part can this be attributed to the Reagan Revolution, for the changes in Social Security taxes as well as those incorporated into the Tax Reform Act of 1986 were fully bipartisan.

Tables 4-11, 4-12, and 4-13 address the second question posed earlier, namely how the tax changes of the 1980s affected the distribution of income in the United States.[48] Table 4-11 shows the distribution of pretax family income (by deciles or tenths) for 1977, 1984 and 1988. Since these data shown in table 4-11 are for *pretax* family income, they do not reflect the impact of tax changes in the 1980s on the distribution of income, but they do reflect the effect of some of the changes in transfer spending on income. This is because the definition of family income used by the Congressional Budget Office in compiling these data includes cash transfers from the federal government, but it does not include in-kind transfers.[49] What these data do show is a definite increase in pretax inequality in family income

Table 4-11.   Distribution of Pretax Family Income by Population Decile: 1977, 1984, 1988 (in Percent)

| Family Decile[a] | 1977 | 1984 | 1988 |
|---|---|---|---|
| Lowest or first[b] | 1.1% | 0.9 | 0.9 |
| Second | 2.5 | 2.3 | 2.2 |
| Third | 3.9 | 3.6 | 3.6 |
| Fourth | 5.5 | 5.0 | 5.0 |
| Fifth | 7.1 | 6.6 | 6.5 |
| Sixth | 8.9 | 8.3 | 8.2 |
| Seventh | 10.9 | 10.2 | 10.2 |
| Eighth | 13.2 | 12.8 | 12.7 |
| Ninth | 16.6 | 16.4 | 16.4 |
| Top tenth | 30.6 | 34.4 | 34.9 |
| Top 5% | 20.1 | 23.7 | 24.2 |
| Top 1% | 8.1 | 11.2 | 11.8 |
| All deciles[c] | 100.0 | 100.0 | 100.0 |

[a] Ranked by size of family income.
[b] Excludes families with zero or negative income.
[c] Includes families with zero or negative incomes not shown separately.

Source: Congressional Budget Office, *The Changing Distribution of Federal Taxes: 1975–1990*, October, 1987.

between 1977 and 1988, part of which can be attributed to the changing structure of transfer spending described in this chapter. Between 1977 and 1988 the income share of all deciles except the top tenth declined; the share of the top tenth increased from 30.6% to 34.9%. The Congressional Budget Office found that this increase resulted from an increase in the top deciles share in all types of income—labor income, property income, and even transfer income![50] The Gini coefficient for pretax family income rose between 1977 and 1988 (table 4-13), a change that indicates an increase in inequality.

The impact of tax changes during the 1980s on the federal tax structure is shown in table 4-12. The Congressional Budget Office calculated for 1977, 1984, and 1988 the effective tax rate applicable to each income decile and for each of the major forms of federal taxes. The table contains these calculations for the personal income tax, the payroll tax, the corporate income tax, and all federal taxes combined for these three years.[51] The rates shown for 1988 are estimates, based upon the analysis of the Congressional Budget Office of how the changes made by the Tax Reform Act of 1986 would affect tax structure. The *effective* tax rate is the ratio of taxes actually

Table 4-12. Effective Federal Tax Rates and Average Family Income by Population Decile: 1977, 1984, 1988 (in Current Dollars and in Percent)

| Family Decile | Personal Income Taxes | | | Payroll Taxes | | | Corporate Income Taxes | | | All Taxes | | | Family Income in Current Dollars | | |
|---|---|---|---|---|---|---|---|---|---|---|---|---|---|---|---|
| | 1977 | 1984 | 1988 | 1977 | 1984 | 1988 | 1977 | 1984 | 1988 | 1977 | 1984 | 1988 | 1977 | 1984 | 1988 |
| Lowest or first | -0.4% | -0.4% | -0.8% | 3.2% | 4.3% | 4.7% | 1.5% | 0.9% | 1.2% | 8.0% | 10.5% | 9.6% | $2,184 | $3,102 | $3,685 |
| Second | -0.1 | 0.2 | -0.5 | 3.7 | 4.7 | 5.3 | 1.7 | 1.0 | 1.4 | 8.7 | 8.5 | 8.3 | 4,435 | 6,769 | 8,064 |
| Third | 1.5 | 2.5 | 1.5 | 5.7 | 7.1 | 8.0 | 2.7 | 1.6 | 2.1 | 12.0 | 13.4 | 13.3 | 6,992 | 10,820 | 12,964 |
| Fourth | 4.0 | 4.7 | 4.0 | 6.9 | 8.1 | 9.0 | 3.3 | 1.8 | 2.4 | 16.2 | 16.3 | 16.3 | 9,810 | 15,130 | 18,108 |
| Fifth | 6.1 | 6.3 | 5.8 | 7.7 | 8.8 | 9.6 | 3.8 | 2.0 | 2.6 | 19.1 | 18.5 | 19.2 | 12,715 | 19,737 | 23,544 |
| Sixth | 7.6 | 7.6 | 7.1 | 8.0 | 9.1 | 10.0 | 4.0 | 2.2 | 2.8 | 21.0 | 20.1 | 20.9 | 15,590 | 24,906 | 29,660 |
| Seventh | 9.0 | 8.7 | 8.2 | 8.3 | 9.5 | 10.3 | 4.4 | 2.3 | 2.9 | 23.0 | 21.5 | 22.3 | 19,371 | 30,756 | 36,625 |
| Eighth | 10.2 | 9.7 | 8.9 | 7.8 | 9.9 | 10.8 | 4.4 | 2.4 | 3.1 | 23.6 | 22.0 | 23.6 | 23,575 | 38,403 | 45,752 |
| Ninth | 11.5 | 10.8 | 10.3 | 7.4 | 9.6 | 10.5 | 4.5 | 2.4 | 3.1 | 24.5 | 21.8 | 24.7 | 54,659 | 103,293 | 125,808 |
| Top 5% | 20.3 | 16.8 | 17.5 | 3.5 | 4.4 | 4.8 | 3.2 | 1.7 | 2.3 | 27.5 | 23.3 | 24.9 | 71,591 | 141,954 | 174,582 |
| Top 1% | 26.7 | 19.8 | 20.9 | 1.5 | 1.8 | 1.9 | 2.3 | 1.3 | 1.9 | 30.9 | 23.1 | 22.9 | 143,696 | 353,392 | 425,440 |
| All deciles | 11.1% | 10.6% | 10.4% | 6.5% | 8.0% | 8.7% | 3.9% | 2.1% | 2.7% | 22.8% | 21.7% | 22.7% | $17,840[a] | $30,022[a] | $36,042[a] |

[a] Average all deciles.

Source: Congressional Budget Office, The Changing Distribution of Federal Taxes: 1975–1990, October, 1987.

paid to family income in each income class. A progressive tax system is one in which the effective rate rises with income. If the tax structure overall become less progressive—that is, the effective rate for the higher income ranges declines—then it is safe to assume that the burden of taxes is being shifted away from the top incomes and toward the middle and lower incomes.

Table 4-12 shows that this is what happened in the 1980s. Overall, the federal tax structure became less progressive. For example, in 1977 the effective rate for all federal taxes (including excises) for the top 1% of families was 30.9%, but by 1988 this rate had fallen to 22.9%, nearly a 26% drop in the rate. For families in the upper 5% of the income scale, the effective rate went from 27.5% in 1977 to 24.9% in 1988, a 9.5% decrease in the rate. For families at the bottom of the income scale, however, the opposite story prevailed. Between 1977 and 1988, the effective rate increased for families in the first, third, fourth, and fifth income deciles. The rate went down for families in the second income decile. There was a slight decrease for families in the sixth and seventh income deciles between 1977 and 1988, no change for families in the eighth income decile, and a slight rise in the effective rate for families in the tenth, or highest, income decile.

The significance of these effective rates and their changes can be gauged by referring to the last column in table 4-12, which shows in current dollars the average family income in each population decile. For example, in 1988 a family in the top 1% of the income distribution would have paid $131,461 in taxes if its income had been taxed at the 1977 effective rate of 30.9% for that income level. But its actual tax at the 1988 effective rate of 22.9% would have been $97,426, a tax savings of $34,035! For a family in the top 5% of the income scale, the tax savings would be $4301 as a result of the decline in the effective rate of taxation for this income level from 27.5% to 24.9%. But consider the family in the lowest income decile, a family with an average income of $3685 in 1988. Its tax bill would go up because of the change in effective rates, from $295 at the 1977 rate to $354 at the 1988 rate. Its tax loss is $59.

A look at what happened to the effective rates for each major type of tax explains why the federal tax structure overall has become less progressive. The personal income tax still retains a progressive structure, but is generally less progressive in 1988 than 1977, especially for the top 5% and 1% of families. Payroll taxes are mildly progressive up through the eighth income decile, where the average family income is $45,752, but become sharply regressive after that. But for *all* income deciles, the effective rate rose for payroll taxes between 1977 and 1988. The story is about the same for the corporate income tax, namely a very slight progression up through the sev-

Table 4-13.   Pretax and Posttax Gini Coefficients and Suits Indexes: 1977, 1984, 1988

|  | Year | | |
|---|---|---|---|
|  | 1977 | 1984 | 1988 |
| 1.  Pretax Gini coefficient | .4427 | .4845 | .4890 |
| 2.  Posttax Gini coefficient | .4185 | .4700 | .4724 |
| 3.  Suits Index | .1025 | .0630 | .0696 |

Note: An increase in the Gini coefficient means an *increase* in income inequality. An *increase* in the Suits Index means the tax system has become *more* progressive.

Source: Congressional Budget Office, *The Changing Distribution of Federal Taxes: 1975–1990*, October, 1987.

enth income decile, then a proportional increase for the next two deciles, and a sharp dropoff in the effective rates for the top 5% and 1% of families. Of course, there is some overlap here between the top 5% and 1% of families and the tenth decile, but the tilt nevertheless is toward a regressive tax structure for the corporate income tax in the upper ranges. This helps explain the declining share of corporate income taxes in the overall tax receipts of the federal government, as well as the general shift of federal taxes in less progressive direction.

Table 4-13 sums up the foregoing discussion in terms of two fairly well-know coefficients—the Gini coefficient and the Suits Index. The Gini coefficient is a commonly used measure of the extent of inequality in the distribution of income. It is based upon the Lorenze curve, which measures the cumulative percentage of income against the cumulative percentage of the population receiving income. It is so constructed that an *increase* in the coefficient means *greater* inequality in the distribution of income. The Suits Index is derived from a curve similar to the Lorenze curve, although in this case the cumulative percentage of taxes paid is compared to the cumulative percentage of total income. In the case of the Suits Index, an *increase* in the number means that the tax system has become *more* progressive. If the index declines, the oppostite has happened, namely the tax system has become less progressive or more regressive. In table 4-13, the Gini coefficient tells us two important things. First, since the coefficient for pretax family income increased between 1977 and 1988 from .4427 to .4890, the distribution of pretax income worsened during these years, a development commented upon earlier. Second, for all three years—1977, 1984, and

1988—the posttax Gini coefficient is lower, which indicates overall that the distribution of family income is less unequal after taxes than before taxes in each of these years. However, the *increase* in the Gini coefficient for posttax income between 1977 and 1988 from .4185 to .4724 shows that posttax income became somewhat more unequal during this period. The latter conclusion is supported by the behavior of the Suits Index. Between 1977 and 1988, this index fell from .1025 to .0696, which indicates that the federal tax system became less progressive during these years. There was a slight improvement in progessivity between 1984 and 1988, but not enough to offset the overall drop for the entire period.

## Summary Observations

We can conclude this chapter with a few brief summary remarks on the Reagan Revolution and America's welfare state, It is fairly clear that the ambitious goal of Mr. Reagan's "revolution" to cut back sharply the contours of the welfare state was not achieved. Overall, transfer spending as a percentage of all federal spending changed hardly at all, even though there were important shifts in its basic composition. As noted earlier in this chapter, the tilt generally was away from people-based programs and direct transfers to people. The goal of cutting back the size of the federal government as measured by its expenditures in relation to the GNP failed completely. Government was larger by this standard when Ronald Reagan left office then when he entered office. This does not mean, however, that Mr. Reagan failed in his drive to halt the further expansion of the welfare state. He may not have been able to roll back its boundaries, but the massive legacy of deficits and debt he bequeathed the economy has probably forestalled for well into the future any new initiatives in social welfare spending. The greatest impact of the Reagan Revolution and Reaganomics was clearly on the tax structure. Not only were there significant cuts in personal and corporate income taxes, but the burden of federal taxes was shifted strongly away from the top ranges of the income scale toward the middle and lower ranges. These changes began before Mr. Reagan took office, but they were accelerated and enhanced during his tenure in the presidency. In general the federal tax structure became less progressive, and the burden was shifted away from business onto individuals. For the first time in the postwar era, a measurable increase in income inequality took place in this nation, a result in part of the spending and tax policies pursued during the Reagan years. There is not much credible evidence, either, that supply-side economics, the intellectual basis for the Reagan Revolution, really worked.

The sharp 1981–1982 recession was caused by putting on the monetary brakes, while the recovery and long expansion since then has largely been sparked by debt, both public and private. Although the overall contours of America's welfare state were not drastically changed by the Reagan "Revolution, formidable and difficult problems lie ahead. It is to a consideration of these that we turn in our final chapter.

## Notes

1. The White House, *A Program for Economic Recovery*, February 18, 1981.
2. *Ibid.*, p. 1.
3. *Ibid.*
4. David A. Stockman, *The Triumph of Politics: Why the Reagan Revolution Failed* (New York, Harper and Row, 1986), p. 49.
5. *The White House, op. cit.*, p. 22.
6. *Ibid.* See table, p. S-1.
7. David A. Stockman, *op. cit.*, p. 72.
8. *Ibid.*, p. 92.
9. *Ibid.*, p. 95.
10. *Ibid.*, p. 96.
11. *Ibid.*, p. 98.
12. See Fred Barnes, "The Story of 'Supply-Side,' a Revolution in Economic Thinking," *The Baltimore Sun*, February 17, 1981, p.
13. *Economic Report of the President* (Washington, D.C., U.S. Government Printing Office, 1989), pp. 308, 401.
14. Bruce Bartlett, *Reaganomics; Supply Side Economics in Action* (Westport, CT, Arlington House Publishers, 1981), P 71.
15. David A. Stockman, *op. cit.*, p. 62.
16. *Ibid.*, p. 8.
17. William Greider, "The Education of David Stockman," *The Atlantic Monthly*, December, 1981, p. 46.
18. David A. Stockman, *op. cit.*, p. 37.
19. *Ibid.*, p. 32.
20. David A. Stockman,, "The Social Pork Barrel," *The Public Interest*, N39, 1975, pp. 5, 13.
21. *Ibid.*, p. 7.
22. *Ibid.*, pp. 15, 19, 29.
23. David A. Stockman, *The Triumph of Politics, op. cit.*, p. 8.
24. *The Wall Street Journal*, December 12, 1980, p. 22.
25. David A. Stockman, *The Triumph of Politics, op. cit.*, p. 72.
26. *Ibid.*, p. 124.
27. *Ibid.*, p. 125. Italics added.
28. *Ibid.*, p. 124.
29. *Ibid.*
30. *Ibid.*, p. 125.
31. *Current Economic Indicators*, December, 1989, p. 31. Joint Economic Committee (Washington, D.C., U.S. Government Printing Office, 1990.)

32. David A. Stockman, *The Triumph of Politics*, *op. cit.*, p. 297.

33. *Ibid.*, p. 109.

34. *Ibid.*, p. 193.

35. *Ibid.*, p. 131.

36. William Greider, *op. cit.*, p. 47.

37. David A. Stockman, *The Triumph of Politics*, *op. cit.*, p. 268.

38. *Ibid.*, p. 228.

39. *Ibid.*, p. 295.

40. *Economic Report of the President* (Washington, D.C., U.S. Government Printing Office, 1990), p. 294.

41. U.S. Department of Commerce, Bureau of the Census, Current Population Series, P-60, *Poverty in the United States, 1987*, p. 9.

42. *Current Economic Indicators*, December, 1989, p. 2.

43. *Economic Report of the President*, 1990, *op. cit.*, pp. 376, 394.

44. *Ibid.*, p. 297.

45. *Ibid.*

46. Congress of the United States, Congressional Budget Office, *The Changing Distribution of Federal Taxes: 1975–1990*, October, 1987, p. 13.

47. *Ibid.*, p. 11.

48. For details on the measure of family income used by the Congressional Budget Office, see the October 1987 CBO study, chapter IV, "Measuring Family Income," pp. 27–38.

49. Congressional Budget Office, *op. cit.*, Chapter II, pp. 5–22. Distribution data for 1988 are estimated.

50. *Ibid.*, pp. 35, 65.

51. Excise taxes play a minor role in the federal tax structure. In 1989 they accounted for only 5.6% of all federal receipts.

# 5  LOOKING TO THE FUTURE

As the nation enters the last decade of the twentieth century, what lies ahead for America's three-tiered welfare state? As noted in the last chapter, the Reagan era ended with the welfare state substantially intact, though somewhat frayed around the edges. It is now tilted more toward its middle-class beneficiaries than it was a decade ago, but the broad contours remain essentially as they have evolved since the 1930s, when the welfare state began. The last major legislative change in the welfare state came in 1987 the Family Support Act, an act properly regarded as an amendment to the AFDC program rather than as a major addition to the structure of the welfare state.

An array of problems lies ahead, not only for the nation's welfare state but for the nation generally. The end of the cold war has not automatically ushered in the millennium—at best, one can hope that now some resources may be freed up for use in coping with domestic problems. Whether this will happen remains to be seen. What can be said with some certainty is that the structure of the classic welfare state, as we have used that term in this book, will not be adequate. It will have to be changed and enlarged. Experience confirms this; the structure was not adequate to solve the problem of the "invisible poor" that surfaced in the 1960s, and it will not be adequate

133

to solve the looming problems of the twenty-first century. Experience also tells us that problems of a social-welfare nature cannot be solved outside the social context—they cannot be resolved by the magic of the market-place. Put bluntly, this means that transfer spending will remain the main vehicle if solutions are to be forthcoming.

So what are the problems to be faced? Within the context of America's welfare state as well as of the objectives of this book, they number three. First, there is the forthcoming and crushing impact of the "baby boomers" on the welfare state, a development that will begin to be felt as early as 2011. Second, there is a growing crisis in health care in the nation, a crisis grounded in the fact that an estimated 37 million Americans have *no* health insurance whatsoever. American is the only modern industrialized nation without a system of national health insurance. In too many instances, famil-ies have no defense against the catastrophic and traumatic financial costs of a major illness. Third, there is the surging and near intractable problem of the *underclass*, a word that refers to an array of social pathologies. This problem comprises the woes afflicting such disparate groups as the poor, both working and nonworking, who fall between the cracks in the safety net of the welfare state, the homeless that roam the streets and alleys of America's big cities, and the blacks and black families fighting for survival in the inner-city ghettos of America. A part of the latter problem is the devastating impact of murder and crime on a growing proportion of young American blacks between the ages of 15 and 30.

This third problem, which is not a single problem, but many related problems, is one that cannot be solved within the traditional structure of the welfare state. Partly for this reason, and partly because the problem is so sweeping that it requires a book in itself for adequate discussion and analy-sis, we shall not discuss it here.[1] The baby boomer and health care problems, however, can and should be discussed within the context of the welfare state.

## The Baby Boomers and the Social Security System

The baby boomers, estimated to number more than 80 million, are the largest single demographic bloc in the nation's population structure. Now (1990) ranging in age from 24 to 44, they will put unheard and unex-perienced strains on the Social Security system when the first boomers reach retirement age in 2011. The last of the Boomer cohort will reach retirement around 2031, assuming that a retirement standard of 65 to 67 years of age still prevails. The nation has only 21 years, from 1990 to 2011, to get ready for this impact. The essential question is this: can the system as now structured deliver the benefits implied by the system when this huge bulge in the population reaches retirement? The enormity of the problem can be seen in the fact that from the end of World War II (1945) through 1987 (42 years), 36.9 million new beneficiaries were brought into the system. In a 20-year period, from 2011 to 2031, the system will have to absorb more than twice as many new beneficiaries as in almost the whole of the post-World War II era.[2] Can it be done?

To answer this question, we must first examine with as much precision as possible the full magnitude of the problem. Tables 5-1, 5-2, and 5-3 do this from two different perspectives and on the basis of several sets of assumptions about economic and demographic behavior between the present and a time two thirds of the way into the next century.[3] Table 5-1 looks at the relationship between covered workers and beneficiaries under the Old Age, Survivors, and Disability Insurance program—OASDI or Social Security. *Covered* workers are those whose jobs come under the Social Security Act and various amendments, and whose wage or salary is subject, consequently, to payroll taxes. Two basic relationships are shown in the table: the number of covered workers per beneficiary, and the number of beneficiaries per 100 covered workers. Since ultimately benefits under the system are paid for in one way or another by the working population, these relationships are crucial for seeing what is likely to happen to the system in the future. The table is organized in two parts. The upper part gives the historical record, showing for selected years since 1950 the values for these relationships. The lower part of the table is predictive, It shows estimated values for these two relationships over the next 75 years on the basis of *four* different assumptions about the behavior of key economic variables over this period. We will discuss these assumptions shortly.

So what is the story from this table? The historical data show that there has been a continuous decline in the ratio of covered workers to beneficiaries ever since the end of World War II. This means simply that in this period, the number of beneficiaries has grown much faster than the numbers of workers, a not-too-surprising development, since the Congress and *all* post-World War II administrations have cooperated in continuously expanding and improving Social Security benefits. In 1950 were 16.5 workers in covered employment for every person receiving OASDI benefits; by 1988 the ratio had fallen to 3.3 covered workers per beneficiary. The same story is told in a slightly different fashion by the figures showing the number of beneficiaries for each 100 workers in covered employment. In 1950 there were a mere 6 beneficiaries for every 100 workers, but by 1988 this number had climbed to 30 beneficiaries per 100 workers. The economic story told by

# Table 5-1. OASDI Workers Per Beneficiary and Beneficiaries per 100 Workers: Selected Years

### A. Past Experience

| Year | Covered Workers Per Beneficiary | Beneficiaries Per 100 Workers |
|---|---|---|
| 1950 | 16.5 | 6 |
| 1960 | 5.1 | 20 |
| 1970 | 3.7 | 27 |
| 1980 | 3.2 | 31 |
| 1988 | 3.3 | 30 |

### B. Projections

| Year | Alternative I | | Alternative II-A | | Alternative II-B | | Alternative III | |
|---|---|---|---|---|---|---|---|---|
| | W/Ben[a] | Ben/100W[b] | W/Ben | Ben/100W | W/Ben | Ben/100W | W/Ben | Ben/100W |
| 1990 | 3.3 | 30 | 3.3 | 30 | 3.3 | 30 | 3.2 | 31 |
| 2000 | 3.4 | 30 | 3.2 | 31 | 3.2 | 31 | 3.1 | 33 |
| 2010 | 3.2 | 31 | 3.0 | 33 | 3.0 | 33 | 2.7 | 36 |
| 2020 | 2.6 | 38 | 2.4 | 42 | 2.4 | 42 | 2.4 | 47 |
| 2030 | 2.3 | 44 | 2.0 | 50 | 2.0 | 51 | 1.7 | 59 |
| 2040 | 2.3 | 43 | 1.9 | 52 | 1.9 | 53 | 1.5 | 65 |
| 2050 | 2.4 | 42 | 1.9 | 53 | 1.9 | 54 | 1.4 | 71 |
| 2060 | 2.4 | 41 | 1.8 | 55 | 1.8 | 55 | 1.3 | 78 |
| 2065 | 2.4 | 41 | 1.8 | 55 | 1.8 | 55 | 1.3 | 80 |

[a] Covered workers per beneficiary.
[b] Beneficiaries per 100 workers.

Source: Board of Trustees of the Federal Old-Age and Survivors Insurance Trust Fund and the Federal Disability Insurance Trust Fund, 1989 Annual Report, (Washington, D.C., U.S. Government Printing Office, 1989), p. 77.

these statistics is straightforward: each worker must "support" a growing number of nonworkers who enjoy benefits provided by the Social Security system. The trend embodied in these figures is also used to justify alarmist conclusions about growing strains on the system and its ability to provide future benefits to the same degree as it has done in the past. Subsequently, we shall examine critically the validity of such assumptions, but they are derived from the data found in the lower portion of the table.

In the lower part of table 5-1 are found projections for the two basic relationships discussed above for the next 75 years, from 1990 through 2065. There are four such projections, labeled Alternative I, Alternative II-A, Alternative II-B, and Alternative III. A word about these is in order. These projections or forecasts are compiled periodically by the Office of Actuary in the Social Security Administration. Alternative I is described as *optimistic*, Alternative III as *pessimistic*, and Alternatives II-A and II-B as *best-guess* alternatives lying between the two extremes. The terms *optimistic* and *pessimistic* as used in this context also require explanation. *Optimistic* refers to developments in the economy that reduce program costs and thereby increase trust fund reserves. If, for example, people chose voluntarily to work longer, this development would affect the optimistic forecast. *Pessimistic*, on the other hand, refers to developments that increase program costs, thus reducing the trust fund balances. An increase in longevity, for example, would have this effect.[4]

All the forecasts shown in the lower half of table 5-1 show the same trend—a reduction in the number of covered workers per beneficiary and an increase in the number of beneficiaries per covered worker. At the optimistic extreme, covered workers per beneficiary are expected to decline to 2.4 by 2065, and beneficiaries per 100 covered workers to increase to 41 in the same period. The pessimistic projection, on the other hand, has the number of covered workers per beneficiary dropping over the next 75 years to 1.3, and the number of beneficiaries per 100 covered workers climbing to 80. The two in-between best-guess projections come out the same— 1.8 covered workers per beneficiary by 2065 and 55 beneficiaries per 100 covered workers by the same year.

*All* the above projections—optimistic, pessimistic and in-between— spell bad news for the Social Security system. Just how bad is demonstrated by the data in table 5-2. This table shows the proportion of OASDI and Hospital Insurance (HI) costs for each set of projections that can be financed by tax rates in place for OASDI and HI in 1990. The percentages in the table are calculated from data on income and cost rates compiled by the Social Security Actuary for the time intervals shown.[5] The income rate is the combined employee-employer OASDI and HI contribution rate expressed

Table 5-2. Proportion of OASDI[a] and HI[b] Benefits that Can be Financed By Scheduled Tax Income, 1989–2063 (Percentage of Taxable Payroll)

| Period | Alternative I | Assumptions | | |
| | | Alternative II-A | Alternative II-B | Alternative III |
| --- | --- | --- | --- | --- |
| *25-year averages* | | | | |
| 1989–2013 | 126.5 | 114.7 | 110.8 | 95.1 |
| 2014–2038 | 102.7 | 80.3 | 76.5 | 55.2 |
| 2039–2063 | 100.1 | 70.0 | 66.6 | 42.6 |
| *75-year average* | | | | |
| 1989–2063 | 110.5% | 87.9% | 83.8% | 62.0% |

[a] Old-Age Survivors and Disability Trust Funds.
[b] Hospital Insurance Trust Fund (Medicare).

Source: Board of Trustees of the Federal Old-Age and Survivors Insurance Trust Fund and the Federal Disability Insurance Trust Fund, *1989 Annual Report* (Washington, D.C., U.S. Government Printing Office, 1989), compiled from table E3, p. 126.

as a percentage of taxable payrolls. It includes income from the taxation of Social Security benefits. The cost rate consists of annual outgo or beneficiary expense expressed as a percentage of taxable payrolls. The actuarial balance is the difference between summaries of the estimated income rates and cost rates for the period under review. If the actuarial balance is negative, the program is said to have an actuarial deficit, and such a deficit is taken as a warning signal that future changes may be needed in either program benefits or financing.[6]

So what do the figures in table 5-2 tell us about the troubles confronting the brightest gem in America's welfare state, the Social Security system? Save for the superoptimistic projections that underlie Alternative I (see table 5-3), the system will find itself in deep trouble beginning around the year 2014. For the first 25-year interval shown in the table (1989 to 2013), funding is more than adequate to finance all benefits paid out by the system except under the most pessimistic forecast, Alternative III. But even there the shortfall in revenue compared to benefits is only 4.9 percentage points. However, for the second (2014 to 2038) and third (2039 to 2063) 25-year intervals, disaster strikes, save again for the highly optimistic assumptions (table 5-3) that undergird Alternative I. By 2063, (Alternative IIB), the shortfall in tax revenues to finance benefits will be 33.4 percentage points. The shortfall reaches 57.4 percentage points in the worst-case scenario in the third 25-year interval. For the entire 75-year forecast period (1989–2063) show in table 5-2, the actuarial deficit (benefit cost in excess of system revenues) is 12.1 percentage points for Alternative II-A, 16.2 percentage points for Alternative II-B, and 38.0 percentage points for Alternative III, the pessimistic forecast.

For a look at the assumptions that underlie the forecast alternatives shown in tables 5-1 and 5-2, examine the figures in table 5-3. This table shows actual annual average rates of increase in *real* GNP, covered wages, and the consumer price index (CPI), the average annual unemployment rates for selected past periods, and forecast or projected values for the same variables through 2065 for each alternative. *Real* GNP, wage increases, the inflation rate (CPI), and the unemployment rate are the key macroeconomic variables that govern what happens to both benefits and Social Security income during the forecast period. To these, the actuaries of the Social Security system add demographic assumptions involving birth, death, and fertility rates, as well as assumptions about net migration. How good are these assumptions and the predictions that flow from them? No one really knows. It is a bold act to project such volatile variables as *real* GNP, inflation, and the unemployment rate so far into the future, but given the hordes of baby boomers waiting in the wings, the attempt must be

Table 5-3. Past Experience and Assumed Values For Selected Economic Variables: 1960–2010 and Later (in Percent)

| | Annual Average Percentage Increase | | | Average Annual Unemployment Rate |
|---|---|---|---|---|
| | Real GNP[a] | Covered Wages | Consumer Price Index | |
| Past Experience | | | | |
| 1. 1960–1964 | 3.9 | 3.4 | 1.3 | 5.7 |
| 2. 1965–1969 | 4.4 | 5.4 | 3.4 | 3.8 |
| 3. 1970–1974 | 2.4 | 6.3 | 6.1 | 5.4 |
| 4. 1975–1987 | 2.7 | 7.1 | 6.6 | 7.5 |
| Projections (1988–2010 and later) | | | | |
| 1. Alternative I | 3.3 | 4.8 | 2.5 | 4.9 |
| 2. Alternative II-A | 2.8 | 5.1 | 3.2 | 5.2 |
| 3. Alternative II-B | 2.5 | 5.6 | 4.2 | 5.6 |
| 4. Alternative III | 1.4 | 5.7 | 5.2 | 6.5 |

[a] In 1982 dollars.

Source: Board of Trustees of the Federal Old-Age and Survivors Insurance Trust Fund and the Federal Disability Insurance Trust Fund, *1989 Annual Report*, (Washington, D.C., U.S. Government Printing Office, 1989), p. 34.

made. Only as time passes will we know how good these projections really are. One point ought to give us pause. Only Alternative III the pessimistic forecast sees a recession happening within the next ten years. If one of the other three forecasts turns out to be right, the nation will have gone 16 years *without* a recession, an unheard-of feat!

## The 1983 "Big Fix"

Forecasts such as those contained in tables 5-1, 5-2, and 5-3 helped trigger a presumed financing crisis for the system in the early 1980s. A slowing of the economy in the 1970s, a growing awareness of the looming Baby Boomer crunch, and actual deficits in the OASDI Trust Funds from 1976 and after contributed to the belief that the system was facing disaster in the next century unless speedy action was taken. Table 5-4 shows the income, outgo, and overall balance of the OASDI Trust Funds for selected years since 1940.[7] Typically, the Trust Funds have had only a modest balance at the end

Table 5-4.  OASDI[a] Trust Funds for Selected Years: 1940–1987[b] (in Millions of Current Dollars)

| Year | Receipts | Expenditures | Net Change | Fund Balance |
|------|----------|--------------|------------|--------------|
| 1940 | 368 | 35 | 333 | 2,031 |
| 1945 | 1,420 | 274 | 1,146 | 7,121 |
| 1950 | 2,928 | 1,022 | 1,906 | 13,721 |
| 1955 | 6,167 | 4,968 | 1,199 | 21,663 |
| 1960 | 12,445 | 11,798 | 647 | 22,613 |
| 1965 | 17,857 | 18,311 | −1,331 | 19,841 |
| 1970 | 36,993 | 33,108 | 3,886 | 38,068 |
| 1975 | 67,640 | 69,184 | −1,544 | 44,342 |
| 1980 | 119,712 | 123,550 | −3,838 | 26,453 |
| 1985 | 203,540 | 190,628 | 11,088 | 42,163 |
| 1987 | 231,039 | 209,093 | 21,946 | 68,807 |

[a] OASI and DI Trust Funds combined.
[b] Before 1955 OASI only.

Source: U.S. Department of Health and Human Services, Social Security Administration, *Social Security Bulletin, Annual Statistical Supplement*, 1988, pp. 121, 123.

of each period, reflecting what has been the essentially pay-as-you-go nature of the system since its founding in the 1930s. Note that from 1960 to 1970, the balance in the funds was only slightly larger than the annual outlay.

In December 1981, President Reagan established by executive order the National Commission on Social Security Reform, a bipartisan blue-ribbon group with five members appointed by the President, five members by the Republican congressional leadership, and five members by the Democratic congressional leadership. The Commission was chaired by Alan Greenspan, now Chairman of the Board of Governors of the Federal Reserve System, and included among the Republicans Senator Robert Dole and House member Barber Conable, since retired, and from the Democrats New York Senator Daniel Patrick Moynihan and the late Claude Pepper of Florida. Noncongressional appointees included Robert A. Beck, Chairman of the Board of Prudential Insurance Company, Alexander Towbridge, president of the National Association of Manufacturers, and Lane Kirkland, President of the AFL-CIO.[8] Although the Commission was weighted heavily in favor of Republicans, its recommendations were essentially bipartisan, and when presented to the Congress in early 1983 they were adopted largely intact. The major reforms in the bill signed into law by the President included accelerating already scheduled payroll tax increases, delaying cost-of-living increases for benefits, and raising the retirement age to take effect in the next century.[9] The package was supposed to make the Social Security system self-financing through the middle of the twenty-first century.

## The Buildup in the Social Security Trust Funds (OASI and DI)

The joker in the deck from the 1983 "big fix" package of Social Security reforms is the anticipated buildup in the two major trust funds for the system, Old Age and Survivors Insurance (OASI) and Disability Insurance (DI). It is this buildup that triggered Senator Moynihan's call in late 1989 for a roll-back in payroll taxes. The bill Senator Moynihan introduced in the Senate would repeal the increase in Social Security taxes that went into effect on January 1, 1990—from 6.06% of covered wages for employees and employers each to 6.2%—and cut the rate further on January 1, 1991 to 5.1%. In his bill, Senator Moynihan essentially sought to roll Social Security taxes back to a level that would maintain a balance in the trust funds roughly equal to one year's outlay.[10]

Unfortunately, when the 1983 bipartisan "big fix" for Social Security was engineered, apparently not much thought was given to either the size of the surplus that would emerge from the reforms, or to what was to be done with the money. Table 5-5 shows in current dollars, and on the basis of Alternative II-A, the expected annual surpluses generated in the combined OASI and DI accounts and the balance in their combined trust funds flowing out of the 1983 "big fix." The figures are staggering.

By 2020—just 30 years distant—the OASDI trust fund balance, measured in current dollars, will reach 36.9% of the GNP! By 2035, the balance in the trust fund will have soared to an incredible $14,797 *billion*. In that year, again in current dollars, the trust fund balance will be nearly six times greater than the expected benefits outflow. Figures 5-1 and 5-2 show in graphic form the projected path of the trust funds from 1990 through 2060. At this point, one cannot help but wonder what the prestigious members of the high-powered blue-ribbon Social Security Reform Commission were thinking. Did they really give any serious thought to the possible disposition of such enormous sums? Merton C. Bernstein and Joan Brodshaug Bernstein, in their excellent book *Social Security: The System That Works*, devote only a few pages to this question, even though Mr. Bernstein served as a consultant to the Commission.[11] Before we can tackle

Table 5-5. Estimated Buildup in Combined OASI and DI Trust Funds and GNP: 1990–2060[a] (Billions of Current Dollars)

| Year | Funds | GNP | Trust Funds As Percent of GNP |
|------|-------|-----|-------------------------------|
| 1990 | $ 241 | $ 5,555 | 4.3% |
| 1995 | 769 | 7,378 | 10.4 |
| 2000 | 1,634 | 9,687 | 16.9 |
| 2005 | 2,963 | 12,711 | 23.3 |
| 2010 | 4,877 | 16,435 | 29.7 |
| 2015 | 7,247 | 20,900 | 34.7 |
| 2020 | 9,734 | 26,353 | 36.9 |
| 2025 | 11,971 | 33,155 | 36.1 |
| 2030 | 13,682 | 41,865 | 32.7 |
| 2035 | 14,797 | 53,060 | 27.9 |
| 2040 | 15,365 | 67,197 | 22.9 |
| 2045 | 15,181 | 84,905 | 17.9 |
| 2050 | 13,466 | 107,143 | 12.6 |
| 2055 | 8,879 | 135,306 | 6.6 |
| 2060 | — | 171,113 | — |

[a] Based upon Alternative II-A assumptions.

Source: Board of Trustees of the Federal Old-Age and Survivors Insurance Trust Fund and the Federal Disability Insurance Trust Fund, *1989 Annual Report* (Washington, D.C., U.S. Government Printing Office, 1989), p. 132.

the crucial and vexing question of what can be done with these funds, a short, historical detour is in order.

## A Historical Note on Social Security

The 1935 Social Security Act was initially hammered out by a Committee on Economic Security, a subcabinet group appointed by Franklin D. Roosevelt and chaired by his Secretary of Labor, Francis Perkins. Roosevelt particularly wanted two things in the system. First, it had to be differentiated from the "dole," which meant that it had to be contributory to some extent. And second, it had to be self-financing, by which Roosevelt meant that no money should come directly from the Treasury to pay for the benefits.[12]

There were, and still are, two interpretations of what is meant by *self-financing*. It could be either *pay-as-you-go* or *pay-for-yourself*. A pay-as-

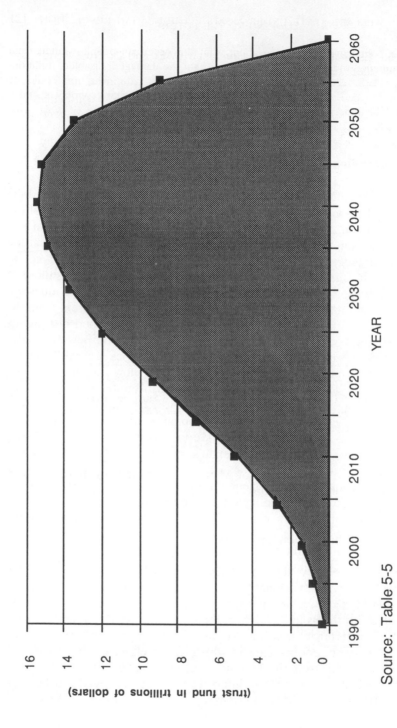

Source: Table 5-5

Figure 5-1 Trust fund balances in trillions of dollars: 1990–2060

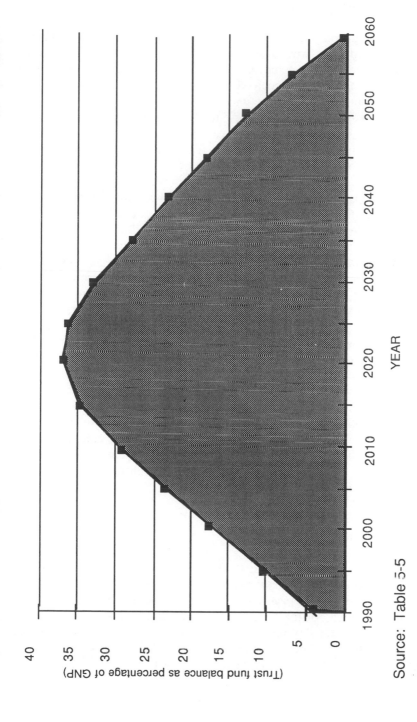

(Trust fund balance as percentage of GNP)

YEAR

Source: Table 5-5

Figure 5-2  Trust fund balances as a percent of the GNP: 1990–2020

you-go system means that the sources of finance for the system have to be identified and *earmarked* for the beneficiaries of the system. Taxes must, of course, be enacted to achieve this. In a pay-as-you-go system, *current* taxpayers pay the benefits received by *current* beneficiaries. Benefits and taxes are in approximate balance each year or over a time period of a few years. A pay-as-you-go system is essentially an intergenerational transfer scheme. People working and being taxed pay the benefits flowing to the retired, their survivors, and the disabled. This is essentially how the Social Security system operated until the 1983 "big fix."

A pay-for-yourself system, on the other hand, is one in which *each* generation of participants pays for its own benefits. In such a system, each participant would pay money into a fund, out of which the benefits would be paid at retirement, for disability, or to survivors. This kind of a system is analogous to systems of private insurance, and, when operating effectively, is said to be *fully funded*. To be actuarially sound, such a system must have a fund of sufficient size that in the event the system was closed down, all future claims of beneficiaries in the system at the time of the shutdown could be paid. Only if the system operated in this way could it be described as being "real" insurance. Most current beneficiaries of Social Security regard it in this way, even though the reality is different.

Originally, President Roosevelt opted for a pay-for-yourself system, believing that pay-as-you-go was simply the dole under another name.[13] Francis Perkins wanted a pay-as-you-go system, but the original legislation took the other route. However, in 1939, just before the outbreak of war in Europe, the Social Security Act was amended to transform Social Security into a pay-as-you-go system. As one critic has said, "The amendments of 1939 adopted a funding orientation that stared an intergenerational transfer on a grand scale and set a precedent that, once established, would become practically inescapable for those who followed."[14]

## Back to the Trust Funds Problem

In retrospect, it appears that the 1983 Reform Commission undertook to shift Social Security from what it has been since 1939—essentially a pay-as-you-go system—toward a pay-for-yourself system *without* fully understanding what it was doing or the serious economic consequences of such a shift. To see this, we need to examine the economic scenarios that could emerge as a result of the mammoth buildup in trust fund reserves shown in table 5-5 and figure 5-1. Two such scenarios are possible; we need to ask ourselves if either is realistic.[15] Only then will we be able to deal adequately with the baby boomer burden confronting the system.

For the sake of keeping the analysis as simple and as straightforward as possible, we shall assume a full employment economy with annually balanced budgets.[16] As table 5-5 shows, the trust funds build to a peak at about the midpoint of the 70-year period and then drop to zero by the end of 2026. In the first scenario, which John C. Hambor calls a *Validation Scenario*, the trust funds are used as a vehicle to channel funds into the private capital markets, from whence they will find their way into new, *real* investment.[17] To the extent that this happens, the nation's capital stock and productive capacity will be increased. Out of such increases will come the additional output needed in the future to provide benefits for the baby boomers as they reach retirement age. Why will there be new investment? The trust fund surpluses are a part of national savings, even though they originate in the public sector, and, as savings increase, interest rates will decline and investment will be stimulated. When the baby boomers begin to retire, benefits paid out will start running ahead of receipts, and the whole process will be thrown into reverse. Selling off the trust fund assets that represent the claims against the *real* capital built up when the trust fund balances were expanding provides the money needed to pay benefits to new beneficiaries. In effect, Hambor says, the Validation Scenario can be thought of as a mechanism by which the current working generation provides partially for its own retirement.[18]

The second possibility is labeled the *Offset Scenario*.[19] It is called *offset* because the regular budget of the federal government would be managed over the next 70 years to offset exactly the rise and fall of the surpluses in the OASDI trust funds. During the buildup of these surpluses, from approximately 1990 through 2040, there would have to be deficits of equal magnitude in the on-budget accounts of the federal government.[20] Overall, the accounts of the federal government, including the trust funds, would be in balance. When the trust fund balances began to decline, which will happen as soon as benefits begin to exceed revenues, the regular or on-budget accounts of the federal government would have to develop surpluses. For the entire 70-year period, the government would spend the trust fund surpluses generated in the first part of the period and would use general tax revenues in the latter part of the period when the assets of the trust funds have to be sold off to pay for benefits flowing to the baby boomers. In principle, at least, the surpluses or deficits of the trust funds would not have any effect upon the national savings rate, and hence upon the rate of investment and new capital creation. Basically, this is a pay-as-you-go scenario in which future taxpayers will have to pay for future benefits. As Hambor says, the trust fund buildup that will result from this approach "...more accurately represents a stack of IOUs to be presented to future generations for payment, rather than a build-up of resources to fund future benefits."[21] This conclusion, it is important to note, rests upon payroll tax changes contained in the 1983 "big fix" not being changed.

From the viewpoint of the logic of macroeconmic theory and analysis, both scenarios are correct. In principle, either could be achieved by acting through the trust funds or by manipulating the overall on-budget accounts of the federal government. From a practical and political perspective, however, both scenarios confront difficulties that are probably insurmountable. The second or offset scenario, assuming the indicated trust funds buildup is allowed to continue, would require continuous and even major adjustments in the tax revenues of the federal government from sources that are not tied to the trust funds, namely personal and corporate income taxes. This simply could not be done. This bring us to the Validation Scenario, the scenario put in place by the 1983 "big fix." For reasons that we shall now explore, this solution, too, is unworkable.


## The Impossible Dream: A Pay-for-Yourself System

In his *Introduction* to the Bush administration's budget for fiscal 1991, Richard G. Darman, Director of the Office of Management and Budget (OMB), opted essentially for the Validation Scenario. The vehicle for this is the proposed Social Security and Debt Reduction Fund, the purpose of which is, in effect, to use an *increasing* proportion of the surpluses building up in the OASDI trust funds to *reduce* the portion of the federal debt held by the public. By 1995, 85% of the Social Security surplus would be used for this purpose, and after 1995 the percentage would rise to 100%.[22] This proposal, the budget document goes on to say, will "...preserve the trust fund buildup for its intended purpose—the payment of benefits to the baby boom generation."[23] The Bush budget not only argues that the 1983 Amendments to Social Security were successful, but one of their major effects was to move the Social Security system away from "...the traditional pay-as-you-go approach and toward a form of 'accrual funding,'" by which is meant building a fund out of which future benefits can be paid.[24]

The logic behind the Bush and Darman proposition is straightforward. Using the OASI trust fund surpluses to retire privately held federal debt will provide bondholders with cash. The funds released by retiring federal debt will presumably flow through the private capital markets into *real* investment, thereby increasing the nation's capital stock and improving productivity. As sketched out in the prior section, the greater output associated with higher productivity would be the real source of retirement benefits for the baby boomer generation. For this scenario to work, however, two things must happen. First, the public or privately held portion of the federal debt *must* be reduced. If that does not happen, then the entire scenario comes unglued. The OASDI surplus will then simply continue to mask the real size of the federal government's deficit, as is now the case. Second, funds released into the economy by the retirement of privately held debt *must* find their way into net *real* capital investment. Instead, if they are used to finance mergers and buyouts, the entire point of the exercise is lost. Whether this second requirement will happen, we simply do not know, although the record of the 1980s is not encouraging. From 1980 through 1986, corporate America spent $689.1 billion on mergers and acquisitions, as compared to $307.8 billion for research and development, and $527.4 billion on net new nonresidential investment.[25]

What of the first requirement, namely, that the size of the privately held portion of the federal debt be reduced? Here we can be more precise, because data showing what is likely to happen do exist. The sad fact is that any hope of using OASDI surpluses to *reduce* the pivately held portion of the federal debt has foundered, and will continue to founder, on the rock of the Reagan era deficits. The figures in table 5-6, which are for 1990–1995, show why this is likely to happen. Column 1 in the table shows the portion of projected on-budget deficits that will be reflected in federal debt held in the private sector. These totals are based upon the past division of the total deficit between private and public ownership.[26] Congressional Budget Office data are the source for the total on-budget deficit for these years.[27] Column 2, the projected privately held debt for the 1990–1995 period, is obtained by adding column 1 for each year to the total of privately held debt for the preceding year. In 1989 this total was $1964 billion, so by adding the projected deficit of $137 billion for 1990 to this figure, we get the privately held debt total at the end of 1990. From these totals for each year we subtract the projected OASDI surpluses each year to get the figures shown in column 4, which are the privately held debt totals to be expected at the end of each year shown in the table. To get the total of $1860 billion shown at the end of 1990, the OASDI surplus of $73 billion for that year was increased by $168 billion, the latter being the expected balance in the OASDI trust funds at the end of 1989 on the basis of the Alternative II-A projection. What is assumed here is that the whole of the trust fund balance

Table 5-6.   Projected Privately Held Federal Debt and OASDI Surpluses: 1990–1995 (in Billions of Current Dollars)

| Year | (1) Projected Deficit[a] | (2) Projected Privately Held Federal Debt[b] | (3) Projected OASDI Surpluses[c] | (4) Privately Held Debt Less OASDI Surpluses |
|------|------|------|------|------|
| 1990 | 137 | 2,101 | 241 | 1,860 |
| 1991 | 142 | 2,243 | 82 | 2,161 |
| 1992 | 148 | 2,391 | 93 | 2,298 |
| 1993 | 160 | 2,551 | 105 | 2,446 |
| 1994 | 162 | 2,713 | 118 | 2,595 |
| 1995 | 165 | 2,878 | 130 | 2,748 |

[a] Congressional Budget Office projection of the baseline on-budget deficit adjusted to reflect proportion of deficit financed by private purchase of government securities.

[b] Privately held federal debt at the end of 1989 increased each year by the projected deficit (Column 1).

[c] For 1990 the figure shown ($241 billion) includes OASDI Trust Fund balances at end of 1989 plus OASDI surplus in 1990 ($168 + $73 billion).

Sources: Congress of the United States, Congressional Budget Office, *The Economic and Budget Outlook: Fiscal Years 1991–1995*, January 1990; *1989 Annual Report*, Board of Trustees of the Federal Old-Age and Survivors Insurance Trust Fund, and the Federal Disability Insurance Trust Fund (Washington, D.C., U.S. Government Printing Office, 1989).

available in 1990 would be used to retire privately held federal debt, and thereafter, only the surpluses of income over outgo in the Social Security trust funds could be used for this purpose.

So what are we to conclude from the figures in table 5-6? Under the most favorable assumptions possible—namely, that *all* of the OASDI operational surpluses generated each year (1990–1995) can be used to retire privately held federal debt—there will not be a net reduction in the amount of outstanding federal debt held by private persons. The reason, of course, is the federal deficit. It is still there, and, according to the Congressional Budget Office projections, the on-budget deficit—the deficit not masked by the Social Security surpluses—will actually increase between 1990 and 1995, Gramm–Rudman–Hollings notwithstanding.[28] But without a net reduction in the privately held portion of the federal debt, the Social Security surpluses cannot be regarded as an addition to the nation's pool of savings. As long as the deficits continue and *exceed* Social Security surpluses, the federal government is drawing more out of the savings pool than it is putting in. Thus, the conclusion seems inescapable: the Bush–Darman idea of using the OASDI surpluses to augment the flow of funds into private capital markets and boost real investment spending simply will not work, given the expected magnitude of the federal deficits.

There are two other things wrong with the Darman scenario. First, it is well recognized that the Social Security tax works out to be regressive. It is also true, although the recognition may not be so wide, that the private owners of the federal debt are mostly found in the upper ranges of the income distribution scale. A 1983 survey of consumer finances by the Federal Reserve System found that 28% of total net worth for all families is held by the upper 2% of families at the top; the upper 10% of all families have 57% of all net worth, while 20% of families have a zero or negative net worth.[29] Bonds of all kinds make up only 4% of the net worth for all families, and their ownership is highly concentrated. The most recent data shows that 30% of all bonds are held by the top 1% of families.[30] It is sometimes argued that bond ownership is more widely distributed than these figures suggest, the reason being that bonds, especially federal bonds, are important in the portfolios of private pension funds. True enough, except that the catch-all category that includes pension funds as well savings and loan associations, credit unions, mutual savings banks, and other similar financial institutions accounts for only 31% of all privately held federal debt.[31] So it is a reasonable conclusion that the individual ownership of federal debt is heavily concentrated in the upper income ranges. So what the Darman scenario involves is using a regressive tax—the Social Security payroll tax—to transfer income on a massive scale from persons and families in the lower income ranges to those at the top. Since privately held debt at the end of 1989 was equal to almost $2 *trillion*, this plan, if actually implemented, would involve a transfer of wealth to the wealthy probably unprecedented in the nation's history.

There is an even more fundamental fault with the Darman scenario, one rooted in standard macroeconomic theory and policy. The question is this: should the federal government use its fiscal powers as an instrument to increase the level of saving in the economy? Or should not this be left to the private capital markets and the private decisions of business firms and households? Of course, the massive deficits of the 1980s absorbed a large share of privately generated savings, but it does not follow that this outcome represented wise or appropriate policy. Table 5-5 shows that by 2020 the OASDI trust fund surplus is expected to equal 36.9% of the GNP. Does it make any economic sense for the federal government to pull money out of the income stream to the extent necessary to build up a trust-fund surplus of this magnitude? This idea flies in the face of all the lessons of Keynesian economics. Ever since publication of *The General Theory*, it has

Table 5-7. The Bush and Reagan Administration Budget Reduction Plans: A Comparison (in Billions of Current Dollars)

| | Reagan Plan | | | Bush Plan | |
|---|---|---|---|---|---|
| Fiscal Year | Estimate Deficit | Actual Deficit | Fiscal Year | Estimated Deficit | CBO[a] Estimates |
| 1981 | −54.5 | −58.5 | 1990 | −123.8 | −138 |
| 1982 | −45.0 | −112.6 | 1991 | −63.1 | −138 |
| 1983 | −22.9 | −186.7 | 1992 | −25.1 | −135 |
| 1985 | +6.9 | −185.5 | 1994 | +10.7 | −130 |
| 1986 | +36.9 | −212.8 | 1995 | +9.4 | −118 |

[a] Congressional Budget Office.

Sources: *Budget of the United States Government, Fiscal Year 1991* (Washington, D.C., U.S. Government Printing Office, 1990); The White House, *A Program for Economic Recovery*, February 18, 1981; *Economic Report of the President* (Washington, D.C., U.S. Government Printing Office, 1990).

been well understood that the main role of a central government as far as fiscal policy is concerned is to create temporary budgetary surpluses or deficits in order to offset cyclical ups and downs in the private economy. It is not the business of fiscal policy to generate savings that may or may not find their way into private capital formation.

There is a another and perhaps more fundamental perspective from which to approach the Validation Scenario, one which will show why, even if the federal budget were balanced, a pay-for-yourself system is an impossibility. We begin this part of the analysis with a brief review of the fiscal 1991 budget. Like President Reagan before him, President Bush foresees in his fiscal year 1991 budget the elimination of the federal deficit in three years. Table 5-7 compares the Bush budget forecasts for a five-year period (1990–1995) with the Reagan forecasts (1981–1986). The Bush forecasts are from the fiscal 1991 budget transmitted to the Congress on January 29, 1990, and the Reagan figures are from the February 1981 *Program for Economic Recovery*. Also shown in the table are Congressional Budget Office projections for the budget (deficit or surplus) for 1990–1995. The Bush budgets, which a cynic might label *Rosy Scenario II*, foresee a balanced budget by the end of 1992, and a surplus emerging in 1993 and ensuing years! The figures in table 5-7 are a starting point for the discussion to follow.

As noted earlier, Budget Director Richard G. Darman said that the Bush Administration plans to use an increasing proportion of the OASDI trust

Table 5-8.  Hypothetical Timetable for OASDI Trust Fund Surplus and Federal
Debt Retirement (in Billions of Current Dollars)

| Year | OASDI Surplus [a] | Federal Debt [b] | |
|------|-------------------|-------------------|---|
| 1989 | — | −1,964.3 | |
| 1990 | 72.5 | −1,723.7 | |
| 1991 | 81.9 | −1,641.8 | |
| 1992 | 93.7 | −1,548.1 | |
| 1993 | 105.2 | −1,442.9 | |
| 1994 | 117.6 | −1,325.3 | |
| 1995 | 130.1 | −1,195.2 | |
| 1996 | 143.5 | −1,051.7 | |
| 1997 | 156.6 | −895.1 | |
| 1998 | 171.4 | −723.7 | |
| 1999 | 187.9 | −535.8 | |
| 2000 | 205.8 | −330.0 | |
| 2001 | 224.3 | −105.7 | |
| 2002 | 244.0 | +138.3 | Federal Assets |
| 2003 | 264.9 | +403.2 | Federal Assets |
| 2004 | 287.2 | +690.4 | Federal Assets |
| 2005 | 310.8 | +1,001.2 | Federal Assets |

[a] Total OASDI Income, including interest, minus OASDI outgo.

[b] Estimated privately held federal debt (−), or assets held by federal government (+).

Sources: Board of Trustees, Federal Old-Age and Survivors Insurance and Disability Insurance Trust Funds, *Annual Report* (Washington, D.C., U.S. Government Printing Office, 1989); *Economic Report of the President* (Washington, D.C., U.S. Government Printing Office, 1990).

fund surplus to retire privately held public debt, the vehicle being the Social Security and Debt Reduction Fund. According to the Darman plan, $14.1 billion (15% of the surplus) will be paid into the fund in 1993, $53.6 billion (50% of the surplus) in 1994, and $101.8 billion (85% of the surplus) in 1995; by 1996 *all* of the surplus will begin flowing into the debt reduction fund.[32]

This raises our first important question: if this scenario is followed, how long will it take to retire the privately held part of the federal debt? To answer this question, let us begin with a simplifying assumption, namely that we start with a balanced budget in 1990 and from then on apply the entire projected surplus in the OASDI trust funds to debt retirement. Then we can adjust the results to reflect the Darman scenario. At the end of 1989, privately held federal debt totaled $1964.3 billion.[33] Table 5-8 shows how long it will take to retire this debt, assuming *all* of the OASDI trust fund surpluses are applied to debt retirement. By the end of 1990, debt outstanding will equal $1723.7 billion. This figure is obtained by first adding together the surplus in the trust funds at the end of 1989 ($168.1 billion) and the estimated 1990 surplus of $72.5 billion, the sum of these two figures being $240.6 billion.[34] The latter figure is then subtracted from the 1989 total of outstanding debt ($ 1964.3 billion) to get the outstanding total at the end of 1990 ($1723.7 billion). Subsequently, the estimated surplus in the trust funds is applied toward debt retirement. If this scheme were followed, the privately held portion of the federal debt would be eliminated between 2001 and 2002, there being a surplus in the trust fund accounts of $138.3 billion at the end of 2002. By the year 2005 the surplus will have grown to $1001.2 billion. Given the assumption we started with—a balanced budget in 1989—it would take 12 years (1990–2001) to retire the debt. As discussed earlier, whether it is good social policy to transfer increasing amounts of tax revenue to current bondholders is another question. But in principle, a debt-free (federal) society could be achieved in a relatively short time. The Darman plan would take a bit longer, for it does not envisage applying the full surplus in the OASDI trust funds to debt retirement until 1996. Thus, under the Darman scenario, the debt would not be retired until 2007.

This brings us to the next question: what will happen after the retirement of the privately held debt? By 2005, according to table 5-9, the surplus in the two Social Security trust funds will have reached $1001 billion (the numbers in this and subsequent tables are rounded to the nearest whole number). This total is obtained by adding the estimated surpluses for the years 2002 through 2005, as shown in table 5-8. Table 5-9 contains two columns. The first column shows the increase or decrease in the trust fund balance at five-year intervals. The second column shows the buildup in the trust funds that will take place on the basis of the simplified assumption made earlier, namely that the budget is balanced in 1989, and thereafter *all* of the surpluses can be applied to debt reduction. Currently any surplus is required by law to be "invested" in interest-bearing obligations of the U.S. Government.[35] This is an important point, for it has a direct bearing on the subsequent discussion of what is to be done with these surpluses, and, further, to what extent the anticipated surpluses will bring the retirement, survivors, and disability part of the Social Security system toward a genuine pay-for-yourself system (tables 5-10 and 5-11). The data in table 5-9 show that the buildup in the assets of the trust funds will peak in 2040; thereafter, the surplus will begin to decline, becoming exhausted by 2060. The increase (or decrease) in the surplus (measured at five-year intervals) reaches a maximum in the year 2020, which is the year that the first of the baby

Table 5-9.  Alternative[a] Estimate of Buildup in Combined OASI and DI Trust
Funds: 2005–2060 (in Billions of Current Dollars)[b]

| Year | Five-Year Interval Increase or Decrease | Balance in Trust Funds |
|------|------------------------------------------|------------------------|
| 2005 | — | 1,001 |
| 2010 | 1,914 | 2,915 |
| 2015 | 2,370 | 5,285 |
| 2020 | 2,487 | 7,772 |
| 2025 | 2,237 | 10,009 |
| 2030 | 1,711 | 11,720 |
| 2035 | 1,115 | 12,835 |
| 2040 | 568 | 13,403 Peak |
| 2045 | −184 | 13,219 |
| 2050 | −1,715 | 11,504 |
| 2055 | −4,588 | 6,911 |
| 2060 | — | — |

[a] Alternative to estimates in table 5-5.
[b] All balances rounded to nearest billion.

Source: Board of Trustees, Federal Old-Age and Survivors Insurance and Disability
Insurance Trust Funds, *Annual Report* (Washington, D.C., U.S. Government Printing Office,
1989).

boomers reach retirement (assuming the retirement age remains at 65), and
becomes negative after 2040, the year in which the last of the boomers
enter into retirement.

The enormous buildup of money in the OASDI trust funds, however
calculated, raises several more crucial questions. The first is this: what is to
be done with this money? Where, in other words, is it to be invested?
According to the data in table 5-8, by the year 2002 (2007 according to the
Darman timetable), privately held federal debt would be eliminated. Thereafter, the surplus in the trust funds would continue to build, reaching a peak
in 2040 as shown in table 5-9. According to the Validation Scenario the
surpluses in the trust funds must be channeled into private capital formation so that the economy's productivity will increase sufficiently to pay for
benefits that begin to flow to the baby boomers as they reach retirement
age. But by 2005 (or shortly thereafter), the mechanism for doing this
assumed by Budget Director Darman will no longer be there, namely the
debt retirement process. Since privately held federal debt will presumably
no longer exist, the surpluses will have to be invested directly by the Social

Security Trustees in private securities. But the law does not permit this; as noted earlier, any trust fund surpluses *must* be invested in interest-bearing securities of the U.S. Government! From the perspective of the Validation Scenario, this does not make sense. If, as is now the case, trust fund surpluses continue to be "invested" in federal securities, the money collected by payroll taxes simply flows back into the U.S. Treasury, to be used as the government (Congress and the Administration) sees fit. There is no assurance that such funds augment savings and flow into private capital formation. This is not to say that the federal government could not manage the process in such a way that the surpluses could be used, say, for investment in the nation's infrastructure, but given the way the law now stands, there is no certainty that this will take place.

This question of what is to be done with the enormous sums locked up in the trust funds—possibly more than $15 trillion in 2024—raises an issue that originally came up in the 1930s when the Social Security Act was being drafted. The issue was whether the system was to be fully funded. A fully funded system raised the fear of a trust fund so gigantic that the federal government might wind up owning a huge portion of the nation's economy. This fear was an important reason why Social Security eventually was put on a pay-as-go basis. The issue remains, however. Given the estimated size of the trust fund buildup (tables 5-5 and 5-9), and given, too, the presumption that a Validation Scenario requires that the balances flow into real capital formation in the private sector, what would be the economic impact of these surpluses? The figures in table 5-10 seek to supply an answer.

What the data in table 5-10 show is a comparison between estimated values for the *net* stock of private wealth and the values of the combined OASDI trust fund balances as shown in tables 5-5 and 5-9. The latter are also shown as a percentage of the *net* stock of private wealth (estimated),[36] the purpose being to show approximately what share of the private economy the federal government might eventually own if Social Security moved toward a fully funded pay-for-yourself system. On the basis of the OASDI Board of Trustees estimates (table 5-5), the balance of the funds would reach a maximum of 19.8% of the net worth of private wealth in 2020, declining thereafter until the fund surpluses were eliminated by 2060. On the basis of the alternative estimate of the fund buildup contained in table 5-9, the peak ratio of trust funds to net private wealth would come in 2025, when assets in the funds would total 16.1% of the net stock of private wealth. If it is assumed that the funds are invested in the private economy, then these data suggest that the danger of the federal government taking over most of the private economy is not so great as was feared back in the 1930s. Aside from the question of whether it makes much economic sense

Table 5-10.  Estimated Balance in OASDI Trust Funds and Net Stock of Private Wealth: 2005–2055 (in Billions of Current Dollars and in Percent)

| Year | Estimated Stock of Net Private Wealth[a] | Estimated Balance In Trust Funds | Trust Funds As Percent of Private Wealth |
|------|------|------|------|
| 2005 | $ 23,770 | $ 1,001 | 4.2% |
| 2010 | 30,733 | 2,915 | 9.5 |
| 2015 | 39,083 | 5,285 | 13.5 |
| 2020 | 49,280 | 7,772 | 15.8 |
| 2025 | 61,999 | 10,009 | 16.1 Peak |
| 2030 | 78,287 | 11,720 | 14.9 |
| 2035 | 99,222 | 12,835 | 12.9 |
| 2040 | 125,658 | 13,407 | 10.7 |
| 2045 | 158,772 | 13,219 | 8.3 |
| 2050 | 200,357 | 11,504 | 5.7 |
| 2055 | 253,013 | 6,916 | 2.7 |
| 2060 | 319,813 | — | — |

[a] Fixed reproducible tangible wealth.

Source: Board of Trustees, Federal Old-Age and Survivors Insuranc and Disability Insurance Trust Funds, *Annual Report* (Washington, D.C., U.S. Government Printing Office, 1989); U.S. Department of Commerce, *Fixed Reproducible Tangible Wealth in the United States, 1925–85* (Washington, D.C., U.S. Government Printing Office, 1989).

for the government to buy into the economy to a maximum of 19.8%, and then turn around and sell off what it acquired, the amounts involved would not necessarily socialize the economy through the back door. Ownership of approximately 20% of the economy's fixed, reproducible assets does not mean a socialized economic system, although the type of assets acquired by the federal government would be a question of paramount economic and social importance.

There is, however, much more to the matter than this. If we assume that the scenario described by the data in table 5-10 is carried out, a new question arises: how far will this carry Social Security toward a fully funded system? Not nearly so far as the figures in tables 5-5, 5-9, and 5-10 might lead one to suspect. To show why this is the case, we need to examine some additional calculations made by the Board of Trustees. These are contained in table 5-11. These data show, for the period 1989 through 2055, estimates of assets held in the OASDI trust funds (same as in table 5-5), interest income from those assets, the rate of return on these assets, benefits to be paid during these years, and, finally, interest income as a percentage of estimated benefits.

Tabel 5-11.  Estimated Balances in OASDI Trust Funds, Interest Income, and OASDI Benefits: 1989–2060 (in Billions of Dollars and in Percent)

| Year | Balance in Trust Funds | Interest Income | Rate of Return | Benefits Payable | Interest as Percent of Benefits |
|------|------|------|------|------|------|
| 1989 | $    168.1 | $ 13.0 | 7.7% | $   235.7 | 5.5% |
| 1990 | 240.7 | 18.7 | 7.7 | 250.4 | 7.5 |
| 1991 | 322.6 | 25.0 | 7.7 | 265.9 | 9.4 |
| 1992 | 415.9 | 31.3 | 7.5 | 280.1 | 11.2 |
| 1993 | 521.1 | 37.6 | 7.2 | 294.6 | 12.8 |
| 1994 | 638.8 | 44.1 | 6.9 | 309.5 | 14.2 |
| 1995 | 768.9 | 50.5 | 6.6 | 325.0 | 15.5 |
| 2000 | 1,634.1 | 91.1 | 5.6 | 417.6 | 21.8 |
| 2005 | 2,963.0 | 152.0 | 5.1 | 543.3 | 28.0 |
| 2010 | 4,877.2 | 252.5 | 5.2 | 735.4 | 34.3 |
| 2015 | 7,246.8 | 378.8 | 5.2 | 1,042.3 | 36.3 |
| 2020 | 9,734.4 | 513.3 | 5.3 | 1,490.1 | 34.4 |
| 2025 | 11,971.2 | 635.9 | 5.3 | 2,069.7 | 30.7 |
| 2030 | 13,682.3 | 730.9 | 5.3 | 2,765.0 | 26.4 |
| 2035 | 14,797.2 | 793.5 | 5.4 | 3,560.0 | 22.3 |
| 2040 | 15,364.9 | 826.2 | 5.4 | 4,470.1 | 18.5 |
| 2045 | 15,181.4 | 820.2 | 5.4 | 5,615.1 | 14.6 |
| 2050 | 13,465.8 | 736.1 | 5.5 | 7,129.9 | 10.3 |
| 2055 | 8,878.6 | 503.6 | 5.7 | 9,109.4 | 5.5 |
| 2060 | Exhausted | None | — | — | — |

Source: Board of Trustees, Federal Old-Age Survivors Insurance and Disability Insurance Trust Funds, *Annual Report* (Washington, D.C., U.S. Government Printing Office, 1989).

The latter is the crucial figure for getting an answer to our earlier question. In 2015 interest income as a percent of benefits paid will reach a maximum at 36.3%. In other words, that the buildup envisaged by the 1983 "big fix" for the Social Security system will, *at a maximum*, carry the system slightly more than one third of the way to a fully funded system. Moreover, this would not be permanent; after 2015, the assets of the system would have to be sold off to finance benefits being paid out as the baby boomers enter retirement in ever increasing numbers.

This brings us back full circle to the fundamental question raised earlier: is a fully funded, pay-for-yourself system really possible? A reasonable answer is theoretically yes, but practically no. Table 5-12 indicates why. This table shows, given the Trustees' estimates of the benefits the Social Security

Table 5-12. Hypothetical Fund Required to Fully Fund OASDI Benefits Compared to Estimated Stock of Net Private Wealth: 2005–2055 (in Billions of Current Dollars and in Percent)

| Year | Estimated Benefits | Hypothetical Fund | Estimated Stock of Private Wealth | Fund as a Percent of Private Wealth |
|------|--------------------|-------------------|-----------------------------------|-------------------------------------|
| 2005 | $  543  | $  10,056 | $  23,770 | 42.3% |
| 2010 | 735     | 13,611    | 30,763    | 44.2  |
| 2015 | 1,042   | 19,296    | 39,083    | 49.4  |
| 2020 | 1,490   | 27,592    | 49,280    | 55.9  |
| 2025 | 2,070   | 38,333    | 61,999    | 61.8  |
| 2030 | 2,765   | 51,203    | 78,287    | 65.4  |
| 2035 | 3,560   | 65,925    | 99,222    | 66.4  |
| 2040 | 4,470   | 82,777    | 125,658   | 65.9  |
| 2045 | 5,615   | 103,981   | 158,772   | 65.4  |
| 2050 | 7,130   | 132,037   | 200,357   | 65.9  |
| 2055 | 9,109   | 168,685   | 253,013   | 66.6  |

Sources: Board of Trustees, Federal Old-Age and Survivors Insurance and Disability Insurance Trust Funds, *Annual Report* (Washington, D.C., U.S. Government Printing Office, 1989); U.S. Department of Commerce, *Fixed Reproducible Tangible Wealth in the United States, 1925–85* (Washington, D.C., U.S. Government Printing Office, 1989).

system will have to pay out for the years 2000 through 2055 (at five-year intervals), the estimated size of a fund yielding a 5.4% rate of return that would be needed to fully finance the stream of benefits.[37] The table also compares the estimated value for this fund with estimates of the size of the net stock of private wealth for the same period. By 2055, the fund would have an estimated value of 66.6% of the worth of the economy's net stock of private reproducible assets. On the basis of these estimates, the fears of the 1930s would be realized, as the federal government could end up owning two thirds of the economy! This simply will not happen.

## A Return to Pay-As-You-Go

The real solution to the future problem of the baby boomers and Social Security is, as Senator Daniel Patrick Moynihan has proposed, to return to a pay-as-you-go basis. We need to understand, first, that Social Security is, and has been since its inception, an income transfer system, and it must

Table 5-13. Actual and Projected OASDI Benefits as a Percent of the GNP: 1945–2055 (in Percent)

| Year | Actual Benefits as a Percent of GNP | Year | Projected Benefits as a Percent of GNP |
|------|------|------|------|
| 1945 | 0.1 | 1990 | 4.5 |
| 1950 | 0.4 | 1995 | 4.4 |
| 1955 | 1.2 | 2000 | 4.3 |
| 1960 | 2.3 | 2005 | 4.4 |
| 1965 | 2.6 | 2010 | 4.5 |
| 1970 | 3.3 | 2015 | 5.0 |
| 1975 | 4.3 | 2020 | 5.7 |
| 1980 | 4.5 | 2025 | 6.2 |
| 1985 | 4.6 | 2030 | 6.6 |
| 1987 | 4.5 | 2035 | 6.7 |
|      |     | 2040 | 6.6 |
|      |     | 2045 | 6.6 |
|      |     | 2050 | 6.7 |
|      |     | 2055 | 6.7 |

Sources: U.S. Department of Health and Human Services, Social Security Administration, *Social Security Bulletin, Annual Statistical Supplement*, 1988, pp 121, 123; *Economic Report of the President*, 1990, p. 294; Board of Trustees of the Federal Old-Age and Survivors Insurance Trust Fund and the Federal Disability Insurance Trust Fund, *1989 Annual Report* (Washington, D.C., U.S. Government Printing Office, 1989), pp. 128, 132, Alternative II-A.

remain such. Accepting this permits us to examine the looming problems of the system from a more realistic perspective. Taking this approach should make it clear that the problems confronting the system, particularly the problem of the baby boomers, are not nearly so formidable as we have been led to believe. Table 5-13 tells us why.

Table 5-13 shows both actual and projected benefits as a percentage of the GNP for the years 1945 thorough 2055. The figures for 1945 through 1985 are derived from actual OASDI outlays and GNP (both in current dollars), while the figures for 1990 through 2055 are based upon estimates made by the OASDI Board of Trustees. These figures put the entire Social Security problem into a proper perspective by telling us what proportion of the nation's current dollar output has been transferred to beneficiaries under the Social Security system and what proportion will probably have to be transferred in the future as the Baby Boomers enter the system. The numbers are not intimidating. As these data in table 5-13 show, OASDI transfers have grown from 0.1% of the GNP in 1945 to 4.7% as the 1980s came to a close. The Board of Trustees estimates show that this percentage will rise to 6.7% by the year 2035, when the full impact of the baby boomers is being felt, and then will remain roughly stable until 2055. By way of comparison, *total* transfers to people on the national income and product accounts basis were 9.0% of the GNP in 1980, 9.1% in 1985, and 8.8% in 1989. Military outlays as a percent of the GNP totaled 5.2% in 1980, 6.4% in 1985, and 5.8% in 1989.[38]

What should we conclude from these figures? First, if the baby boomer problem is viewed in its proper context as a *transfer* problem and in relation to the probable growth in the nation's output (GNP), the problem is manageable. Transferring 6.7% of the national output to OASDI beneficiaries is a larger problem than transferring 4.5% (as in 1987), but it is in no way an unmanageable problem. The *real* solution to the baby boomers lies with what happens to the nation's productivity in the years that lie ahead. In the Alternative II-A assumption being used in this discussion, the OASDI Board of Trustees assumed an annual average rate of growth in real GNP for 2010 and beyond of 2.1%.[39] This is a modest projection, entirely within the range of the nation's historic experience and not beyond attainment in the decades ahead. What is dubious, however, is the proposition, embodied in the 1983 "big fix" and the Bush Social Security Integrity and Debt Reduction Fund, that nation's real capital formation and worker productivity can be significantly advanced by attempting to channel huge quantities of funds into the nation's capital markets through surpluses in the OASDI accounts. It is the federal government's responsibility to use current deficits or surpluses in its overall budget as instruments of stabilization, not to generate money savings for the private capital market.

There is another major question to be addressed, namely, the troublesome issue of how we should finance the portion of the nation's GNP to be transferred to beneficiaries of the Social Security system, including the baby boomers as they reach retirement age. As Senator Moynihan noted in making his proposal for a rollback in Social Security tax rates, "The tax structure of the United States is fast becoming one of the most regressive of any Western nation. The 1980s have witnessed a decline in the progressivity of federal taxes as a whole...."[40] Payroll taxes are regressive, and they now finance an increasing share of federal revenues. In 1980 their share was 33.7% of all federal revenue; by 1989 this percentage had jumped to 40.4%.[41] This is not so much an economic problem as a political problem. The challenge is to move away from excessive reliance upon a regressive payroll tax for financing the system, and yet preserve the widespread belief—myth, if you will—that Social Security is a contributory arrangement in which beneficiaries have paid for the benefits they are drawing from the system. Meeting this challenge may be impossible.

## Health Care in America

The second major problem confronting America's welfare state in the 1990s is the problem of health care. Like the worsening problem of the underclass, the crisis in health care facing the nation is one so vast that an adequate analysis discussion of it is well beyond the scope of this book.[42] What we shall do in this section, however, is sketch out in broad outline the dimensions of the problem, relating these dimensions to the framework followed throughout this study in discussing the evolution of America's welfare state. This procedure permits us to point toward a solution to the problems of health care, a solution that can and should be developed within the framework of the classic welfare state, as that term has been used in this book.

*Crisis* is a much overworked word, even though it is being used with increasing frequency to describe the problems facing the provision of medical care to Americans. No matter how the situation is described, however, there is little doubt that some exceedingly difficult problems confront what economists and others describe as the nation's *medical care delivery system.* If we cut through most of the rhetoric surrounding the "crisis," the health care problem reduces itself to the following. First, there are now at least 37 million Americans—adults and children—without any medical insurance whatsoever.[43] Second, there is general agreement that the United states spends a higher proportion of its GNP for medical care than any other major industrial nation. And yet, millions of persons have no financial protection from the expenses of medical care, and millions more have inadequate protection. Third, the system, if it can be called a system, is in a near-chaotic state. As *Newsweek* magazine economic columnist Robert J. Samuelson has commented, "You can't describe our system, let alone control it. It's not socialized medicine. It's not private medicine.... Our health-care system is a jumble of groups (doctors, hospitals, government agencies, health-maintenance organizations, private insurers) working under a bewildering array of regulations and pursuing different objectives. No one is in charge...."[44] Finally, there is little agreement about what can and should be done to resolve the crisis, even though almost everyone involved in the system is dissatisfied to some degree.

Much of the foregoing discussion is summarized in statistical form in table 5-14. These data show basically for the 1980s—the years of the

Table 5-14. Total Spending[a] in the U.S. for Medical Care: 1980, 1984, and 1988 (in Billions of Current Dollars and in Percent)

| | 1980 | 1984 | 1988 | Percent Change 1980 to 1988 |
|---|---|---|---|---|
| **Federal spending** | | | | |
| 1. Health and hospitals, of which grants-in-aid to | $ 9.4 | $ 10.2 | $ 14.1 | 50.0% |
| state and local govts. | ($ 3.3) | ($ 3.3) | ($ 4.3) | 30.0 |
| 2. Medicare | 36.7 | 64.2 | 88.8 | 142.0 |
| 3. Medicaid | 14.3 | 20.6 | 31.5 | 120.3 |
| 4. Veterans (primary hospitals) | 6.2 | 10.3 | 13.1 | 111.3 |
| Total federal | $ 66.6 | $ 105.2 | $ 147.5 | 121.5% |
| Percent of GNP | 2.4% | 2.8% | 3.2% | — |
| **Private spending** | | | | |
| 1. Prescription drugs | $ 17.7 | $ 23.6 | $ 34.5 | 95.0% |
| 2. Orthopedic appliances | 4.7 | 7.3 | 10.2 | 117.0 |
| 3. Physicians and dentists | 55.9 | 91.2 | 132.0 | 136.1 |
| 4. other professional services[b] | 5.6 | 12.2 | 54.3 | 869.6 |
| 5. Private hospitals[c] | 70.6 | 110.0 | 182.3 | 158.2 |
| 6. Health insurance | 11.4 | 14.1 | 29.8 | 161.4 |
| Total private | $ 165.9 | $ 258.4 | $ 443.1 | 167.2% |
| Less: Transfers to Persons from Governments | 49.9 | 84.4 | 120.6 | |
| Adjusted total | $ 116.0 | $ 174.0 | $ 322.5 | 178.0% |
| Percent of GNP | 4.2% | 4.6% | 7.0% | — |
| **State and local spending** | | | | |
| 1. Health | $ 8.7 | $ 13.0 | $ 18.3 | 110.3% |
| 2. Hospitals | 25.6 | 35.4 | 42.9 | 67.6 |
| Total state and local | $ 34.3 | $ 48.4 | $ 61.2 | 78.4% |
| Less: Federal grants-in-aids | 3.3 | 3.3 | 4.3 | 30.0 |
| Adjusted total | $ 31.0 | $ 45.1 | $ 56.9 | 83.5% |
| Percent of GNP | 1.1% | 1.2% | 1.2% | — |
| **Total for federal, private, and state and local** | $ 213.6 | $ 324.3 | $ 526.9 | 146.7% |
| *Percent of GNP* | 7.8% | 8.6% | 11.5% | — |
| *GNP* | $2732.0 | $3777.2 | $4580.6 | 67.7% |

[a] Goods and services and transfers.

[b] Consists of osteopathic physicians, chiropractors, private duty nurses, chiropodists, podiatrists, and other health care professionals.

[c] Consists of current expenditures of nonprofit hospitals, sanitariums, and nursing homes, and payments by patients to proprietary hospitals, sanitariums, and nursing homes.

Sources: U.S. Department of Commerce, *Survey of Current Business*, July, 1981, 1984, 1989; *Economic Indicators*, February, 1990.

Reagan Revolution—what happened to spending for medical care in the United States. The data are broken down into three major categories: spending by the federal government, private spending adjusted for transfers to persons, and spending by state and local governments—and cover *all* government expenditures for medical purposes, including the buying of goods and services and transfer outlays. They also show the percentage increases over the period for these three major categories, as well as the increases for the subcategories within these classifications.

In 1980 private and public health care spending was equal to 7.8% of the GNP. By 1988, this percentage had increased to 11.5%, a 47% percent increase in the relative share of the nation's output going for health care. Overall, total federal, private, and state and local spending for medical purposes grew by 146.7%, more than twice the 67.7% increase in current-dollar GNP in the same period. Medical spending grew faster than any of the three major components of the GNP, namely consumption, investment, and government buying of goods and services. In the 1980–1988 period, consumption grew by 92.5%, investment (gross) by 71.6%, and government (federal, state, and local) purchases of goods and services by 82.7%. Government spending for all purposes, including transfers, grew by 86.5% in this period.[45]

As between the three major categories of health care spending, private spending less transfers from government grew the most, rising by 178.0%. Adjusted private spending was equal to 7.0% of the GNP in 1988, compared to 4.2% in 1980. In relative terms, this was a 67% increase. Federal outlays for health purposes increased by 121.5% from 1980 to 1988. Overall, federal spending for *all* purposes rose by 81.8% during these years.[46] The federal health care spending share of the GNP went from 2.4% in 1980 to 3.2% in 1988, a 33% gain in relative terms. State and local health care expenditures adjusted for federal grants-in-aid rose the least over the period. Adjusted state and local health care spending increased 83.5%, slightly less than the increase overall in government spending for all purposes. State and local health expenditures continue to absorb only a small fraction of the GNP, 1.1% in 1980 vs. 1.2% in 1988. In the overall picture, price increases played a major role in these changes in health care spending. Between 1980 and 1988, the consumer price index rose by 43.6%, but the medical care component of the index rose by 85.0%.[47] What may come as a surprise to some in view of the public attention directed toward federal spending is the change in the overall mix of public vs. private spending between 1980 and 1988. In 1980 federal plus state and local spending for health care accounted for 46 cents out of every dollar spent for medical purposes. Private spending accounted for 54 cents. By 1988, however, the private share of the medical expense dollar had increased to 61 cents and the public share had fallen to 39 cents.[48]

The foregoing is the statistical story on health care spending in the United States in the 1980s. As a nation, we spent an increasing share of output on health with increasingly unsatisfactory results. The fact that the number of Americans without any health insurance continues to increase is testimony to this.[49] There is no simple explanation for why this has happened—there are, no doubt, enough villains in the picture to satisfy the most demanding critic. No attempt will be made here to identify them, but we will try to point the way toward a solution.

There is a saying: "If it ain't broke, don't fix it." Unfortunately, this does not apply to America's health care delivery system. It is "broke." It is not beyond repair, but it can't be fixed within the confines of the existing patchwork, crazy-quilt system, which includes hundreds, if not thousands, of different medical plans, The solution lies in some form of national health insurance, a direction that even the medical profession is beginning to realize the nation must take.

Early in 1989 the prestigious *New England Journal of Medicine* published two important articles that set forth in detail how the nation could move to a system of universal health insurance.[50] One plan, which was described in a two-part article, was developed by Alain Enthoven and Richard Kronick of the Graduate School of Business, Stanford University, whereas the second plan was drafted by a Working Committee of Physicians from the Harvard Medical School, and endorsed by 412 other physicians representing almost every state and medical specialty. More important, perhaps, the editor (and presumably the editorial board and the Massachusetts Medical Society, which owns and publishes *The New England Journal of Medicine*) endorsed the idea of a comprehensive plan, without specifically endorsing either proposal. As the editor, Dr. Arnold S. Relman, said, "In my view, nothing short of a comprehensive plan, which includes improved technology assessment and malpractice reform as well as other reforms in medical practice, is likely to achieve the goals of universal access, cost containment, and preservation of quality that everyone seems to want."[51]

The two proposed plans are not identical. What both have in common is a belief that the present system is failing, that we as a nation spend a larger percent of our GNP on health care than do other modern nations but fail to provide care for everyone, and that the time for comprehensive reform is at hand. The Enthoven–Kronick proposal is the less radical of the two. It would retain to a degree the existing pluralistic insurance network by keeping Medicare, Medicaid, and other successful public programs, but make affordable coverage available to everyone not covered by these plans through a strategy of "managed competition." By means of the impetus of federal legislation, each state would create a "public sponsor" agency to take competitive bids from health plan suppliers and offer health care coverage to persons and families not otherwise covered through employment. The coverage would be subsidized, with the public sponsor paying 80% of the cost for an average health care plan. Basically, the public sponsor would act as a broker for the many small and even medium-sized employers who are not large enough to manage competition among health care plans effectively. Employers would be mandated to cover all full-time employees with a health insurance plan, and would pay an 8% payroll tax on the first $22,500 of wages and salaries for employees *not* covered. Without the mandate and tax, employers would have a powerful incentive to stop providing health care coverage and to send their employees to the public sponsor.[52] To encourage universal health care coverage, the Enthoven–Kronick plan would provide for a federal subsidy for the portion of the health insurance premium that individuals and families would have to pay if their adjusted gross income was below 120% of the poverty level for a family of their size.[53]

The alternative plan, the one advanced by the committee of Harvard physicians, is much less complex but far more radical. Basically, their plan proposes a single national health program that would fully cover all persons and families and would be funded from a common pool of money, to be drawn initially from the same sources now being used to finance the current medley of health care plans. Eventually the federal government would take over full responsibility for the program, with private insurance gradually being phased out. At the state level, "National Health Program Payment Boards" would be created that would have the responsibility of negotiating payments and fees with all health care providers, including hospitals and physicians. "Fee-for-service" payments for physicians could continue, but these would be on the basis of a negotiated fee schedule and mandatory acceptance of payment through the national health program.[54]

Neither proposal involves socialized medicine, because neither envisages the federal government owning and operating health care facilities—that is, hospitals—or being the major (or sole) employer of physicians and other health care professionals. But these plans would, as will any other plan for a system of national health insurance, change significantly the way in which most physicians are paid. Fee-for-service would continue, but salaried group practice would, no doubt, become the primary arrangement for the compensation of physicians.

No attempt will be made in this book to describe what kind of a national health insurance scheme the nation should undertake. That is too ambitious a project to undertake in a work of this scope and purpose. The question to be addressed is whether the nation can afford national health insurance. If we seek to create an entirely new system and impose it on top of existing schemes, the answer is obviously no. With the federal deficit running near $200 billion, there obviously isn't any money for new social welfare programs. If we look, however, at what we are now spending for medical care in relation to the nation's output (table 5-14), the answer is yes. Neil Pierce, columnist and writer for *The National Journal*, estimates that the administrative costs for our fragmented health care system average 5.4% a year, compared to Canada where such costs in their single-payer system are 1.4% a year.[55] Moving to a single and unified national system would yield enormous savings in administrative costs alone. The issue is not primarily one of costs, however. We are now spending more than enough to provide adequate and decent medical care for every citizen. It is a matter of how we spend the money, a question of the inefficient structure of the health care system. In the final analysis, this is *not* an economic problem. It is a problem of vision and will, a problem of politics and change. We can afford a decent and workable system, but we shall not get it until political leaders emerge with the knowledge, the vision, the skill, and the determination to change the way things are done. It will not be easy, but the fact that the existing system is moving toward a breaking point means that it will have to be done.

## A Concluding Comment

In concluding this short study of the evolution of America's welfare state, primarily during the post-World War II era, a few observations are in order. It is clear that the American welfare state works, if by "works" we mean the effective transfer of income from one segment of society to another. As we have shown, approximately two thirds of federal spending is transfer spending and hence is linked to a broadened definition of the welfare state. In a different sense, if we look at it from the perspective of the Beveridge Report as a scheme to eliminate "want" among the poorest members of society, America's three-tiered welfare state does not work very well. Generally speaking, the poor fare less well than do the middle and upper classes. This seems to be the kind of structure the American people want— one does not sense any great political pressure for immediate change. Change is not an impossibility, however: witness what happened in the Tax Reform Act of 1986. Major changes were made in eliminating and reducing corporate tax expenditures, something many would not have thought possible.

A second matter to note is this: programs that are universal rather than selective work best, especially with respect to the reduction or elimination of poverty. There is enormous political support in the nation for Social Security—a near universal entitlement program—in contrast to selective programs targeted at the poor, such as AFDC and food stamps. Few of America's poor are regarded as "deserving," so support for public-assistance-type programs is grudgingly given at best. Reducing or eliminating want or poverty cannot be achieved without spending money, contrary to the sloganeering by conservatives that you "can't solve problems by throwing money at them." Most of the time there is no other way, as is attested to by the nation's success in reducing poverty in the over-65 segment of the population. In 1966 nearly 30% of persons over 65 were "in poverty," but by 1987 this percentage had fallen to 12%. In contrast, the poverty rate among children has climbed back to 20% (one fifth of all American children live in poverty), after dropping to near 14% in the early 1970s.[56] The difference is between Social Security, a non-means-tested entitlement program directed at *all* eligible persons, and the means-tested social insurance programs for AFDC families, where most of American's poor children are found. The former has the political support necessary for generous funding; the latter does not. The problem with universal-type programs is that the benefits go to rich and poor alike, which in the United States seems to be a necessary condition for political support. This probably will not change, but this defect, if it is so considered, can be overcome by a properly designed tax system. The latter means progression. If the tax system is progressive, then society can readily recapture benefits that flow through the welfare state to those at the upper ends of the income scale. Unfortunately, America has moved in the opposite direction in the last decade. This trend needs to be reversed.

Finally, there probably will not be any grand restructuring of America's welfare state to bring it more into conformity with the classical ideal discussed earlier. Change and politics in America rarely work that way. Reform will come, as it always does, but it will be piecemeal, gradual, and rarely with a welfare label attached. The earned income tax credit in the federal tax code is a case in point. This really is a different name for a rudimentary family allowance system, a descendent of the ill-fated schemes for a negative income tax proposed by both Richard Nixon and George McGovern about two decades ago. Child care legislation wending its way through the Congress at this writing is another case in point. It does not constitute a full-blown system of allowances for children, as is found in most other western nations, but it is a step in that direction, even though not called that or necessarily considered as a formal part of the welfare state.

Irrespective of the direction that reform may take in the future, a clear understanding of the distinction between government spending for goods and services and government transfer spending is essential. Most of our problems that require some action by the federal government involve transfer spending in one form or another, whether we are talking about welfare state reform, the reconstruction of the nation's health care system, or the problems of the underclass. Intelligent debate and discussion cannot take place unless the distinction is both made and understood. It is hoped that this book makes some contribution to that end.

## Notes

1. See William Julius Wilson, *The Truly Disadvantaged* (Chicago, The University of Chicago Press, 1987).

2. The number of live births between 1946 and 1966 was 83.3 million.

3. Board of Trustees, Federal Old Age and Survivors Insurance and Disability Insurance Trust Funds, *Annual Report* (Washington, D.C., U.S. Government Printing Office, 1989), pp. 33 ff; U.S. Department of Health and Human Services, Social Security Administration, *Social Security Bulletin*, Vol. 50, No. 7, pp. 31 ff.

4. Merton C. Bernstein and Joan Brodshaug Bernstein, *Social Security: The System That Works* (New York, Basic Books, 1988), pp. 33 ff.

5. Board of Trustees, *op. cit.*, p. 126.

6. *Ibid.*, pp. 4, 5.

7. Old age (retirees) and survivors (OASI) and disabled (DI) have separate trust funds, as does Medicare (MI). The DI trust fund was started in 1956 and the Medicare trust fund in 1965.

8. Berstein and Berstein, *op. cit.*, pp. 36 ff.

9. *Ibid.*

10. Office of Senator Daniel Patrick Moynihan, "Statement," January 23, 1990.

11. Bernstein and Berstein, *op. cit.*, p. 84.

12. Herman B. Leonard, *Checks Unbalanced: The Quiet Side of Public Spending* (New York, Basic Books, 1986), p. 57.

13. *Ibid.*, p. 54.

14. *Ibid.*, p. 57.

15. John C. Hambor, "Economic Policy, Intergenerational Equity, and the Social Security Trust Fund Buildup," *Social Security Bulletin*, Vol. 50, No. 10, pp. 13–18.

16. *Ibid.*, p. 16.

17. *Ibid.*

18. *Ibid.*

19. *Ibid.*, p. 17.

20. *On-budget* in this context means the regular income and outgo of the federal government, *excluding* the many trust fund accounts. For the purposes of the Gramm–Rudman–Hollings law, however, trust funds are included in the budget for calculating the deficit.

21. Hambor, *op. cit.*, p. 17.

22. Congress of the United States, *Budget of the United States Government* (Washington, D.C., U.S. Government Printing Office, 1990), pp. 20, 225, 266.

23. *Ibid.*, p. 226.

24. *Ibid.*

25. Walter Adams and James W. Brock, *Dangerous Pursuits: Mergers and Acquisitions in the Age of Wall Street* (New York, Pantheon Books, 1989), p. 123.

26. *Economic Report of the President* (Washington, D.C., U.S. Government Printing Office, 1990), pp. 392, 394.

27. Congress of the United States, Congressional Budget Office, *The Economic and Budget Outlook: Fiscal Years 1991–1995* January, 1990, p. xix.

28. *Ibid.*

29. *Federal Reserve Bulletin*, December, 1984, p. 863.

30. *Statistical Abstract of the United States* (Washington, D.C., U.S. Government Printing Office, 1983), p. 481.

31. *Economic Report of the President*, 1990, *op. cit.*, p. 394.

32. *Budget of the United States Government*, *op. cit.*, pp. 225, 226.

33. *Economic Report of the President*, 1990, *op. cit.* p. 394.

34. Board of Trustees, *op. cit.*, p. 132. In the discussion that follows, the Alternative II-A assumption is used in every instance.

35. *Ibid.*, pp. 15, 16.

36. The net stock of private reproducible wealth is estimated by computing the ratio of this stock to the GNP for the period 1970 through 1987, and then applying this ratio to the Board of Trustee' estimates of the GNP for the years 1990 through 2055.

37. The fund size is estimated by capitalizing the expected benefits each year at an interest rate of 5.4%.

38. *Economic Report of the President*, 1990, *op. cit.*, pp. 294, 389.

39. Board of Trustees, *op. cit.*, p. 34.

40. Senator Daniel Patrick Moynihan, *op. cit.*

41. *Economic Report of the President*, 1990, *op. cit.*, p. 389.

42. Eli Ginzberg, *The Medical Triangle* (Cambridge, MA, Harvard University Press, 1990), forthcoming.

43. *The New York Times*, July 30, 1989, National Section, p. 1.

44. Robert J. Samuelson, *Newsweek*, October 2, 1989, p. 52.

45. *Economic Indicators*, February, 1990, p. 1; *Economic Report of the President*, 1990, *op. cit.*, p. 388.

46. *Economic Report of the President*, 1990, *op. cit.*, p. 389.

47. *Economic Indicators*, *op. cit.*, p. 23.

48. From table 5-14.

49. According to the Employee Benefit Research Institute, there were 28 million Americans without health care in 1980, 35 million in 1984, and 37 million at last count. See *Business Week*, November 10, 1986, p. 32, and *The New York Times*, *op. cit.*

50. *The New England Journal of Medicine*, January 5, 12, 1989, pp. 29–37, 94–101, and 102–107.

51. *Ibid.*, January 12, 1989, p. 118.

52. *Ibid.*, January 5, 1989, pp. 31, 32.

53. *Ibid.*

54. *Ibid.*, January 12, 1989, p. 118.

55. Neil R. Peirce, syndicated column, *The National Journal*, April 7, 1990.

56. U.S. Department of Commerce, Bureau of the Census, P-60, *Poverty in the United States, 1987*, pp. 7, 9.

# INDEX